NEW FORMATIONS

EDITOR:
Judith Squires

CONSULTING EDITORS:
James Donald
Erica Carter

EDITORIAL BOARD:
Homi Bhabha
Lesley Caldwell
Tony Davies
Simon Frith
Jim Grealy
Stuart Hall
Dick Hebdige
Graham Murdock
Ali Rattansi
Denise Riley
Jenny Bourne Taylor
Valerie Walkerdine

OVERSEAS EDITORS:
Ien Ang
Angelika Bammer
Tony Bennett
Jody Berland
Victor Burgin
Hazel Carby
Iain Chambers
Joan Copjec
Lidia Curti
Cora Kaplan
Noel King
Colin Mercer
Kobena Mercer
Edward Said
Renata Salecl
Gayatri Chakravorty Spivak
John Tagg

New Formations is
published three times
a year by
Lawrence & Wishart
144a Old South Lambeth Road
London SW8 1XX
Tel 0171–820 9281
Fax 0171–587 0469

CW00969903

ADVERTISEMENTS
for enquiries/bookings con
Ruth Borthwick, Lawrenc

SUBSCRIPTIONS
For 1995, subscription ra
Wishart are, for 3 issues
UK: Institutions £55, Ind
Rest of world: Institution.
£38.
Single copies: £14.99

CONTRIBUTIONS, CORRESPONDENCE AND BOOKS
FOR REVIEW
should be sent to
The Editor, *New Formations*,
Dept of Politics, University of Bristol,
12 Priory Road, Bristol BS8 1TU

Prospective writers are encouraged to contact
the editors to discuss their ideas and to obtain
a copy of our style sheet.
Manuscripts should be sent in triplicate. They
will not be returned unless a stamped,
self-addressed envelope is enclosed.
Contributors should note that the editorial
board cannot take responsibility for any
manuscript submitted to *New Formations*.

ISSN 0 950-2378
ISBN 0 85315 765 0

Text design by Jan Brown Designs, London
Photoset in North Wales by
Derek Doyle & Associates, Mold, Clwyd
Printed in Great Britain
at the University Press, Cambridge

NOTES ON CONTRIBUTORS

Ien Ang teaches in the School of Humanities at Murdoch University, Western Australia and is the author of *Watching Dallas* (1985) and *Desperately Seeking the Audience* (1991).

Ghassan Hage teaches Social Anthropology at the University of Sydney. He is currently completing a work entitled *Strategies of Domestication: Multiculturalism, Racism and the Spatial Imaginary of the Dominant Culture*.

C.J.W.-L. Wee teaches Literature and Cultural Theory at the School of Arts, Nanyang Technological University in Singapore.

Neil Roughley teaches Philosophy at the University of Constance, Germany, where he is working on a 'Habilitation' on pragmatist ethics. He has published articles on hermeneutics and aesthetics, is the author of *Philosophische Anthropologie* and co-editor of *Identitat, Normativitaet, Leiblichkeit* (both forthcoming).

Julia Emberley is an Assistant Professor of Women's Studies at the University of Northern British Columbia. Her publications include *Thresholds of Difference: Feminist Critique, Native Women's Writings, Postcolonial Theory* and articles in *Cultural Critique, The Canadian Journal of Social and Political Theory, Feminist Studies* and *Canadian Woman Studies*.

Johan Fornäs teaches Media and Communication Studies at Stockholm University, Sweden. He is editor of the journal *Young: Nordic Journal of Youth Research* and of *Moves in Modernity* (1992).

Iain Chambers teaches at the Istituto Orientale, Naples, and is author of *Border Dialogues: Journeys in Postmodernity* (1990) and *Migrancy, Culture, Identity* (1994).

Rob Wilson teaches English at the University of Hawaii in Honolulu. A member of the *boundary 2* and *Bamboo Bridge* collectives and contributor to *Korean Culture*, he is author of *Waking In Seoul (1988)* and *American Sublime: The Genealogy of a Poetic Genre (1991)*. He is co-editor of a special issue of *boundary 2* on 'Asia/Pacific as Space of Cultural Production' Spring 1994.

Gillian Swanson teaches in the Humanities Department at Griffith University, Australia.

CONTENTS
NUMBER 24 WINTER 1994

On Not Speaking Chinese: Diaspora and Identity

EDITORIAL

This issue of *New Formations* had no initiating theme, no prior agenda. The articles published here are simply the most interesting of the many diverse articles that have arrived on my desk over the past year. My editorial comments then, will neither attempt to draw out the common theme in the articles, nor to articulate a unified project of the contributors. Rather, I want to reflect briefly upon the strengths of transnational and interdisciplinary work, and the potential dangers.

The contributors in this issue are geographically and disciplinarily dispersed: based in Australia, Canada, the United States, Italy, Germany, Sweden, Singapore and Hawaii; located in departments of women's studies, cultural studies, intercommunal studies, media and communication studies, English literature and philosophy. Most moved at least once between submitting the article and its publication, and many are in more than one department simultaneously ... A small reminder, lest we forget, that cultural theory debates are increasingly held at a global level, that academic disciplinary boundaries are becoming ever more hazy and that academics are increasingly mobile and flexible.

As we theorise the globalization of the economy – changing production processes necessitating flexibility, transience and mobility – so we ourselves are increasingly required to develop precisely these skills in order to compete in the international market-place of ideas. One recognises a deep uncertainty about the nature of departmental disciplines, doubt about the status of the 'canon', confusion over disciplinary methodologies, as symptomatic of wider social change and institutional organisation. The flexibility and multiplicity of the global economy are, for better or for worse, manifestly evident in the pages of the ever burgeoning number of academic journals.

The global economy is a given in our life now: transnational corporations cross borders to maximise productivity and transnational intellectuals cross academic boundaries to maximise knowledge. The academic discipline, along with the national state, is subject to powerful forces of change. And, as we might acknowledge the failings of the old model of state sovereignty and hegemonic nationalism but nonetheless remain deeply sceptical about the gains to be had from the free movement of international capital around the globe in pursuit of profit, so we must be attuned to the benefits of jettisoning the status of empirical area studies, the constricting patriarchal academic canons and oppressive hierarchical departments structures, but also the pitfalls.

The fear of course is that the undermining of disciplinary boundaries may simply produce blurriness; and that scholarly discourse, even of those deeply engrossed with the issues of postcoloniality, multiculturalism and difference is conducted within the insiders' globe. It is undeniably true that ideas rapidly circulate the globe, skimming the scholarly consciousness which is ever ready to invest resources if the return looks high, or to move on swiftly as the intellectual return dwindles, and that articles are becoming increasingly self-referential, attention firmly focused on one another's footnotes. The time-space compression of academic life condenses the intellectual process, pressurising academics to begin publishing and editing ever sooner, to find niche markets, to attend and organise ever more conferences, to produce ever more journals. Recent developments within academia and current shifts in the production process are far from distinct: both are driven by the urgent need to erode barriers to the free circulation of capital/ideas and accumulate territory/knowledge in distant worlds in order to gain unhindered access to its raw materials.

If theorists of cultural and political studies are to avoid the narcissistic opportunism accompanying the fate of becoming just one more manifestation of the imperialist globalization process, it will surely be through the attempt to locate our theorising in the grounded sites of cultural and political resistance. Otherwise the global celebration of difference may prove to be little more than a western hymn in praise of undifferentiation.

In her article 'On Not Speaking Chinese', Ien Ang notes, reflecting on her diasporic identity: 'if I am inescapably Chinese by descent, I am only sometimes Chinese by consent. When and how is a matter of politics.' Her point is 'to critique the formalist, poststructuralist tendency to over generalise the global current of so-called nomadic, fragmented and deterritorialized subjectivity'. Such 'nomadology' is rife in the pages of international cultural journals: decontextualising specific experiences of difference within a global analysis of the postmodern world.

In similar vein, Benita Parry has noted that the historical specificity of analyses of imperialism is increasingly sacrificed to the desire to produce accounts of empire's ubiquity, to map shared idioms across distinct periods. One consequence is that, whereas Edward Said has always been careful to 'delineate colonialism as one incarnation of a more extensive and variable process which he names "imperialism" ', the terms imperialism and colonialism are increasingly used interchangeably. This is no quibble about terminology: it is symptomatic of the ubiquitous desire to find a unified discursive form in imperialist texts, disconnected from their social conditions of possibility. Whilst the strength of much recent post-colonial criticism has been to afford an understanding of how tropes of domination inflect each other and can be transposed from one situation to another, the dilemma is that at the same time, these interpretations divert attention from the singularities of colonialist and later imperialist enunciations. Hence the need to address the specificities of imperialist rhetoric, diasporic experiences, racist practices; to develop, what Ang calls a critical diasporic cultural politics which avoids 'the most facile forms of postmodernist nomadology' by remaining contextual and political.

Only by so doing can we celebrate the globalisation of intellectual debates and the erosion of disciplinary boundaries whilst avoiding the spectre of dedifferentiated blandness and an easy nomadology.

Judith Squires, November 1994

ON NOT SPEAKING CHINESE
POSTMODERN ETHNICITY AND THE POLITICS OF DIASPORA

Ien Ang

'No ancestors, no identity'
(Chinese saying)

'The world is what it is; men who are nothing, who allow
themselves to become nothing, have no place in it.'
(V.S. Naipaul, *A Bend in the River*)

I

I only went to China once, for one day only. I crossed the border by speedboat
from Hong Kong, where I had booked for a daytrip to Shenzhen and
Guangzhou, the so-called New Economic Zone, with a local tourist company.
'This is the most well-off part of China. Further north and inland it is much
worse', the arrogant Hong Kong guide warned. It was, obviously, the
arrogance of capitalism. Our group of twelve consisted mainly of white,
western tourists – and me. I didn't have the courage to go on my own since I
don't speak any Chinese, not even one of the dialects. But I had to go, I had no
choice. It was an imposed pilgrimage.

'China', of course, usually refers to the People's Republic of China, or more
generically, 'mainland China'. This China continues to speak to the world's
imagination – for its sheer vastness, its huge population, its relative
inaccessibility, its fascinating history and culture, its idiosyncratic embracement
of communism, all of which amounts to its awesome difference. This China
also irritates, precisely because its stubborn difference cannot be disregarded,
if only because the forces of transnational capitalism are only too keen to finally
exploit this enormous market of more than a billion people. Arguably this was
one of the more cynical reasons for the moral high ground from which the
West displayed its outrage at the crushing of the students' protests at
Tiananmen Square in June 1989, discourses of democracy and human rights
notwithstanding.

My one-day visit occurred nine months after those dramatic events in Bejing.
At the border we were joined by a new guide, a twenty-seven-year old woman
from Bejing, Lan-lan, who spoke English in a way that revealed a 'typically
Chinese' commitment to learn: eager, diligent, studious. It was clear that
English is her entry to the world at large (that is, the world outside China), just
as being a tourist guide means access to communication and exchange with

foreigners. It shouldn't come as a surprise, therefore, as Lan-lan told us, that it is very difficult for young Chinese people to become a tourist guide (they must pass through a huge number of exams and other selection procedures): after all, these guides are the ones given the responsibility of presenting and explaining China to the foreign visitors. International tourism emphasizes and reinforces the porousness of borders – and is thus potentially dangerous for a closed society like China which nevertheless, paradoxically, needs and promotes tourism as an important economic resource.

How Lan-lan presented and explained China to us, however, was undoubtedly not meant for the ears of government officials. Obviously aware that we all had the political events of the year before in mind, she started spontaneously to intersperse the usual touristic information with criticism of the current communist government. 'The people *know* what happened last year at Tiananmen Square', she said as if to reassure us, 'and they don't approve. They are behind the students. They want more freedom and democracy. We don't talk about this in public, but we do among friends.' She told us these things so insistently, apparently convinced that it was what we *wanted* to hear. In other words, in her own way she did what she was officially supposed to do: serving up what she deemed to be the most favourable image of China to significant others – that is, westerners.

But at the same time it was clear that she spoke *as a Chinese*. Typically, she would begin her sentences with 'We Chinese ...' or 'Here in China we ...' Despite her political criticism, then, her identification with China and Chineseness was by no means in doubt. On the contrary, voicing criticism of the system through a discourse that she knew would appeal to western interlocutors, seemed only to strengthen her sense of Chinese identity. It was almost painful for me to see how Lan-lan's attempt to promote 'China' could only be accomplished by surrendering to the rhetorical perspective of the western other. It was not the content of the criticism she expounded that I was concerned about.[1] What upset me was the way in which it seemed necessary for Lan-lan to take up a *defensive* position, a position in need of constant self-explanation, in relation to a West that can luxuriate in its own taken-for-granted superiority. My pain stemmed from ambivalence: I refused to be lumped together with the (other) westerners, but I couldn't fully identify with Lan-lan either.

We were served a lunch in a huge, rather expensive-looking restaurant, complete with fake Chinese temple and a pond with lotus flowers in the garden, undoubtedly designed with pleasing international visitors in mind, but paradoxically only preposterous in its stereotypicality. All twelve of us, members of the tourist group, were seated around a typically Chinese round-table. Lan-lan did not join us, and I think I know why. The food we were served was obviously the kind of Chinese food that was adapted to European taste: familiar, rather bland dishes (except for the delicious crispy duck skin), not the 'authentic' Cantonese delicacies I was subconsciously looking forward to now that I was in China. (Wrong assumption: you have to

1. How the political present and future of the People's Republic of China should be judged in the light of what has come to be known worldwide as the 'Tiananmen Massacre' is a complex issue, too easily schematized in the complacent West in terms of good and bad, heroic students and a villainous communist dictatorship – a schematization that only enhances feel-good smugness, not nuanced analysis.

be in rich, decadent, capitalist Hong Kong for that, as I found out.) And we did not get a bowl and chopsticks, but a plate with spoon and fork. I was shocked, even though my chopstick competence is not very great. An instant sense of alienation took hold of me. Part of me wanted to leave immediately, wanted to scream out loud that I didn't belong to the group I was with, but another part of me felt compelled to take Lan-lan's place as tourist guide while she was not with us, to explain, as best as I could, to my fellow tourists what the food was all about. I realized how mistaken I was to assume, since there is a Chinese restaurant in virtually every corner of the world, that 'everybody knows Chinese food'. For my table companions the unfamiliarity of the experience prevailed, the anxious excitement of trying out something new (although they predictably found the duck skin 'too greasy', of course, the kind of complaint about Chinese food that I have heard so often from Europeans). Their pleasure in undertaking this one day of 'China' was the pleasure of the exotic.

But it was my first time in China too, and while I did not quite have the freedom to see this country as exotic because I have always had to see it as somehow *my* country, even if only imaginarily, I repeatedly found myself looking at this minute piece of 'China' through the tourists' eyes: reacting with a mixture of shame and disgust at the 'thirdworldliness' of what we saw, and with amazement and humane wonder at the peculiarities of Chinese resilience that we encountered. I felt caught in-between: I felt like wanting to protect China from the too harsh a judgement which I imagined my fellow travellers would pass upon it, but at the same time, I felt a rather irrational anger towards China itself – at its 'backwardness', its unworldliness, the seemingly naive way in which it tried to woo western tourists. I said goodbye to Lan-lan and was hoping that she would say something personal to me, an acknowledgement of affinity of some sort, but she didn't.

II

I am recounting this story for a number of reasons. First of all, it is my way of explaining why I am writing this paper in English, not in Chinese. Perhaps the very fact that I feel like explaining is interesting in itself. Throughout my life, I have been implicitly or explicitly categorized, willy-nilly, as a 'Chinese'. I look Chinese. Why then don't I speak Chinese? I have had to explain this apparent oddity countless times, so I might just as well do it here too, even though I might run the risk, in being 'autobiographical', of coming over as self-indulgent, of resorting to personal experience as a privileged source of authority, uncontrollable and therefore unamendable to others. However, let me use this occasion to shelter myself under the authority of Stuart Hall: 'Autobiography is usually thought of as seizing the authority of authenticity. But in order not to be authoritative, I've got to speak autobiographically.'[2] If, as Janet Gunn has put it, autobiography is not conceived as 'the private act of a self writing' but as 'the cultural act of a self reading',[3] then what is at stake in autobiographical discourse is not the narcissistic representation of the subject's

2. Stuart Hall, 'Cultural Studies and its Theoretical Legacies', in Lawrence Grossberg, Cary Nelson and Paula Treichler (eds), *Cultural Studies*, Routledge, New York 1992, p277.

3. Janet V. Gunn, *Autobiography: Towards a Poetics of Experience*, University of Pennsylvania Press, Philadelphia 1982, p8.

4. *Ibid.*, p23.

authentic 'me', but the narrative construction of a subject's social location through the active interpretation of experiences that one calls one's own in particular, 'worldly' contexts,[4] that is to say, a reflexive positioning of oneself in history and culture. In this respect, I would like to consider autobiography as a more or less deliberate, rhetorical construction of a 'self' for *public*, not private purposes: the displayed self is a strategically fabricated performance, one which stages a *useful* identity, an identity which can be put to work. It is the quality of that usefulness which determines the politics of autobiographical discourse. In other words, what is the identity being put forward *for*?

So I am aware that in speaking about how it is that I don't speak Chinese, while still for the occasion identifying with being, and presenting myself as, an 'Overseas Chinese', I am committing a political act. I care to say, however, that it is not my intention to just carve out a new niche in what Elspeth Probyn dismissively calls 'the star-coded politics of identity',[5] although I should confess that there is considerable, almost malicious, pleasure in the flaunting of my own 'difference' for critical intellectual purposes. But I hope to get away with this self-empowering indulgence, this exploitation of my ethnic privilege, by moving beyond the particulars of my mundane individual existence. Stuart Hall has proposed a theorization of identity as 'a form of representation which is able to constitute us as new kinds of subjects, and thereby enable us to discover places from which to speak'.[6] To put it differently, the politics of self-(re)presentation as Hall sees it reside not in the establishment of an identity *per se*, full-fledged and definitive, but in its use as a strategy to open up avenues for new speaking trajectories, the articulation of new lines of theorizing. Thus, what I hope to substantiate in staging my 'Chinese identity' here – or better, my (troubled) relationship to 'Chineseness' – is precisely the notion of *precariousness* of identity which has preoccupied cultural studies for some time now. As Gayatri Chakravorty Spivak has noted, the practice of 'speaking as' (for example, as a woman, an Indian, a Chinese) always involves a distancing from oneself since one's subjectivity is never fully steeped in the modality of the speaking position one inhabits at any one moment.[7] In this vein, my autobiographical tales of Chineseness are meant to illuminate the very *difficulty* of constructing a position from which I can speak *as* an (Overseas) Chinese, and therefore the *indeterminacy* of Chineseness as a signifier for 'identity'.

At the same time, I want to mobilize the autobiographic – that is, the narrating of life as lived, thereby rescuing notions of 'experience' and 'emotion' for cultural theorizing[8] – in order to critique the formalist, postmodernist tendency to overgeneralize the global currency of so-called nomadic, fragmented and deterritorialized subjectivity. This 'nomadology' only serves to decontextualize and flatten out difference, as if 'we' were all in fundamentally similar ways always-already travellers in the same postmodern universe, the only difference residing in the different itineraries we undertake.[9] Epistemologically, such a gross universalization of the metaphor of travel runs the danger of reifying, at a conveniently dehistoricized level, the infinite and permanent flux in subject formation, thereby foregrounding what Lata Mani

5. Elspeth Probyn, 'Technologizing the Self', in Lawrence Grossberg, Cary Nelson, Paula Treichler (eds), *op.cit.*, p502.

6. Stuart Hall, 'Cultural Identity and Diaspora', in Jonathan Rutherford (ed), *Identity: Community, Culture, Difference*, Lawrence & Wishart, London 1990, pp222-237.

7. Gayatri Chakravorty Spivak, *The Post-Colonial Critic*, ed. Sarah Harasym, Routledge, New York & London 1990, p60.

8. See for a good example of the use of the autobiographical method for cultural theorizing, Carolyn Steedman, *Landscape for a Good Woman*, Virago, London 1986.

calls an abstract, depoliticized, and internally undifferentiated notion of difference.[10] Against this tendency, which paradoxically only leads to a complacent *in*difference toward real differences, I would like to stress the importance of paying attention to the particular historical conditions and the specific trajectories through which actual social subjects become incommensurably different *and* similar. That is to say, in the midst of the postmodern flux of nomadic subjectivities we need to recognize the continuing and continuous operation of 'fixing' performed by the categories of race and ethnicity, as well as class, gender, geography and so on in the formation of 'identity'. Although it is never possible, as determinist theories would have it, to decide ahead of time *how* such markers of difference will inscribe their salience and effectivity in the course of concrete histories, and which meanings accrue to them in the context of specific social, cultural and political conjunctures. It is some of the peculiarities of the operative dynamics of 'Chineseness' as a racial and ethnic category which I would like to highlight here. What I would like to propose is that 'Chineseness' is a homogenizing label whose meanings are not fixed and pregiven, but constantly renegotiated and rearticulated, both inside and outside China.

But this brings me also to the *limits* of the polysemy of Chineseness. These limits are contained in the idea of diaspora, the (imagined) condition of a 'people' dispersed throughout the world, by force or by choice. Diasporas are transnational, spatially and temporally sprawling sociocultural formations of people, creating imagined communities whose blurred and fluctuating boundaries are sustained by real and/or symbolic ties to some original 'homeland'. As the editors of *Public Culture* have put it, 'diasporas always leave a trail of collective memory about another place and time and create new maps of desire and of attachment.'[11] It is the myth of the (lost or idealized) homeland, the object of both collective memory and of desire and attachment, which is constitutive to diasporas, and which ultimately confines and constrains the nomadism of the diasporic subject. In the rest of this essay, I will describe some moments of how this pressure toward diasporic identification with the mythic homeland took place in my own life. In the end, what I hope to unravel are some of the possibilities and problems of the cultural politics of diaspora. But this, too, cannot be done in general terms: not only is the situation different for different diasporas (Jewish, African, Indian, Chinese and so on), there are also multiple differences within each diasporic constituency. Let me start, therefore, from my own perspective, my own peculiar positioning.

III

I was born in post-colonial Indonesia into a middle-class, Peranakan Chinese family. The term 'Peranakan', meaning 'children of the country', is generally used by people of Chinese descent born and bred in South-east Asia.[12] The status of the Peranakans as 'Chinese' has always been somewhat ambiguous. This is what I know about their received history. I present it in the form of an

9. James Clifford, 'Travelling Cultures', in Lawrence Grossberg, Cary Nelson and Paula Treichler (eds), *op.cit.*, pp96–112.

10. Lata Mani, 'Cultural Theory, Colonial Texts: Reading Eyewitness Accounts of Widow Burning', in Lawrence Grossberg, Cary Nelson & Paula Treichler (eds), *op.cit.*, pp392-3.

11. 'Editors' Comment: On Moving Targets', *Public Culture*, 2 (1) 1989: 1.

12. The word 'peranakan' is derived from the Malay world for child, 'anak', which is also the root of, for example, 'beranak', to give birth. Other terms used to designate Peranakan Chinese in Malaysia and Singapore are 'Baba' (for the males), 'Nyonya' (married female) and 'Nona' (unmarried female), or 'Straits Chinese'.

all too simplified – and selective – linear narrative. They arrived in what is now known as Indonesia, Malaysia and Singapore centuries ago. Having settled as traders and craftsmen in this South-east Asian region long before the European colonialists did – in the case of Indonesia, the Dutch – they tended to have lost many of the cultural features usually attributed to Chinese, including everyday practices related to food, dress and language. Most Peranakans lost their command over the Chinese language a long time ago and actually spoke their own brand of Malay, a sign of their intensive mixing with the locals, not least through intermarriage. This orientation toward integration and assimilation in the newly adopted place of residence was partly induced by their exclusion from the homeland by an Imperial Decree of China, dating from the early eighteenth century, which formally prohibited Chinese from leaving and re-entering China: after 1726 Chinese subjects who settled abroad would face the death penalty if they returned.[13] This policy only changed with the weakening of the Qing dynasty at the end of the nineteenth century, which prompted a mass emigration from China, and signalled the arrival of the so-called Totok Chinese in Indonesia, who understandably had much closer personal and cultural ties with the ancestral homeland.[14]

However, so the history books tell me, even among the Peranakans a sense of Chineseness prevailed throughout the centuries. If this is the case, then a sense of 'ethnic naturalism' seems to have been at work here, for which I have not found a satisfactory explanation so far. Why is it that these early Chinese traders and merchants still maintained their sense of difference from the locals? This is something that the history books do *not* tell me. Tineke Jansen, speaking about the early colonial period, has this to say: 'The "Chineseness" of the earlier [Peranakan] settlers could survive through the creation of a separate ethnic community, whereby especially the registration of the Chinese names functioned to peg down what was left of [their] cultural "Chineseness" '.[15] Jansen indicates that before the Dutch arrived, the term Peranakan already circulated on Java to refer to people with a Chinese father who were culturally Javanese, but that the term's explicitly racial association with 'Chineseness' was articulated only by the Dutch rulers. Does this suggest that before European colonialism, the Peranakan did not identify themselves in essentialist ethnic or racial terms? If this is so, then we can concur with Dipesh Chakrabarty's forceful argument that 'ethnicity' as an objectivist, absolutist means of categorizing people is a modern concept, introduced by the Europeans into the colonized world as an instrument of control and governmentality.[16] But the question still remains: what is the relation between external, political pressures and internal or 'spontaneous' forms of tribal identification?

So much seems to be clear: the construction of the Indonesian-Chinese as a separate ethnic group was reinforced considerably by the ever stricter divide-and-rule policies in the three hundred years of Dutch colonialism. Dubbed 'foreign Orientals' by the Dutch colonizers, both Peranakans and Totoks – categorized together as 'Chinese' – were subjected to forms of surveillance and control which set them apart from both the Europeans and

13. Leo Suryadinata, *Primubi Indonesians, the Chinese Minority and China*, Heinemann, Kuala Lumpur, 1975, p86; Stephen Fitzgerald, *China and the Overseas Chinese*, Cambridge University Press, Cambridge 1975, p5.

14. 'Totok' is an Indonesian term meaning 'pure blood foreigner'. The Peranakans used the term 'singkeh' to designate this category of Chinese, meaning 'newcomers'.

15. Tineke E. Jansen, *Defining New Domains: Identity Politics in International Female Migration: Indonesian-Chinese Women in the Netherlands*, Working Paper Series no.121, Institute of Social Studies, The Hague, 1991, p23.

16. Dipesh Chakrabarty, 'Modernity and Ethnicity in India', in: *Communal/Plural 1: Identity/Community/Change*, University of Western Sydney, Nepean: 1993, pp1-16.

Eurasians in the colony on the one hand, and from the indigenous locals on the other. For example, increasingly strict pass and zoning systems were enforced by the Dutch on the Chinese in the last decades of the nineteenth century, requiring them to apply for visas whenever they wanted to travel outside of their neighbourhoods. Moreover, those neighbourhoods could only be established in strict districts, separate residential areas for Chinese.[17] Arguably, the widespread resentment caused by such policies of apartheid accounted for the initial success of the pan-Chinese nationalist movement which emerged in the early decades of the twentieth century. In this period diverse and dispersed Chinese groups (Hokkiens, Hakkas, Cantonese, as well as ethnic Chinese from different class and religious backgrounds) were mobilized to transform their self-consciousness into one of membership in the greater imagined community of a unified pan-Chinese nation – a politicization which was also a response to the imperialist assault on China, the distant 'homeland', in the late 1890s. According to Lea Williams, Overseas Chinese Nationalism was the only possible way for ethnic Chinese at that time to better their collective conditions as a minority population in the Dutch Indies. However, animosity and cultural differences continued to divide Totoks and Peranakans. The Peranakans only partly responded to calls for their resinification, predominantly in the form of education in Chinese language, values and customs. This made the Totoks regard the Peranakan Chinese as 'unpatriotic' and behaving like 'non-Chinese'.[18]

Peranakan Chinese identity then is, and has always been, a thoroughly hybrid identity. In the period before World War Two Chinese Malay (bahasa Melayu Tionghoa) was Malay in its basic structure, but Hokkien and Dutch terms were extensively used.[19] My grandmother was sent to a Dutch-Chinese school in Batavia, but her diary, while mainly written in Dutch, is interspersed with Malay words and Chinese characters I can't read. In the late 1920s, encouraged by the Chinese nationalist mood of the day, my grandfather decided to go 'back' to the homeland and set up shop there, only to realize that the mainland Chinese no longer saw him as 'one of them'. Upon his return to Indonesia, he sent his daughters (my mother and her sister) to study in the Netherlands. At the same time other Peranakans were of the opinion that 'it was in the interests of Peranakan Chinese to side with Indonesians rather than with the Dutch'.[20] It is not uncommon for observers to describe the Peranakan Chinese situation in the pre-World War Two period as one caught 'between three worlds'. Some more wealthy Peranakan families invested in the uncertain future by sending one child to a Dutch school, another to a Chinese one, and a third to an Indonesian school.[21]

However, so the story continues, all this changed when Dutch colonialism was finally defeated after World War Two. Those who were previously the ruled in the power structure, the indigenous Indonesians, were now the rulers. Under these new circumstances, most Peranakans, including my parents, chose to become Indonesian citizens, although they remained ethnic Chinese. But it was a Chineseness which for political reasons was not allowed to be cultivated.

17. Lea E. Williams, *Overseas Chinese Nationalism*, The Free Press, Glencoe, Ill.: 1960, pp27-33. It should be noted that the practices of the Dutch colonizers were particularly oppressive in this respect. A fundamental principle of British colonialism, universal equality before the law, was conspicuously absent in the Dutch system. Singapore Chinese under British rule, for example, were not burdened with hated pass and zoning systems. (Williams, *op.cit.*, p43). Such historical specificities make it difficult to generalize over all Peranakans in the South-East Asian region: the differential western colonialisms have played a central role in forming and forging specific Peranakan cultures.

18. Suryadinata, *op.cit.*, p94.

19. *Ibid.*

20. *Ibid.*, p57. This view was expressed, for example, by the Partai Tionghoa Indonesia (the Indonesian Chinese Party), founded in 1932, which was Indonesia-oriented and identified itself with Indonesia rather than China or the Netherlands. Suryadinata does not say how popular this position was.

21. Leonard Blussé, *Tribuut aan China*, Cramwinckel, Amsterdam 1989, p172.

22. Suryadinata, *op.cit*, p45. See for the rise of Indonesian nationalism also Benedict Anderson, *Imagined Communities*, Verso, London 1983.

Indonesian nationalism has always tended to define the Indonesian nation as comprising only the indigenous peoples of the island, excluding the Chinese – and other 'non-natives' such as the Arabs – who were considered an 'alien minority'.[22] To this day the pressure on the Chinese minority to assimilate, to erase as many traces of Chineseness as possible, has been very strong in Indonesia; for example, in the late sixties my uncle, who chose to stay and live in Indonesia, Indonesianized his surname into Angka.

It would be too easy, however, to condemn such assimilationist policies as just the result of ordinary racism on the Indonesians' part. This is a difficult point as I am implicated in the politics of memory here. How can I know 'what happened' in the past except through the stories I hear and read? And the stories don't cohere: they are a mixture of stories of oppression and opportunism. I was told stories about discrimination, about how the Indonesians didn't like 'us' Chinese because 'we' were more well-off (and often by implication: because 'we' worked harder). But I also heard stories about how the Chinese exploited the indigeneous Indonesians: how, under the rule of the Dutch, the Chinese felt safe because the Dutch would protect them from the ire of the Indonesians, and became rich in the meantime. Yes, the retort goes, but 'we' were forced into the trading professions because we were not allowed to do other jobs ...

In retrospect, I am not interested in reconstructing or fabricating a 'truth' which would necessarily put the Chinese in an unambiguously favourable light – or in the position of victim. But neither am I interested in accusations such as the one made by a self-declared, morally superior black anti-racist a few years ago: 'Your parents were collaborators.' History, of course, is always ambiguous, always messy, and people remember – and therefore construct – the past in ways that reflect their present need for meaning. I am not exempt from this process. So, baggaged with my intellectual capital, I resort to Benedict Anderson's 'explanation' of the origins of Indonesian nationalism: it was precisely by the separating of the 'foreign Orientals' and the 'natives' in the colonial administration that a space was opened up for the latter, treated as lowest of the low by the Dutch, to develop a national consciousness which excluded the former.[23] So this is why the Chinese in Indonesia could never become 'true' Indonesians: it is a consequence of the modern ideology of the nation-state. But while this theoretical narrative is enabling at the general level of political and historical understanding, it has little therapeutic value at the subjective level. Concrete social subjects are cornered into contradictory and conflict-ridden conditions of existence in the turmoil of these historical developments. How do they negotiate and carve out a space for themselves in the confusion created by these conditions of existence?

23. Anderson, *op.cit.*, especially p112.

My mother, who was born in 1926 and spent part of her youth in China (as a result of my grandfather's brief romance with the homeland) and who speaks and writes Chinese fluently, carefully avoided passing on this linguistic heritage to me. So I was cut off from this immense source of cultural capital; instead, I learned to express myself in *bahasa Indonesia*. Still, it was in my early youth in

Indonesia that I was first yelled at, 'Why don't you go back to your own country?' – a remark all too familiar to members of immigrant minorities anywhere in the world. Trouble was, to my own best knowledge as a young girl, Indonesia *was* my own country. In Sukarno's Indonesia (1945-1965) all schoolchildren were heavily exposed to the discourses and rituals of Indonesian nationalism through compulsory 'civics lessons' (as is the case in all nations having just gained independence from colonial rule), and during that time the singing of *Indonesia Merdeka* (the nation's anthem) did make me feel intensely and proudly Indonesian. Therefore, to be told – mostly by Javanese kids – that I actually didn't belong there but in a faraway, abstract, and somewhat frightening place called China, was terribly confusing, disturbing, and utterly unacceptable. I silently rebelled, I didn't *want* to be Chinese. To be sure, this is the kind of denial which is the inner drive underpinning the urge towards assimilation. That is to say, cultural assimilation is not only and not always an official policy forced and imposed by host countries upon their non-native minorities; there is also among many members of minority groups themselves a certain *desire* to assimilate, a longing for fitting in rather than standing out, even though this desire is often at the same time contradicted by an incapability or refusal to adjust and adapt completely.

Chineseness then, at that time, to me was an imposed identity, one that I desperately wanted to get rid of. It is therefore rather ironic that it was precisely our Chinese ethnicity which made my parents decide to leave Indonesia for the Netherlands in 1966, as a result of the rising ethnic tensions in the country. This experience in itself then was a sign of the inescapability of my own Chineseness, inscribed as it was on the very surface of my body, much like what Frantz Fanon has called the 'corporeal malediction' of the fact of his blackness.[24] The 'corporeal malediction' of Chineseness, of course, relates to the more general 'fact of yellowness', characterized amongst others by those famous 'slanted eyes'. During the Los Angeles 'riots' in 1992 my uncle, who lives there, felt threatened because, as he said, he could be mistaken for a Korean. However, I should point to the odd trajectories of labelling that are involved even here: when I was in Hong Kong my (Hong Kong Chinese) host assured me that people wouldn't expect me to be able to speak Chinese because I would surely be mistaken for a Filipina. That is to say, racial categories obviously do not exist outside cultural and spatial context, but are thoroughly framed by and within it.

Anyway, in the new country, the former colonizer's country, a new cycle of forced and voluntary assimilation started all over again. My cherished Indonesian identity got lost in translation, as it were, as I started a life in a new language.[25] In the Netherlands I quickly learned to speak Dutch, went to a Dutch school and a Dutch university and for more than two decades underwent a thorough process of 'Dutchification'. However, the artificiality of 'national identity' – and therefore the relativeness of any sense of historical truth – was brought home to me forever when my Dutch history book taught me that Indonesia became independent in 1949. In Indonesia I had always

24. Frantz Fanon, *Black Skin, White Masks*, Paladin, London 1970, Chapter 5.

25. I derive this phrase from Eva Hoffman, *Lost in Translation*, Penguin, Harmondsworth 1989. In this book Hoffman tells the story of her own migration from Poland to Canada.

been led to celebrate 17 August 1945 as Independence Day. The disparity was technical: Sukarno *declared* Indonesia's independence in 1945, but the Dutch only *recognized* it in 1949, after four years of bloody war. But it's not the nuances of the facts that matter; what is significant is the way in which nations choose to construct their collective memories, how they narrate themselves into pride and glory.[26] The collision of the two versions of history in my educational experience may have paved the way for my permanent suspicion toward any self-confident and self-evident 'truth' in my later intellectual life. As Salman Rushdie has remarked, those who have experienced cultural displacement are *forced* to accept the provisional nature of all truths, all certainties.[27]

At the level of everyday experience, the fact of my Chineseness confronted me only occasionally in the Netherlands, for example when passing ten year old redhaired boys triumphantly shouting behind my back, while holding the outer ends of their eyes upwards with their forefingers: 'Ching Chong China China', or when, on holiday in Spain or Italy or Poland, people would not believe that I was 'Dutch'. The typical conversation would run like this, as any non-white person in Europe would be able to testify:

'Where are you from?'

'From Holland.'

'No, where are you *really* from?'

To this usually insistent, repetitive and annoying inquiry into origins, my standard story has become, 'I was born in Indonesia but my ancestors were from China' – a shorthand (re)presentation of self for convenience's sake. Such incidents were disturbing signals of the impossibility of complete integration (or perhaps 'naturalization' is a better term), no matter how much I (pragmatically) strived for it. As Paul Gilroy puts it, '[s]triving to be both European and black requires some specific forms of double consciousness'.[28] That is, it is the very question 'where are you from' – a question so easily thrown up as the bottomline of cultural identity (thereby equating cultural identity with national identity) – which lacks transparency here. Of course, this is a problem shared by millions of people throughout the world today, where migration has become an increasingly common phenomenon.

The experience of migration brings with it a shift in perspective: to paraphrase Gilroy, for the migrant it is no longer 'where you're from', but 'where you're at' which forms the point of anchorage.[29] However, so long as the question 'where you're from' prevails over 'where you're at' in dominant culture, the compulsion to explain, the inevitable positioning of yourself as deviant *vis-à-vis* the normal, remains – especially for those migrants marked by visible difference. In other words, the relation between 'where you're from' and 'where you're at' is a deeply problematic one. It is this very problem which is constitutive of the idea of diaspora, and for which the idea of diaspora attempts to be a solution, where the adversity of 'where you're at' produces the cultivation of a lost 'where you're from'. As William Safran has put it, 'diaspora consciousness is an intellectualization of an existential condition',[30] an existential condition – which is always socially and politically determined – that

26. Cf. Homi Bhabha (ed), *Nation and Narration*, Routledge, London 1990.

27. Salman Rushdie, *Imaginary Homelands*, Granta Books, London 1991, p12 (emphasis mine).

28. Paul Gilroy, *The Black Atlantic: Modernity and Double Consciousness*, Verso, London 1993, p1.

29. Paul Gilroy, 'It Ain't Where You're From, It's Where You're At ... The Dialectics of Diasporic Identification', in *Third Text*, 13, Winter 1990/91, pp3-16.

30. William Safran, 'Diasporas in Modern Societies: Myths of Homeland and Return', in *Diaspora* 1 (1) 1991: p87.

becomes understood and reconciled through the myth of a homeland from which one is removed but to which one actually belongs. But I would argue that this solution, at least at the cultural level, is by no means sufficient or unambiguously gratifying: in fact, the diasporic imagination itself creates and articulates a number of new problems.

However much Peranakan Chinese families who migrated to the cold and windy Netherlands were determined to 'make it' in the new country, the regime of ethnicity has made it increasingly inevitable for many of them, including me, to call ourselves 'Chinese'. However, such (self)ethnicization, which is in itself a confirmation of minority status in white, western culture, can paradoxically serve as an alibi for what Rey Chow has called 'prescribed "otherness" ',[31] a sign of not-belonging, a declaration of actually belonging somewhere else. If this happens, the discursive conditions are established for the credentials of this diasporic identification with being 'Chinese' to be routed back to essentialist and absolute notions of 'Chineseness', the source of which can only originate in 'China', to which the ethnicized 'Chinese' subject must adhere to acquire the stamp of 'authenticity'. So it was one day that a self-assured, Dutch, white, middle-class Marxist, asked me, 'Do you speak Chinese?' I said no. 'What a fake Chinese you are!', was his only mildly kidding response, thereby unwittingly but aggressively adopting the disdainful position of judge to sift 'real' from 'fake' Chinese. In other words, in being defined and categorized diasporically, I was found wanting.

31. Rey Chow, *Woman and Chinese Modernity*, University of Minnesota Press, Minneapolis 1991, pxvi.

'Not speaking Chinese', therefore, has become a personal political issue to me, an existential condition which goes beyond the particularities of an arbitrary personal history. It is a condition that has been hegemonically constructed as a lack, a sign of loss of 'authenticity'. This, then, is the reason why I felt compelled to apologize that I have to speak to you in English – the global lingua franca which is one of the clearest expressions of the pervasiveness of western hegemony. Yet it is precisely this urge to apologize which I would now like to question and counter as well. In order to do this, however, I need to come to terms with my ambiguous relationship to 'Chineseness', the complexities and contradictions of which were dramatized in the story about my one-day visit to China and my encounter with Lan-lan. It was, of course, a drama born precisely of a diaspora problematic.

IV

If the 'Indonesian Chinese' can be described as a distinctive 'people' – one which, as I have sketched above, has its historical birth in colonial Dutch East Indies, – then they in turn have become diasporized, especially after the military coup of 1965. While my parents, among many thousands, chose for the relative wealth and comfort of a life in Holland ('for the sake of the education of the children'), I was recently informed by an aunt that I have some distant relatives in Brazil, where two hundred Indonesian Chinese families live in Sao Paulo. There is also a large Indonesian Chinese community

32. Michael R. Godley
and Charles A.
Koppel, 'The
Indonesian Chinese in
Hong Kong: A
Preliminary Report in
a Minority Community
in Transition', *Issues &
Studies: A Journal of
Chinese Studies and
International Affairs*,
July 1990, pp94-108.

in Hong Kong, many of whom ended up there after a brief 'return' to the 'homeland'; they then escaped from Mao's China (where they found, like my grandfather earlier in the century, that their very 'Chineseness' was cast in doubt).[32] Nevertheless, while generally well-integrated in Dutch society, the Indonesian Chinese in the Netherlands have re-ethnicized themselves tremendously in the last decade or so, and it is 'Chineseness', not 'Indonesianness' which forms the primary focal point of ethnic identification, especially for the older generation. There are now Peranakan Chinese associations, sports and entertainment clubs, discussion evenings; lessons in Chinese language and culture, and special trips to China are being organized. Over the last five to ten years or so, my parents have built up a large video collection of films and documentaries about China and China-related subjects, all taped from television (and it is amazing how often European public television features programmes about China!). Whenever I visit them these days, I am ensured of a new dose of audio-visual education in Chineseness, as it were, as we together watch films about the Yellow River, the Silk Route, Taoism, Confucian values, Chinese village life, the Great Wall, the Chinese Red Army, the history of Chinese Communism, the Tiananmen Square Massacre, or whatever is available, or otherwise any Chinese feature film that was recently televized (the Fifth Generation films loom large here), and so on and so on. So my familiarization with the imputed 'homeland', and therefore my emotional subjection to the homeland myth, has been effected rather informally, through intimate and special family rituals and practices. In other words, I felt I already 'knew' China, albeit a mythic China, a fetishized China, when I went there for that one day visit.

In her book *Sons of the Yellow Emperor*, Lynn Pan describes how many overseas Chinese cling to a place they have left behind, sometimes even centuries ago:

> China has repeatedly dashed their hopes, and remains to this day a country to occasion despair, a country to get away from ... Even so, the millions who live outside it will never cease to wish it well, to want for it a place among the great nations, not only for the sake of their own pride and dignity, but because they find it hard to resist its power to compel tribal feeling. If they revolt against it, that itself is a reference and a tribute to the potency of what has been left behind.[33]

33. Lynn Pan, *Sons of
The Yellow Emperor*,
Mandarin, London
1990, p379.

And indeed, it is well known that strong institutional links continue to connect China intimately with overseas Chinese communities in South-East Asia, the Americas, Australia and elsewhere. The current economic boom in southern China, for example, is largely due to capital investments of overseas Chinese entrepreneurs.[34] As Pan says, it is 'not philosophy but money and methods [that] have been the chief contribution of the emigrant Chinese to China'.[35] But if this orientation toward the 'homeland' is, at least in part, effected by China's 'power to compel tribal feeling', how does it complicate the problem of identity in the diaspora?

The symbolic construction of 'China' as the cultural/geographical core of

34. 'Chinese Diaspora
Turns Homeward',
The Economist, Number
329, November 1993,
pp33-4.

35. Pan, *op.cit.*, p379.

'Chinese identity' forces 'westernized' overseas Chinese to take up a humble position, even a position of shame and inadequacy over her own 'impurity'. As Rey Chow has observed, 'Chinese from the mainland are [often felt to be] more "authentic" than those who are from, say, Taiwan or Hong Kong, because the latter have been "Westernized".'[36] But the problem is exacerbated for more remote members of the Chinese diaspora, say for the Indonesian Peranakan Chinese or for second-generation Chinese Americans, whose 'Chineseness' is even more diluted and impure. In this situation the overseas Chinese is in a no-win situation: she is either 'too Chinese' or 'not Chinese enough'. In the West, she will never be able to erase the traces of her 'Chineseness' – no matter how 'westernized', she can never pass as white – but in China, the first thing thrown at her is her lack of 'Chineseness', especially if 'she doesn't even speak Chinese!'

Of course, this double-bind problem is not unique to migrants of Chinese descent. In a sense, it enters into the experience of all diasporic peoples. What is particular to the Chinese diaspora, however, is that the extraordinarily strong originary pull of the 'homeland' colludes with the prominent place of 'China' in the western imagination. The West's fascination with China as a great, Other civilization began with Marco Polo and remains to this day.[37] In the western imagination China cannot be an ordinary country, so that everything happening there is invested with more than 'normal' significance, as most recently testified by the intense and extreme dramatization of the Tienanmen Massacre in the western media. There is, in other words, an excess of meaningfulness accorded to 'China'; 'China' has often been useful for western thinkers as a symbol, negative or positive, for that which the West was not. As Zhang Longxi has noted, even Jacques Derrida, the great debunker of binary oppositions, was seduced into treating the non-phonetic character of the Chinese language as 'testimony of a powerful movement of civilization developing outside of all logocentrism', that is, as the sign of a culture totally different from what he conceives as western culture.[38] Worse still, this powerful Othering is mirrored by an equally strong and persistent tendency within Chinese culture itself to consider itself as unique within the world, exemplified by the age-old Chinese habit to designate all non-Chinese as 'barbarians', 'foreign devils' or 'ghosts'.[39] This is a form of narcissistic self-Othering expressed in the famous inward-looking aloofness of Chinese culture recently criticized (but simultaneously reproduced), within China itself, in the controversial television series *River Elegy*, and which I also sensed in Lan-lan's ultimate insistence, through a paradoxical, assertive defensiveness in relation to the West, on China's self-sufficient, Absolute Difference.[40]

When the issue of identity is at stake, overseas Chinese people often find themselves inevitably entangled in the interlocking of this mutually exclusionary discursive oppositioning of 'China' and 'the West'. China's elevated status as a privileged Other to the West has the effect of depriving them of an autonomous space in which they can determine their own trajectories for constructing cultural identity. In this sense, Rey Chow's

36. Chow, *op.cit.*, p28/9.

37. See Colin MacKerras, *Western Images of China*, Oxford University Press, Hong Kong 1991.

38. Zhang Longxi, 'The Myth of the Other: China in the Eyes of the West', in *Critical Inquiry* 15, Autumn 1988, p127.

39. See Frank Dikötter, *The Discourse of Race in Modern China*, Stanford University Press, Stanford 1992.

40. Rey Chow points to the narcissistic tendency in Chinese cultural production in the Introduction to her *Writing Diaspora*, Indiana University Press, Bloomington 1993.

observation that there is, among many Chinese people, an 'obsession with China' is an astute one. What connects the diaspora with the 'homeland' is ultimately an emotional, almost visceral attachment – a relationship which Amitav Gosh, in discussing the Indian diaspora, has characterized as an *epic* one.[41] It is the strength of this epic relationship which invests the homeland myth with its 'power to compel tribal feeling': it is this epic relationship to 'China' which made millions of overseas Chinese all over the world feel so inescapably and 'irrationally' sick and nauseous when the tanks crushed the students' movement at Tienanmen Square on June 4th, 1989, as if they felt the humiliation in their own bodies, despite the fact that many, if not most of them would never think of actually 'returning' to this distant 'motherland'. The desires, fantasies and sentimentalisms that go into this 'obsession with China', says Chow, should be seen at least in part as 'a *response* to the solicitous calls, dispersed internationally in multiple ways, to such a [collective, 'Chinese'] identity'.[42] In other words, the subjective processes of diasporic ethnic identification are often externally instigated, articulating and confirming a position of subordination in relation to western hegemony. To be sure, I think that it is this structure of dominance and subjection which I internalized when I found myself caught between my western co-tourists and Lan-lan – an *impossible* position, a position with no means of its own to assert itself.

41. Amitav Ghosh, 'The Diaspora in Indian Culture', *Public Culture* 2:1, 1989, pp73-78.

42. Chow, *Woman and Chinese Modernity*, p25.

The contradictions and complexities in subject positioning that I have tried to explicate are neatly summed up in the memoirs of Ruth Ho, a Malaysian Peranakan Chinese woman who grew up in colonial Malacca before the Second World War. In one chapter of her book, called 'On learning Chinese', she complains about the compulsory lessons in Chinese that she had to undergo as a young girl:

> Mother always felt exceedingly guilty about our language deficiency and tried to make us study Chinese, that is Mandarin, the national dialect... [But] I suppose that when I was young there was no motivation to study Chinese... 'But China was once the greatest and most cultured nation in the world! Weren't you proud to be Chinese? Wasn't that reason enough to study Chinese?' Many people felt this way but unfortunately we just didn't feel very Chinese! Today we are described by one English writer as belonging to 'the sad band of English-educated who cannot speak their own language'. This seems rather unfair to me. Must we know the language of our forefathers when we have lived in another country (Malaysia) for many years? Are the descendants of German, Norwegian and Swedish emigrants to the USA, for instance, expected to know German Norwegian or Swedish? Are the descendants of Italian and Greek emigrants to Australia expected to study Italian and Greek? Of course not, and yet overseas Chinese are always expected to know Chinese or else they are despised not only by their fellow Chinese but also by non-Chinese! Perhaps this is due to the great esteem with which Chinese history, language and culture are universally regarded. But the European emigrants to the USA and Australia also have a not

insignificant history, language and culture, and they are not criticized when they become English speaking![43]

Ho's comparison with the European immigrants to the USA and Australia is well-taken. Isn't the double standard she refers to an expression of the desire to keep western culture white? Wouldn't this explain why an English-speaking Chinese is seen, from a western perspective, as so much more 'unnatural' than an English-speaking Norwegian or Italian? From such a perspective, the politics of diaspora serves as a ploy to keep non-white, non-western elements from fully entering, and therefore contaminating, the centre of white, western culture.[44] That is, no matter how long Chinese people have lived in the West, they can only become western*ized*, never pure and simply 'western'. Ho's heartfelt indignation then should be read as a protest against such an exclusion – an exclusion effected by imposing the identification with a fetishized and overly idealized 'Chineseness'. It exemplifies the fact that when the question of 'where you're from' is made to overwhelm the reality of 'where you're at', the politics of diaspora becomes a disempowering rather than an empowering one, a hindrance to 'identity' rather than an enabling principle.

V

I am not saying here that the politics of diaspora is intrinsically oppressive, on the contrary. It is clear that many members of ethnic minorities derive a sense of joy and dignity, as well as a sense of (vicarious) belonging from their identification with a 'homeland' which is elsewhere. But it should also be noted that this very identification with an imagined 'where you're from' is often a sign of, and a surrender to, a condition of actual marginalization in the place 'where you're at'. Khachig Tölölyan has defined diasporas as 'the exemplary communities of the transnational moment' which interrogate the privileged homogeneity of the nation-state.[45] At the same time, however, the very fact that ethnic minorities within nation-states are defining themselves increasingly in diasporic terms, as Tölölyan indicates, raises some troubling questions about the state of intercultural relations in the world today. The rise of militant and separatist neo-nationalisms in Eastern Europe and elsewhere in the world signals an intensification of the appeal to an ethnic absolutism which underpins the homeland myth. This exclusionary scenario is based on the fantasy of, and desire for, a complete juncture of 'where you're from' and 'where you're at' so that, ideally, all diasporized peoples should return 'home'.[46] It is not only that such a fantasy is at odds with the forces of increasing transnationalization and globalization in world economy, politics, and communications.[47] At a more fundamental, cultural level, the fantasmatic vision of a 'new world order' consisting of hundreds of self-contained, self-identical nations – constituted by a homogenizing equivalence of race/language/ethnicity/culture – strikes me as a rather disturbing duplication of the divide-and-rule politics deployed by the colonial powers to ascertain control and mastery over the subjected. It is against

43. Ruth Ho, *Rainbow Round My Shoulder*, Eastern Universities Press, Singapore 1975, pp97-99.

44. This desire might be at the basis of the ambivalence of western policies and discourses in relation to immigration: on the one hand there is the demand for the immigrant to 'integrate' if not 'assimilate', but on the other hand there is always the denial of the very possibility of 'integration', the insistence on (residual) difference, contained in 'multiculturalism'.

45. Khachig Tölölyan, 'The Nation-State and its Others', *Diaspora*, 1 (1) 1991, pp3-7.

46. Of course, the constitution of modern Israel is based on this scenario.

47. See for a discussion of the paradox between the increasing appeal of nationalism, on the one hand, and the decline of the significance of the nation-state, on the other, E.J. Hobsbawm, *Nations and Nationalism Since 1780*, Cambridge University Press, Cambridge 1990, Chapter 6.

48. See Etienne
Balibar, 'The Nation
Form: History and
Ideology', in E. Balibar
and I. Wallerstein,
Race, Nation, Class,
Verso, London 1991.

49. Safran, *op.cit.*,
p95.

50. Homi Bhabha,
'The Third Space',
Rutherford, *op.cit.*,
pp207-221.

51. Rushdie, *op.cit.*,
p17.

such a vision, which is the ultimate dream of the principle of nationalist universalism, that the politics of diaspora can play a critical cultural role.[48]

Since diasporas are fundamentally and inevitably transnational in their scope, always linking the local and the global, the here and the there, past and present, they have the potential to unsettle essentialist and totalizing conceptions of 'national culture' or 'national identity' and to disrupt their presumption of static roots in geography and history. But in order to seize on that potential, diasporas should make *the most* of their 'complex and flexible positioning (...) between host countries and homelands', as it is precisely that complexity and flexibility which creates the vitality of diaspora cultures.[49] In other words, a critical cultural politics of diaspora should privilege neither host country nor (real or imaginary) homeland, but precisely keep a creative tension between 'where you're from' and 'where you're at'. I emphasize *creative* here to foreground the multiperspectival *productivity* of that position of in-between-ness. The notions of 'biculturality' and 'double consciousness', often used to describe this position, hardly do justice to this productivity. Such notions tend to construct the space of that ambivalent in-between-ness as an empty space, the space that gets crushed in the cultural translation from one side to the other in the bipolar dichotomy of 'where you're from' and 'where you're at'. But the productivity I am referring to precisely fills that space – what Homi Bhabha calls 'the third space' – with *new* forms of culture at the collision/collusion of the two: *hybrid* cultural forms borne out of a productive, creative syncretism.[50] This is a practice and spirit of turning necessity into opportunity, the promise of which is eloquently expressed by Salman Rushdie: 'It is normally supposed that something always gets lost in translation; I cling, obstinately, to the notion that something can always be gained.'[51]

What a recognition of the productivity of the third space of hybridity enables us to come to terms with is not only that the diasporic subject can never return to her/his 'origins', but also, more importantly, that the cultural context of 'where you're at' always informs and articulates the meaning of 'where you're from'. This is, to speak with Rushdie, what the diasporic subject gains. In this sense, hybridity marks the emancipation of the diaspora from 'China' as the transparent master-signified of 'Chineseness': instead, 'Chineseness' becomes a signifier invested with resource potential, the raw material for the construction of syncretic identities suitable for 'where you're at'.

It is by recognizing the irreducible productivity of the hybrid practices in the diaspora that 'Not speaking Chinese' will stop being held against overseas Chinese people. 'China', the mythic homeland, will then stop being the absolute norm for authentic 'Chineseness' against which all other Chinese cultures of the diaspora are measured. Instead, 'Chineseness' becomes an open signifier which acquires its peculiar form and content in dialectical junction with the diverse local conditions in which ethnic Chinese people have constructed new lives and syncretic social and cultural practices. Nowhere is this more vigorously evident than in everyday popular culture. Thus, we have the fortune cookie, a uniquely Chinese-American invention utterly unknown elsewhere in the Chinese diaspora or, for that matter, in China itself. In Malaysia one of the culinary attractions is *nyonya* food, a cuisine developed by the Peranakan Chinese out of their encounter with local, Malay spices and ingredients. A few years ago I was at a Caribbean party in Amsterdam full of immigrants from the Dutch West Indies; to my surprise the best salsa dancer there was a young man of Chinese descent who grew up in the Caribbean. There I was, facing up to my previously held essentialist prejudice that Chinese bodies cannot dance like a Latino!

Hamid Naficy is skeptical about the cultural politics of hybridity.[52] For Naficy, a celebration of the ambivalent positionalities created in the liminal space of hybridity, validated by Homi Bhabha as sites of resistance against the assimilatory impositions of the dominant culture, will only result in a postmodern proliferation of indifferent differences, of 'unattached and weightless hybrids' who are neither this nor that, neither here nor there.[53] Naficy suggests that diasporic subjects must move 'out of liminality and into ethnicity', which is 'equivalent to crossing the threshold of liminality and "entering the room" of the host culture, in order to move out of irony and into struggle to become an instrumental part of social formation of the host country'.[54] In this sense, Naficy opts unambiguously for an ultimate self-location in 'where you're at' over and above a nostalgic identification with a dreamt about 'where you're from'. As a strategy of self-empowerment, the diasporic subject had better renounce the defensiveness of hybridity, which he considers ultimately self-defeating, and create 'a third syncretic culture' in which the 'split subject may become partially whole again as a syncretic being'.[55] I would argue however that the conceptual gap between liminal hybridity and ethnic syncretism Naficy proposes here is in fact not so: rather, they are inextricably intertwined, precisely because, as I have noted earlier, the ethnicization of subjects in diaspora signals the impossibility of their complete nationalization within the dominant culture of the adopted new country.[56] The 'ethnic' subject highlights the fact that s/he does not (quite) belong to the 'host country' – or at least, s/he is positioned as such.[57] The very name with which the 'ethnic' is referred to – in this case, 'Chinese' – already transposes her or him to, and conjures up the received memory of, another site of symbolic belonging, a site which is not 'here'. In this sense liminality is the ineradicable space in-between, the structural borderzone from where the diasporic subject is compelled to construct herself into a syncretic cultural being. In other words, it is her very positioning in the hybrid borderzone of 'neither this nor that' that provides the diasporic subject with both the urgency and the resources to transform herself into a syncretic 'bit of this and a bit of that' – governed by the unerased traces of 'where you're from', no matter how mediated, but ultimately framed by the possibilities and limits offered by 'where you're at'.

The examples I have given above make it very clear that the syncretic meanings of diasporic Chineseness are the result of the irreducible *specificity* of diverse and heterogeneous hybridisations in dispersed temporal and spatial contexts. This in turn means that the unevenly scattered imagined community

52. Hamid Naficy, *The Making of Exile Cultures*, University of Minnesota Press, Minneapolis 1993.

53. Homi Bhabha, 'Signs Taken for Wonders: Questions of Ambivalence and Authority under a Tree Outside Delhi, May 1817', in: Henry Louis Gates, Jr. (ed), *'Race', Writing, and Difference*, University of Chicago Press, Chicago 1986, pp163–184.

54. Naficy, *op.cit.*, p195.

55. *ibid*.

56. Arjun Appadurai, 'Postnationalism and Its Futures', in: *Public Culture*, 5: 3, 1993, pp411-429.

57. The very term 'host country' signals the fact that 'where you're at' can not be signified simply and unproblematically as 'home' for 'ethnic' migrants.

58. What is now called 'the Chinese diaspora' purportedly consists of 'about 30 million [ethnic Chinese residing] outside China proper and Taiwan, dispersed in some 130 countries on the 6 continents' (from the brochure for 'Luodi-Shenggen: The Legal, Political, and Economic Status of Chinese in the Diaspora', an International Conference on Overseas Chinese, held in San Francisco, November 1992).

59. Chakrabarty, *op.cit.*

60. Gayatri Chakravorty Spivak, *In Other Worlds*, Routledge, London 1987, p205.

61. Stuart Hall, 'The Meaning of New Times', in Stuart Hall and Martin Jacques (eds), *New Times*, Lawrence & Wishart, London 1989, p133.

62. This distinction has been made by Werner Sollors in his *Beyond Ethnicity*, Oxford University Press, Oxford 1986.

of the diaspora itself cannot be envisioned in any unified or homogeneous way. Chinese ethnicity, as a common reference point for overseas Chinese people throughout the world,[58] cannot presume the erasure of internal differences and particularities, as well as disjunctures, as the basis of unity and collective identity. What then is still its use? Why still identify ourselves as 'overseas Chinese' at all?

The answer to this question depends on context: sometimes it is and sometimes it is *not* desirable to stress our Chineseness, however defined. In other words, the answer is political. In this thoroughly mixed-up, interdependent, mobile and volatile postmodern world, clinging to a primordial notion of ethnic identity has become one avenue for displaced peoples in their search for certainty, for a secure sense of origin and belonging, for 'roots'. Unfortunately, such a 'solution' is complicit with, and carries through, the effects of the divide-and-rule politics of colonial modernity and its aftermath, where categorical 'ethnicity' has been produced to control and contain peoples.[59] Inasmuch as the stress on 'ethnicity' provides a counterpoint to the most facile forms of postmodernist nomadology, however, we might have to develop a postmodern (rather than modern) notion of ethnicity. This postmodern ethnicity can no longer be experienced as naturally based upon tradition and ancestry; rather, it is experienced as a provisional and partial site of identity which must be constantly (re)invented and (re)negotiated. In this context, diasporic identifications with a specific ethnicity (such as 'Chineseness') can best be seen as forms of what Gayatri Spivak calls 'strategic essentialism':[60] 'strategic' in the sense of using the signifier 'Chinese' for the purpose of contesting and disrupting hegemonic majoritarian definitions of 'where you're at'; and 'essentialist' in a way which enables diasporic subjects, not to 'return home', but, in the words of Stuart Hall, to 'insist that others recognize that what they have to say comes out of particular histories and cultures and that *everyone* speaks from positions within the global distribution of power'.[61]

In short, if I am inescapably Chinese by *descent*, I am only sometimes Chinese by *consent*.[62] When and how is a matter of politics.

This paper was first presented at *Trajectories: Towards an Internationalist Cultural Studies*, a symposium held in Taipei, Taiwan, July 1992. I would like to thank the symposium participants for their inspiring and passionate comments on my reflections on 'Chineseness', as presented in this paper. An earlier version of this paper was published in the *Southeast Asian Journal of Social Science*.

LOCATING MULTICULTURALISM'S OTHER:
A CRITIQUE OF PRACTICAL TOLERANCE

Ghassan Hage

INTRODUCTION

As forms of fundamentalism, ethnic particularism and intercommunal conflict appear to be increasing, notions such as 'cultural pluralism' and 'the tolerant society' become particularly attractive. They are used both as descriptive categories of societies that maintain a semblance of social cohesion despite being 'ethnically' and 'racially' diverse, and as prescriptive categories for the many, not so lucky, conflict ridden post-colonial formations. In a paper presented at the 1992 British Sociological Association conference, the Ukrainian sociologist Tanya Koshechnika[1] argued:

> There are several reasons for the importance of studying and promoting political tolerance in post-Soviet republics. One of them is the deepening of the inter-ethnic conflicts; the increasing national and religious prejudice creates a situation in which tolerance could be seen if not as a solution at least as a possibility to alleviate the communication between the ex-Soviet republics and different ethnic groups.

1. Tanya Koshechnika, *Political Tolerance and Ex-Soviet Society*, Paper presented at the BSA Conference, University of Canterbury, Kent, 1992, p2.

She goes on to point out that: 'The claim that the free market promotes tolerance by eroding particular non-economic discrimination is very popular in ex-Soviet society now'.

In Australia notions of both cultural pluralism and the tolerant society are fused together in the policy of multiculturalism. Here too we hear of tolerance and markets, but linked in a rather different way. As a self congratulatory discourse about the success of multiculturalism in saving Australia from the pains of ethnic conflicts is emerging, voices are heard about the need to 'market the policy'. With both demand and supply available, the commodification of multiculturalism as a mode of managing post-coloniality is not unlikely.

In this essay, I shall play the contextually suitable role of a consumer protection agent and offer a critical evaluation of the new commodity. I shall question the way the discourse of tolerance within Australian multiculturalism is portrayed as an adequate attempt at promoting cultural pluralism and transcending the Anglocentric racism of the policies that preceded it. I shall argue that the very existence and social relevance of a discourse of tolerance implies the continuing presence of dominant and subjugated cultural/political formations. In particular, I shall propose that multicultural tolerance should be understood as a mode of spatial management of cultural difference while reproducing the structuring of this difference around a dominant culture.

THE PARADOXES OF PRACTICAL (IN)TOLERANCE

The theme of tolerance first makes its appearance as a political/practical state policy in the Muslim empires that followed the Islamic expansionary wars, and much later in Europe during the Enlightenment. In both cases, tolerance or toleration emerged as a state policy with an anti-discriminatory intent, aimed at regulating relations between various religious communities.

Given the religious foundations of the Islamic state, the policy of tolerance was a result of an automatic translation of the Islamic *Shari'a* law towards religious minorities. Under the *Shari'a*, Christians and Jews, being 'people of the book', were to be tolerated. They were the *dhumma* or those to be protected, albeit for an extra tax which no doubt provided the rulers with another incentive for their toleration. In Christian Europe, laws advocating tolerance such as the English Toleration Act of 1689 appeared after centuries of religious intolerance epitomised by the Inquisitions. The calls for tolerance came both from inside and outside the Church. However, while some commentators argued for tolerance by appealing to 'reason', the more influential, like Locke in *A Letter Concerning Toleration* (1689) and Voltaire in *Traité sur la Tolerance* (1763), base most of their argument on a return to Christian religious texts.

What is striking about these early periods of state-advocated tolerance is how often they remain marked by *intolerance*. In England, the introduction of the Toleration Act in 1689, while easing some of the penalties imposed on dissenting clergy by the 'Clarendon Code' of the 1660s[2] co-existed with a whole series of discriminatory practices against Nonconformists, who continued to be shut out of public offices, both civil and military,[3] while discrimination against Roman Catholics remained in full force, including restrictions on their freedom of movement.[4] Some of these restrictions remained till much later, even after the Roman Catholic Emancipation Act introduced in the beginning of the nineteenth century (1829). The latter contained 'provisions against Catholics exercising certain rights of patronage, enjoying named offices, and even a clause – never carried into effect – for the suppression of religious orders of men.'[5]

This co-existence of tolerance and intolerance is best exemplified by the politics of tolerance under Islamic law. Under Muslim rule, the *dhumma* status of Christians and Jews legitimised a whole range of discriminatory measures aimed at establishing the superiority of Islam and its protection. The 'tolerated ones' were to wear special clothing; they were forbidden to ride horses or to carry guns; they could not build new churches or synagogues, or practise their religion publicly in front of Muslims. These laws aimed at the marginalisation of the non-Islamic communities, and although not always strictly implemented, the latter suffered in certain circumstances what Maxime Rodinson describes as 'outbreaks of intolerance on the part of the Muslim mob'.[6]

What is important about this co-existence of tolerance and intolerance, whether in the early Islamic period or in today's multicultural societies, is not

2. M. Ashley, *England in the Seventeenth Century*, (eighth edition), Hutchinson, London, 1978, pp133-134.

3. *Ibid.*, p188.

4. *Ibid.*, p40.

5. E.R. Norman, *Anti-Catholicism in Victorian England*, George Allen and Unwin, London 1968, p131.

6. Maxime Rodinson, *Marxism and the Muslim World*, Monthly Review Press, New York 1981, p8.

that tolerance was somehow not forcefully implemented. Rather, it is that those who were and are asked to be tolerant seem to remain *capable* of being intolerant, or to put it differently, that the advocacy of tolerance left people *empowered* to be intolerant. When they wished and felt capable of exercising their power to be intolerant, people did, since the advocacy of tolerance never really challenged *their capacity* to exercise this power.

This is something a number of those who have critically reflected on the term have well understood: Mirabeau once declared: 'Je ne viens pas prêcher la tolérance ... le mot tolérance ... me paraît, en quelque sorte, tyrannique lui-même, puisque l'autorité qui tolère pourrait ne pas tolérer'[7]; Lyotard argues in *Heidegger and 'the Jews'* that: 'Today, hatred comes softly as integration of "the jews" into a permissive collectivity in the name of the "respect for differences" ... The modern version of the church can lend itself to this show of tolerance. One has to keep in mind that ... *tollere* and *aufheben* connote, at the same time, the supression as well as the elevation of what one tolerates.'[8] Preston King in his work *Toleration* gives us an elaborate examination of the many vicissitudes of the term. He begins his analysis by pointing out that:

> There is something intolerable about the concept of 'tolerance'. For if one concedes or promotes a power to tolerate, one equally concedes a power not to tolerate ... Where we empower an agent to be tolerant, we empower him equally to be intolerant.[9]

When those who are intolerant are asked to be tolerant, their power to be intolerant is not taken away from them, they are simply requested not to exercise it. In fact, the very existence of a policy advocating tolerance implies the continuing existence of the power to be intolerant: why would anyone bother asking someone who has no power to be intolerant to be tolerant?

It is this 'power' dimension that has been continuously mystified by liberal writing on tolerance exemplified by Locke and Voltaire's classical texts. In the latter, the mystification occurs as a result of an emphasis on an abstract/philosophical relation between 'religions' rather than on actual practical relations between religious groupings. It is from such a perspective that Voltaire can make pronouncements on 'universal tolerance', implying a kind of communism of tolerance whereby the capacity and the power to tolerate is equally distributed among all those doing the toleration.[10] Likewise Locke is capable of beginning his *A Letter Concerning Toleration* by advocating the concept of 'mutual tolerance', presupposing a rather absurd relation between 'tolerators' without any 'tolerated'.[11] In the absence of a sociological perspective which grounds the possibility of tolerance in the existing social relations of power, this possibility is idealistically located in the prescribed adoption of a rational/ethical ('truly' religious) attitude.

Yet, the sociological dimension of the relations of power in which the discourse of tolerance is grounded manages to escape out of the many fissures of the moral/prescriptive writings of both Locke and Voltaire. This happens,

7. Cited in Preston King, *Toleration*, George Allen & Unwin, London 1976, p8.

8. Jean-François Lyotard, *Heidegger and 'the Jews'*, University of Minnesota Press, Minneapolis 1991, pp39-40.

9. King, *op.cit.*, p6.

10. Voltaire, 'Traité sur la Tolerance' in *L'Affaire Calas*, Éditions Gallimard, Paris 1763 (1975 edition), p176.

11. John Locke, *Letters on Toleration*, Education Society Press, Byculla 1689 (1867 edition), p1.

12. Voltaire, *op.cit.*, pp.135-136.

13. Locke, *op.cit.*, p7.

for example, when Voltaire slips into a more sociological language to talk explicitly of 'the dominant religion';[12] and more implicitly, when Locke, urges toleration since 'it is only light and evidence that can work a change in men's opinions; and that light can in no manner proceed from corporal sufferings, or any other outward penalties', he reveals that those he is urging to be tolerant are necessarily those who have the power to inflict on others penalties and corporal sufferings.[13]

It is, however, the more explicit abstract/philosophical elements of Locke and Voltaire's writings on tolerance that liberal theory has strived to develop, continuing to treat tolerance in complete abstraction from the relations of power it presupposes and embodies. Thus, in a recent article entitled 'Communitarianism and the question of tolerance', in a recycling of the Lockian mystificatory notion of 'mutual tolerance', the author sees his work as concerned with 'the very preconditions of civil coexistence, namely, the ability on the part of individuals and groups belonging to different cultures and traditions to tolerate and respect one another.'[14] It is also from within this tradition that multicultural tolerance is conceived. Even some otherwise very critical analysts continue to use it as defined by such a tradition.[15]

14. Maurizio P. d'Entrèves, 'Communitarianism and the Question of Tolerance', *Journal of Social Philosophy*, Vol. XX1, Number 1, 1990, p77.

15. See for example L. Jayasuriya, 'Multiculturalism: Fact, Policy and Rhetoric' in M.E. Poole *et.al.*, *Australia in Transition*, Harcourt Brace Jovanovich, Sydney, 1985, p23, and, Jock Collins, *Migrant Hands in a Distant Land*, Pluto Press, Sydney 1988, p198.,

16. Non-English Speaking Background. This is the official mode of categorising those who are seen as the primary beneficiaries of the policy of muticulturalism.

17. See Collins, *op.cit.*

MULTICULTURAL TOLERANCE AS A STRATEGY OF REPRODUCTION

Multiculturalism emerged in Australia as a state-sponsored ideology in the early 1970s. Since that time, it has been portrayed as marking a radical break with a previously racist Australian past characterised by the promotion of the 'White Australia' policy, which barred 'Asians' from entering the country, and with the more recent policies of assimilation and integration. It is argued that the policy of assimilation, embraced by successive Australian governments from the end of World War Two until the late 1960s, was an extension of the White Australia policy in its dealings with the wave of post-colonial (NESB)[16] migration that arrived in Australia to meet the country's post-war reconstruction needs.[17] Assimilationist Australia could not tolerate cultural differences and promoted instead the primacy of its Anglo-Celtic heritage. It explicitly required non-British migrants to adopt the language, the culture and the values that are part of this heritage and to relinquish the distinct cultural practices and attitudes of their home countries.

The policy on integration, which followed that of assimilation, is seen as characterising a transitional period. It was briefly pursued by the Snedden government in the late 1960s and entailed a recognition that recently arrived migrants could not possibly assimilate in the way it was previously assumed. Migrants would be allowed to maintain their cultural identity for some time after their arrival, and though eventually they would become integrated in mainstream Anglo culture, transitional, culturally specific, services would be necessary to ensure that this integration, along with the complete 'Australification' of the second generation, was a smooth process.

If in its recognition of the existence of needs specific to the migrant population, integration foreshadowed multiculturalism, its upholding of the ultimate primacy of Anglo culture showed it still to be a product of an assimilationist mentality. It was multiculturalism, or so the story goes, that ushered in the truly pluralist 'cultural egalitarian' era where migrants were not only allowed, but were positively encouraged, to keep the cultural traditions of their home country alive. Australia was a nation where various cultural groups co-existed in one big 'family', as the first state ideologue of multiculturalism, Al Grasby, put it. Australians were from different cultural backgrounds and no culture or cultural group could claim to be 'better' than the others. As an ideology, multiculturalism, everyone was told, was both the description of a reality (the existence of cultural diversity in Australia was a fact), and an attitude that needed to be promoted (Australians should accept this diversity and see it as something positive). Australia had moved from being an intolerant to being a tolerant society. In *The Tyranny of Prejudice*, Al Grasby recalls how he aimed, when he was a Minister, to 'turn the classrooms of the nation into crucibles of tolerance.'[18]

Despite its fairy-tale-like progression and 'happy ending', this (hi)story does account for an important aspect of the social reality reflected and promoted by multiculturalism. Even though it cannot but operate with a 'soft' notion of culture which excludes, for instance, political and legal traditions, multiculturalism has opened up a space which permits the articulation of diverse cultural forms, as well as facilitating the interaction between them. At the level of social policy, the services provided to migrants have increased in quantity and quality. Furthermore, a redistribution of state resources in favour of NESB-Australians allows the latter to create various structures that help them in their continuing struggle for equality within Australian capitalism. Undoubtedly, as far as NESB-Australians are concerned, multicultural tolerant Australia is a better place to be than its historical predecessors.

However, as with all the tolerant societies before it, it has also remained marked by continuing intolerance, prejudice and racism. As Jock Collins has argued in a comparison of Australian and Canadian multiculturalism, revealing similar problems with the latter: 'The Australian and Canadian experience suggests that prejudice co-exists with tolerance, as does racism with social harmony and multiculturalism with ethnic inequality.[19]

While petty prejudices and racism co-exist continually in everyday life with non-prejudiced forms of interaction, sometimes these petty prejudices become reflected at the level of state policy and action, or take on a generalised mass character. Thus, the 1970s saw incidents such as police raids on the houses of hundreds of Greek migrant workers, aiming to uncover a mythical Greek social security conspiracy constructed out of stereotypes of the migrant proneness to dishonesty.[20] The early 1980s saw a particularly powerful resurgence of populist racism against various sections of the Australian community. A series of explicit attempts at re-asserting the 'Britishness' of Australian society has led to an increased questioning of the viability of multiculturalism as a state

18. Al Grasby, *The Tyranny of Prejudice*, Sydney, 1984,, p64.

19. Jock Collins, 'Cohesion with diversity? Immigration and multiculturalism in Canada and Australia', Working Paper Series, School of Finance and Economics, University of Technology, Sydney, no. 28, March 1993, pii.

20. See Andrew Jakubowicz, 'Ethnic affairs policy in Australia: the failure of multiculturalism' in M.E. Poole *et.al.*, *op.cit.*, pp271-278.

ideology. It began with a reactionary and populist history professor, Geoffrey Blainey, accusing the government of allowing into Australia 'too many' 'Asian' migrants. Following the re-election of the Labor government in 1989, the departing Minister of Finance, Senator Peter Walsh, concluded the decade with a critique of the 'hijacking' of immigration policy by 'migrant lobby groups'. More recently, there was an upsurge of racism against Australians of Arab descent following Australia's uncritical involvement in the Gulf Crisis indicating that the 1990s promise to be very much like the 1980s.[21]

It could be quite correctly argued at this point that, despite all this, it is better for the State to advocate tolerance than intolerance. However, one needs to remember that State policy is not restricted to an option between allowing intolerance to flourish and advocating tolerance. As Preston King argues, if one wishes to challenge someone's power to be intolerant, one can go further:

21. See Ghassan Hage, 'Racism, Multiculturalism and the Gulf War', *Arena*, no. 96, Spring 1991.

> Although it might be desirable that one tolerate the lily of the valley, the fox in the snow, the child in the alley, the caw of the crow, it might also be equally or more desirable that one enjoy no such power to tolerate in the first place. In short, given the power to tolerate, it may be well to do so. But calling that power into question it may be better to destroy it.[22]

22. King, *op.cit.*, p9.

Though King himself, for reasons I shall examine below, does not see power relationally, his argument can be used and extended in the context of relations between 'ethnic' or 'racial' communal formations to differentiate between three states of intercommunal relations:

a. Intercommunal intolerance: Group A has the power to be intolerant towards (deploy its racism, discriminate against, harass, intimidate) Group B and actually does so.

b. Intercommunal tolerance: Group A has the power to be intolerant towards Group B but refrains from doing so and tolerates it.

c. Intercommunal egalitarian relation: Group A has no power to be either tolerant or intolerant towards Group B.

While relation *c* is perhaps a utopia that egalitarian struggles yearn for rather than an actual possibility, positing it allows us to grasp an important aspect of the advocacy of multicultural tolerance. It is not just that multiculturalism by advocating relation *b* allows Group A to retain the capacity to be intolerant towards Group B. More importantly, it does so by fictitiously presenting the divide between relation *a* and relation *b* as if it was in itself a change from an inegalitarian to an egalitarian intercommunal setting. That is, it mystifies the inegalitarian nature of relation *b* by presenting it as if it was relation *c*. Even more, it actually uses the advocacy of relation *b* to counter the egalitarian struggles aimed at bringing about relation *c*. In the 1960s in Britain, for example, the existence of 'tolerance' was used to attempt to stop the introduction of anti-racist legislation. As Holmes relates: 'a leading backbencher opposed any attempt to introduce a bill to outlaw racial discrimination in the confident expectation that this matter was best left to the "tolerance and common sense" which abounded in British society.'[23] It is a similar logic which leads Australian multiculturalism to be unproblematically equated with anti-racism by many State officials, while the advocacy of tolerance, equated with the notion of cultural pluralism, assumes a power-free co-existence between cultures.

One can open the paper and read that a number of school kids 'attacked Ms. Rafida Ali, (while) still wearing their school clothes'. Furthermore, 'the victim was threatened with a gun, subjected to the most degrading abuse, and physically attacked.'[24] And while the reporter asks: 'Why did they do it? With what wickedness are they possessed that they are able to set upon a defenceless woman with such absence of conscience, with such callousness', we can read another report about a school where '35 percent of the students are from non-English-speaking backgrounds and (the school) is fine-tuning a program called 'Talking tolerance to teenagers ...'[25]

In the wake of the racist persecution of Arab Australians during the Gulf War, and after several months of silence, this is what the Australian prime minister at the time, Bob Hawke, had to say following the visit of an Arab-Australian delegation: 'I appeal to all my fellow Australians to be understanding, to be charitable and to appreciate that these are loyal Australians entitled to differences of view but they must be protected.'[26]

Such a declaration is a quintessential exemplification of the theme of tolerance masquerading as anti-racism. Instead of saying: 'there are some Australian citizens who are capable of terrorising other Australian citizens and getting away with it. We must not allow them to have this power', the prime minister ends up implying that: 'there are some Australian citizens who are capable of terrorising other Australian citizens and getting away with it. Be charitable and protect their victims'. Not only does this kind of statement leave the power of the racist unchallenged, it does not even empower the victims of racism to resist. It reduces them to helpless people one is encouraged to protect and be charitable to. The essential question that the prime minister's statement raises but fails to confront is: protect them from whom? The unconscious unwillingness to confront this issue directly lies in the fact that many of the people being asked to be charitable are the very uncharitable ones from whom the victims need to be protected! It is here that the nature of this 'anti-racism' reveals itself most: it is not about making the powerful powerless, it is about inviting them not to exercise their power. It invites those who have been uncharitable to be charitable but it does not remove from them the power to be uncharitable. On the contrary, it indirectly consecrates and *reproduces* this power.

To treat the advocacy of tolerance as a mode of reproduction is to reach some of the limits of Preston King's stimulating analysis. Despite his insights into the power-laden nature of tolerance, King's critique does not conceive tolerance in terms of reproduction because it does not see the power to tolerate/not tolerate as grounded in a relation of power. In an astonishingly

23. C. Holmes, *A Tolerant Country? Immigrants, Refugees and Minorities in Britain*, Faber and Faber, London 1991, p16.

24. *Telegraph Mirror*, 13 May 1993.

25. *Sydney Morning Herald*, 26 July 1993.

26. *Sydney Morning Herald*, 12 January 1991.

ideological – in the sense of advocating a specific ideology – passage he argues that:

> The promotion of toleration basically presupposes an inequality, but an inequality that has to be accepted. The promotion of democracy basically presupposes an inequality, but one that can and should be removed. It should be clear that these two types of promotion, where they obtain in different spheres, are not necessarily incompatible. But there is an important type of difference between them which it is perhaps always useful to remain aware of. Where one perceives a lack of toleraton, and encourages it, what one is basically encouraging is a change in *attitude*. Where one perceives a lack of democracy, and encourages it, what one is basically encouraging is a change of *structure*. Thus a predominant feature of the commitment to toleration is the concern with psychology, while a predominant feature of the commitment to democracy is a concern with institutions.[27]

27. Preston King, *op.cit.*, p15.

While the argument correctly sees that the advocacy of tolerance does not change structures (relations of power), it wrongly slips into arguing that it has no effect on structures and should be merely treated as a psychological (non social/structural) phenomenon. One effect of such an approach is that the 'tolerant attitude' is conceived of, in a continuation of the liberal tradition, as the product of an adherence to a belief or a principle that one values more than the action of ridding oneself through intolerance of an undesirable object:

> It is clear that tolerance is not merely a matter of suspending action against an item that is objected to. Crucial to it is the rationale for the suspension of such action. In the event, this rationale consists in the introduction of a competitive and incompatible objection, one that is accorded higher status, and one which accordingly prohibits the operationalisation of the objection first advanced.[28]

28. *Ibid.*, p32.

From such a perspective King fails to see the importance of the *interest* of the dominant in the advocacy of tolerance. He does not ask the question: what does one gain, generally, from the relation of power one is positioned within as the dominant, and more particularly, what does one gain from reproducing this relation of power through tolerance? Thus, those who tolerate do not gain anything from their toleration except maybe some broad sense of satisfaction from adhering to their principles.

Yet, when Locke argues that 'it is only light and evidence that can work a change in men's opinions; and that light can in no manner proceed from corporal sufferings, or any other outward penalties',[29] he is not only shown, as argued above, to be addressing himself to the dominant. He is also revealing that tolerance is a strategy: its aim, 'light', is the same as that of subjecting people to corporal suffering; it is merely perceived to be more efficient in

29. Locke, *op.cit.*, p7.

achieving such an aim. Locke is here following a long tradition of writers from Sebastien Castalion in his *Conseil à la France désolée* (1562) onward who saw the advocacy of tolerance in terms of the opposition between coercion and consent/ hegemony, and the strategic desirability of the latter over the former.[30]

King comes face to face with this strategic intent while examining the work of Castalion and many others. He examines, for example, Michel de L'Hôpital's work *Le bout de la guerre et de la paix* (1570) where the author advocates tolerance almost solely on the basis of the impossibility of winning the war against the enemy (the Huguenots). Here King acknowledges that: 'L'Hôpital's book is primarily argued on the grounds of utility, not principle.'[31] Nevertheless, King tries to 'save' his theory by arguing that: 'ultimately, the principle is always there. This essentially reduces to the notion that a man's conscience is inviolable, that one cannot meaningfully be compelled to believe what one regards as false.'[32] The weakness of King's argument does not lie in that no such principle can be found in L'Hôpital's work. It lies in his inability to perceive that the principle that 'one cannot meaningfully be compelled' itself can derive from the experience of the *inability* to compel.

The above also highlights the question of the social conditions of the possibility of tolerance, and gives us a further insight into its complexity. While it remains true, as I have been arguing, that the advocacy of tolerance reproduces the same relation of power that existed in the period of officially sanctioned intolerance that usually precedes it, it is nevertheless also true that it results from a re-assessment by the dominant of their ability to dominate, usually due to the capacity of the dominated to resist/challenge domination. This was something clearly seen by Renan in his study of the rise of 'clerical liberalism'. Renan argues that the main reason the Church adopted tolerance was that it found itself unable to use force against its enemies.[33] So, while tolerance reproduces the same relation of power, it is the product of a change in the balance of forces between the dominant and dominated, in the interest of the latter. What is even more important, however, is that an essential aspect of the advocacy of tolerance as a strategy of reproduction by the dominant, is that the latter strives to mystify that element of coercion and to present tolerance as if it was a mere benevolent choice on their part.

The official history of multiculturalism in Australia, as presented above, is a clear example of this. Multicultural tolerance is presented as the result of a mere choice of policy made by an enlightened government, mystifying the important fact that it is *as well* the product of the increased power, the resistance and the struggle of NESB Australians. By theorising tolerance into a mere choice based on a disinterested principled attitude, King does not only leave out the problematic of the social conditions of its possibility, he also presents a theory that is complicit in reproducing the very mystification with which the dominant consciously or unconsciously envelop the representation of their advocacy of tolerance.

Multicultural tolerance, like all tolerance, is not, then, a good policy that happens to be limited in its scope. It is a strategy aimed at reproducing and/by

30. See in this regard Joseph Lecler, *Toleration and the Reformation*, 2 volumes, Longman, London 1960.

31. King, *op.cit.*, p82.

32. *Ibid.*

33. See Ernest Renan, *Du liberalisme clerical* (Oeuvres, vol. 1), Paris 1947.

34. See Pierre Bourdieu, *Outline of a Theory of Practice*, Cambridge University Press, Cambridge 1977.

disguising relations of power in society. It is a form of symbolic violence in which a mode of domination is presented as a form of egalitarianism.[34] More formally, it is very close to what Bourdieu has called 'strategies of condescension'. These are the strategies

> by which agents occupying a higher position in one of the hierarchies of objective space symbolically deny the social distance which does not thereby cease to exist, thus ensuring they gain the profits of recognition accorded to a purely symbolic negation of distance ('he's unaffected', 'he's not stand-offish', etc.) which implies the recognition of a distance (the sentences I have quoted always have an implicit rider: 'he's unaffected for a duke', 'he's not stand-offish for a university professor', etc.). In short, one can use the objective distances so as to have the advantages of proximity and the advantages of distance, that is, the distance and the recognition of distance that is ensured by the symbolic negation of distance.[35]

35. Pierre Bourdieu, *In Other Words: Essays Towards a Reflexive Sociology*, Polity Press, Cambridge 1990, pp127-128.

In much the same way, as I have argued throughout the above, to say of someone 's/he is tolerant' always implies a 'rider' ('s/he is tolerant for someone who has the power not to be'). Likewise, it gives the tolerator the advantages of proximity not given to the overt intolerant and the advantage of distance residing in the very power to be (in)tolerant.

BOUNDARIES, NUMBERS AND LOCATIONS: THE PRACTICE OF TOLERANCE

What does one do when one tolerates? To ask this question is to emphasise that the perception of tolerance as a strategy of reproduction entails seeing it as an active practice. This is in opposition to its theorisation as an attitude where it is perceived passively as a suspension of action rather than an action in itself; it is to 'not engage in an act' of intolerance. Thus, King argues that 'to tolerate generally means to endure, suffer or put up with a person, activity, idea or organisation of which one does not really approve.'[36] In this final section, I wish to show that tolerance is an active practice of positioning the Other – the tolerated – in social space.

36. King, *op.cit.*, p21.

To begin with, all tolerance necessarily involves an acceptance of the presence of the Other in a social space within which we have a power to accept or reject. There is no sense for an Australian, say, to declare his/her tolerance of the presence of the Sikhs in India. The tolerated Others are by definition present within our 'sphere of influence'. They are part of our 'world' (society, nation, neighbourhood) but only insofar as we accept them. That is, the tolerated Others are never just present, they are positioned. Their belonging to the environment in which they come to exist is always a precarious one, for they never exist, they are allowed to exist.

The discourse of acceptance has always been present along with the discourse of tolerance within Australian multiculturalism, and the way it positions the 'migrant' is a good example of the precarious positioning of the tolerated/accepted Other.

The theme of acceptance obtains its positive non-racist value within multiculturalism through its opposition to rejection. If the White Australia policy and assimilation were about treating the NESB-Australian as an outsider, multiculturalism is about fully accepting them as Australians. However, outside this opposition, the 'non-racist' claims of such a discourse become much more ambiguous and contradictory. To begin with, the popular language of acceptance, often encountered in the form 'they're just as Australian as we are' or 'they're Australian too', reinforces the placing of the Anglo-Celtic Australians in the position of power they acquire within the discourse of tolerance. As importantly, the very act of acceptance operates as an exclusionary force on the accepted. For why is it, one might ask, that it is the NESB person that needs to be accepted and reassured about the nature of his or her identity in an already established multicultural society?

Seen from this perspective the accepting enunciation 'you're Australian' becomes similar to the 'you're a grown up now' directed from parents to teenagers. Not only does the identity become granted – that is, it can be withdrawn – and a power relation is drawn between those who do the accepting and those who are accepted, but, as importantly, a question mark is put over the suitability of this identity and its genuineness: if *it goes without saying* that the migrant is Australian there would be no need to say it. Acceptance translates into doubt.

The multicultural discourse of acceptance is complemented by a long tradition of what can be defined as 'immigration-speak': linguistic strategies and power-laden ways of talking about the NESB population. The most cherished occasions for the flourishing of immigration-speak are the immigration opinion polls. The fact that no other federal policy has been polled more than immigration policy, while, at the same time, no other policy has evolved more blatantly in disregard of public opinion, makes one wonder about the polls' real function. Maybe, rather than being perceived as a meaningful tool for the formulation of policy, the immigration poll should be seen in a more anthropological spirit as a *ritual of empowerment*, a seasonal festival where Anglo-Australians renew the belief in their possession of *the power to talk and make decisions about* NESB-Australians.

A quick look at the questions asked in the immigration polls gives us a clear indication of the kind of power the Anglo-Celtic Australians are invited to think they have: positioned in the role of masters of the earth's population movements, they are enabled to give opinions on whether the number of migrants that arrived the year before was to their liking or not, and even to venture an opinion about what would be just right for them.[37] By its very nature the immigration opinion poll is an invitation to judge those who have already immigrated as well as those who are about to immigrate. This is facilitated through the use of the word 'migrant' whose meaning slides freely between the two categories; moreover, and inescapably, to pronounce a

37. X. Marcus and X. Ricklefs (eds), *Surrender Australia?*, George Allen & Unwin, Sydney 1985, p18.

judgment on the value of future migration is to pronounce a judgment on the value of the existing NESB-Australians' contribution to Australia's development. It is in the conditions created by all these discursive effects that immigration-speak flourishes: 'they should come and they shouldn't', 'they have contributed and they haven't', 'there are too many and there aren't', 'they are and they aren't', 'they will and they won't'.

Tolerant acceptance, then, is never a passive acceptance, a kind of 'letting be'. It is very different from that described by King who argues that:

> The consequence involved in tolerance, on balance, is acceptance, and it flows from an interruption of the objection. Thus the tolerant consequence is necessarily equivocal – involving either the surrender of some negative impulse or the indulgence of some *limited* act of association. When we tolerate an *x* we accept it in the sense either that we associate with it or do not interfere with it in some limited sphere (emphasis in the text).[38]

38. King, *op.cit.*, p52.

King's passive acceptance ('interruption of an objection', 'not interfering') is contradicted by the very word he emphasises: 'limited'. For to say 'not interfere with it in some limited sphere' means necessarily that in accepting one is not merely engaging in a passive act. One is actively interfering by putting limits. It is precisely this setting of limits that constitutes the active component of tolerance: there is no tolerance without limits. To tolerate is not just to accept, it is to accept and position the Other within specific limits or boundaries.

Writing from the standpoint of the dominant religious groupings of their respective countries, Locke and Voltaire's pleas for tolerance do not stop them from feeling empowered to set the *limits* of tolerance. While this sub-discourse of limits reveals in itself the power of the dominants to set their own limits, it also reveals the line where the tolerant can legitimately become intolerant, such as towards fanatics (Voltaire and Locke) or atheists (Locke). In France the notion of limits has become officially enshrined by the government's promotion of the concept of *seuil de tolerance*, the threshold of tolerance, a category of govermentality aimed at the spatial control of the presence of the tolerated Other, mainly people of African origin, whereby white French citizens are considered to be capable of tolerating a certain number of Africans in their neighbourhood beyond which they can become intolerant.[39]

39. C. Lloyd and H. Waters, 'France: one culture, one people?', *Race & Class*, Number 3, Volume 32, 1991, pp60-61.

To tolerate, then, is to accept and position Others in our sphere of influence within specific limits that we set for them. The question that remains to be answered is: how are these limits determined? As noted above, it is necessary to go beyond the idea that all that tolerance involves is a disinterested 'enduring'. Conceiving of tolerance as an interested mode of acceptance, as we have, necessarily means that the object of tolerance cannot be seen in purely negative terms. It is because some benefits are derived from the objects of toleration, or at least from the act of toleration itself, that we tolerate them – go through the trouble of dominating them through tolerance – and accept them within our sphere of influence. Rather than involving a negative evaluation of its objects, tolerance is guided by a process of evaluating both the benefits accruing from the act of toleration *and* what is perceived as negative and needing to be endured. What defines the object of tolerance is not that it is valued negatively, it is that it is an object of evaluation *as such*.

It is because this evaluating process involves both the negative and the positive, what is appreciated and what needs to be endured, that the positioning of the tolerated Other and the setting of the boundaries within which it can exist is a far more complex affair than a mere search for protection from negativity. Often the history of tolerance as a practice is to be found in the history of *exploitation* even more so than in the history of grand statements about the toleration of other 'religions'. It is slaves, domestic servants, and other forms of exploited labourers – people who are seen as inferior, or in negative terms, by the dominant – who, because of their value as objects of exploitation, are accepted and included within the dominant's 'sphere of influence' (their home, their domain, etc.), while, at the same time, the limits of their inclusion are carefully traced.

This valuing and this exploitation is not restricted to the exploitation of labour. Often the discourse of tolerance is linked to a discourse of cultural value/usage. The black servants that accompanied white middle-class women, and that the latter tolerated in their proximity merely because they served to empasise their paleness, is a good example of such valuing/positioning/ toleration.[40] Voltaire, also, argues for the tolerance of the Calvinists on the basis of their cultural value. If tolerated, Voltaire argued, they would be 'enriching'.

It is this same discourse of 'enrichment' that one finds along with the discourse of tolerance within Australian multiculturalism. And in much the same way, cultural enrichment is closely linked to multiculturalism's emphasis on the recognition of the *value* of the various cultures present in Australia and the value of the interaction between them. '*Carnivale* offers the people of NSW the opportunity to celebrate multiculturalism and to learn from others who have joined our society from other lands'.[41] This official perception of the state of New South Wales' most important multicultural festival in terms of what people can learn/what other cultures have to offer is the most common way in which the discourse of 'cultural enrichment' circulates. It is a central theme of cultural pluralism and is stressed in opposition to ethnocentrism. Thus, Australian multiculturalism is portrayed as transcending one of the major defects of the assimilationist period: its unwillingness to accept that non-Anglo cultures have a contribution to make to the development of a more general Australian culture.

But it is only in its opposition to such ethnocentrism that the notion of enrichment appears in such a nice pluralist garb. Left to itself, it reveals an important opposition inherent to it, which is the opposition between enriched and enriching cultures. For the Anglo-Celtic Australian who accepts it, the discourse of enrichment still positions him or her in the centre of the Australian cultural map. Far from putting 'migrant cultures', even in their 'soft'

40. S.C. Maza, *Servants and Masters in Eighteenth Century France: The Uses of Loyalty*, Princeton University Press, Princeton 1983, p206.

41. *Sydney Morning Herald*, 23/9/91.

sense (as food, dance, etc.), on an equal footing with Anglo culture, this theme conjures the familiar images of the multicultural fair where the various stalls of migrant cultures are exhibited and where blond, blue-eyed men and women, bearers of Anglo-culture, positioned in the central role of the touring subjects, walk around and enrich themselves.

Consequently, the discourse of enrichment operates by establishing a break between valuing negatively and valuing positively, similar to the break the discourse of tolerance establishes between tolerance and intolerance. In much the same way as the tolerance/intolerance divide mystifies the more important divide between holding the power to tolerate and not holding it, the distinction between valuing negatively/valuing positively mystifies the deeper division between holding the power to value (negatively or positively) and not holding it.

Heidegger's critique of the discourse of value perfectly brings out the less than egalitarian assumptions underlying it. As he put it:

> It is important finally to realize that precisely through the characterisation of something as 'a value' what is so valued is robbed of its worth. That is to say, by the assessment of something as a value what is valued is admitted only as an object of man's estimation. Every valuing, even when it values positively, is a subjectivizing. It does not let things: be. Rather, valuing lets things: be valid.[42]

42. Martin Heidegger, *Basic Writings*, Routledge & Kegan Paul, London 1978, p226.

In the context of Australian multiculturalism, the point being made is not that the discourse of enrichment places Anglo-Celtic culture in a more important position than other migrant cultures. If this was the case, it would simply be reflecting an obvious reality. More importantly, this discourse assigns to migrant cultures a different *mode of existence* to Anglo-Celtic culture. While Anglo-Celtic culture merely and unquestionably *exists*, migrant cultures *exist for* the latter. Their value, or the viability of their preservation as far as Anglo-Celtic Australians are concerned, lies in their function as enriching cultures. It is in this sense that the discourse of enrichment contributes to the precarious positioning of NESB Australians within the Australian national space.

TOLERANCE, POST-COLONIAL RACISM AND THE 'POST-CONQUERED' OTHER

To give a more complete answer to the question asked in the beginning of the previous section – what does one do when one tolerates? – we can now say that tolerance is the practice of accepting and positioning the Other in the dominant's sphere of influence according to their value (for the dominant).

In light of the above answer, and in light of the other aspects of practical tolerance revealed in the previous sections, I shall conclude by making a number of observations, first, concerning the general nature of the practice of tolerance, and second, concerning its historical specificity.

In the first section of this essay, I showed that tolerance is a practice that *cannot but* emanate from a position of dominance. In the second section, I positioned tolerance in the context of race and ethnic relations and showed it to be a reproductive practice. From such a perspective, rather than being an anti-racism, tolerance was shown to be *a different modality of racism*. It is an equally racist practice because, like 'intolerant racism', it reproduces, but in a different way, the same racist ethnic/racial relations of power that constitute its condition of possibility.

This demystification of the anti-racist pretensions of tolerance is obviously important politically and analytically. It is all the more important since 'tolerant racism' is far more dominant historically than 'intolerant racism'. In this regard, I think that the constant theorisation of racism as 'intolerance', as 'exclusion' and as 'extermination' is, at least partly, the product of the weight of the history of Nazi extermination camps on the western imaginary of what constitutes 'racism'. In Australia, there is the further weight of the white settlers' exterminatory practices towards the indigenous population. In fact, despite the tragic power of these events, tolerant racism is far more pervasive historically and has constituted, and continues to constitute, the core of most racist *regimes*, from slave societies to societies structured by the exploitation of ethnic/racial industrial, domestic and cultural labour and 'value'. Even Nazi racism involved elements of tolerance, albeit minimal, in so far as it tolerated in some instances the presence, usage and exploitation – not just the extermination – of the 'otherified' Jew.

But while it is necessary, then, to show the continuity between intolerant and tolerant racism, it is also necessary to examine the significance of the latter's specificity as a racist practice. This is what establishes the importance of answering the question we asked in the last section – what does one do when one tolerates?

Intolerant racism, in being an exterminatory racism, puts no *value* on otherness and aims to simply eradicate it from, or neutralise it within, social space. Tolerant racism, on the other hand, by being concerned, as we have seen, with the acceptance, positioning and, most importantly, the *valuing* of otherness, is a practice that aims at creating and managing an 'economy of otherness'. To put it differently, it delineates a political economy of otherness through an ensemble of practices and techniques aimed at regulating the acceptance, positioning and valuing of otherness – which is also the practice of creating the Other as a value. It is in this sense, I believe, that the thematic of tolerance reveals itself to be a thematic of 'governmentality' as Foucault defined it.

In fact, it can also be argued that intolerant racism stands to tolerant racism in the same way as the power of the sovereign stands to governmental power in Foucault's theorisation.[43] While intolerant racism is a power defined solely through its negativity, tolerant racism, through its emphasis on positioning and valuing, embodies the essence of 'government' as presented by Guillaume de la Perrière's *Mirroir de la politique* (1567), in a passage quoted by Foucault, where

43. Michel Foucault, 'Right of Death and Power Over Life' (from *The History of Sexuality, Vol. 1*) in Paul Rabinow (ed), *The Foucault Reader*, Pantheon Books, New York 1984, pp258-272.

44. Michel Foucault, 'Governmentality' in Graham Burchell *et. al* (eds), *The Foucault Effect: Studies in Governmentality*, Harvester, Hemel Hempstead, 1991, p93.

he states that: 'Government is the right disposition of things arranged so as to lead to a convenient end.'[44]

Putting the above in a historical context, it can also be argued that while tolerant racism is the racism of the government of Otherness, intolerant racism is the racism of the conquest of this Otherness. Intolerant racism has historically dominated at the points of colonial territorial expansion, such as in the process of colonising Australia or the US – which again points to Foucault's analysis of sovereignty in terms of a dominant territorial problematic.

From this perspective an important linkage between tolerant and intolerant racism emerges. To say that tolerant racism is a racism of government is to argue that its object is *governable*. But what does it mean to say that an object is governable other than that it is always already *conquered*? It seems to me, then, that intolerant racism constitutes the very condition of possibility of tolerant racism. Not only in a historical sense of precedence, in that one needs to conquer 'others' before governing them, and therefore, the governable other is always 'post-conquered'. But also in a structural sense, in the sense that, tolerant racism is always grounded within intolerant racism, which is what makes its object securely 'tolerable'.

The above can lead us to further conclude that the current *dominance* of tolerant racism is a specifically post-colonial phenomenon. It is within post-coloniality that the colonial problematic of conquest has been almost totally superseded by the problematic of governing post-conquered post-colonial subjects. The latter, by having their conquest constantly inscribed on their bodies, can be safely 'valued' and tolerated.

GOODBYE PARADISE:

GLOBAL/LOCALISM, HAWAII,
AND CULTURAL PRODUCTION IN THE AMERICAN PACIFIC

Rob Wilson

'A frightening type of *papalagi* architecture is invading Oceania: the super-stainless, super-plastic, super-hygenic, super-soulless structure very similar to modern hospitals; and its most nightmarish form is the new-type tourist hotel – a multi-story edifice of concrete, steel, chromium and air-conditioning.'

Albert Wendt, *Towards a New Oceania*

(Ever wonder why there is a McKinley Street and a McKinley High School, but no Cleveland *anything* in Hawai'i?)

H. K. Bruss Keppeler, *Native Hawaiian Claims*

'Our visitors [tourists] come here with a perception of what Hawaii is to them – Paradise.'

Visitors Experience Task Force, 1993 Tourism Congress[1]

CYBORGS ACROSS THE ASIAN/PACIFIC

The post-World War Two formations of global capitalism, often associated with the rise of postmodernism into first-world cultural dominant and the dispersed heteroglossia of postcolonial contentions, has been driven by various material forces which, at a macro-level of analysis, would include: a telecommunications revolution in media, transnationalization of production and rise of the transnational corporation as the locus of economic activity, and the change of the modernist nation-state from manipulator of internal conflict and territorial paranoia over NATO and the Pacific to just-in-time manager of what Kenichi Ohmae pronounces a new 'borderless interlinked economy'.[2] Accelerated during the creative-destruction dynamic of the 1980s, cybernetic technologies and more global modes of production/representation have generated what cultural critics and management gurus alike now recognize as 'the globalization of capitalism' on a sweeping scale of global/local interaction that is source 'at once of unprecedented unity globally, and of unprecedented fragmentation' as Arif Dirlik has outlined.[3] We are only just now beginning to come to terms with the post-national geopolitics and cultural implications of this new global/local interface, entrenchments of community and power into forms of place-bound identity, and what Arjun Appadurai has called 'the global

1. My first epigraph is taken from what is considered the most powerful re-assertion of Pacific regional identity against hegemonic modernity, by the Samoan novelist Albert Wendt: reprinted in *Writers in East-West Encounter: New Cultural Bearings*, Guy Amirthanayagam (ed), Macmillan, London, 1982, p210. The second, which depends upon knowledge that President Grover Cleveland and his Blount commission opposed the illegal overthrowal of Queen Lili'uokalani by an oligarchy of American businessmen in 1892, is taken from *The Price of Paradise: Lucky We Live Hawaii?*, Randall W. Roth (ed), Mutual Publishing, Honolulu 1992, p198. The third expresses the position of the third Tourism Congress sponsored by the Hawaii Department of Business, Economic Development and Tourism: quoted in Stu Glauberman, 'Tourism Congress to seek solutions', *Honolulu Advertiser*, 13 December 1993.

2. See Kenichi Ohmae, *The Borderless World: Power and Strategy in the Interlinked Economy*, Harper, New York 1990.

3. See Arif Dirlik, *Waking to Global Capitalism*, forthcoming, Wesleyan University Press. On transcultural configurations in this intensified global/local world-system, see Arjun Appadurai, 'Disjuncture and Difference in the Global Cultural Economy,' *Public Culture* 2 (1990): pp1-24.

4. Masahiro Mori, *The Buddha In the Robot: A Robot Engineer's Thoughts on Science and Religion*, Kosei, Tokyo 1981, p13.

5. Philip K. Dick, *Blade Runner (Do Androids Dream of Electric Sheep?)*, Ballantine, New York 1991), p24.

production of locality'.

There has been a spectacular rise of contemporary Asian/Pacific interzones, 'global cities', and global/local export zones, fusing transnational technologies to local customs, as in the re-articulation of Confucian spiritualism to the labour of microchip production and fashion semiotics from Singapore to Taiwan and Seoul, for example, or Masahiro Mori's much more technoeuphoric claim that transnational cyborgs 'have the buddha-nature within them',[4] not to mention the ongoing transformation of the Pacific Ocean into a region of dematerialized cyberspace linking the Pacific coast of California to postmodern Hong Kong and Japan (as foreshadowed in transnational spectacles like *Blade Runner*). Pacific Rim nations are said to play a vanguard part in this global/local restructuring and, in effect, are helping to decentre settler countries like the United States, Canada, and Australia from narratives of national identity that would look back to western Europe-as-old-world capitalism model. *Globloc* is the new coinage in postmodern Japan, I have heard: the intensified permeability of any locale in the age of our global economy makes for the world shopping-mall culture of a consumption-oriented novel rooted in brand-glutted subjectivity like Banana Yoshimoto's *Kitchen*, or Douglas Coupland's North American world drifters and global 'mcjob' hunters in *Generation X*.

The United States of America, a fast dissolving and refiguring Cold War nation-state claiming the last phases of military hegemony in the Pacific region, now spreads and struts across the Asia/Pacific Ocean like some clunky old world (nuclearized, Fordist, military-industrialized) First World godzilla. By diverse accounts, the local as ground and space of cultural identity is increasingly being integrated into – if resistant to – global agents and transcultural forces across this new Pacific in ways, I shall claim, that challenge and undermine the imagined community of the settler nation-state.

As cultural premonition, recall that in Philip K. Dick's geoimaginary vision of San Francisco in the year 2018, *Do Androids Dream of Electric Sheep?* (1968), the Rosen Association, which engineers and produces the 'Nexus-6' android, has already spread across the Pacific coast of the United States, to a passive Russia, as well as to an offworld colony of 'New America' on Mars. This transglobal corporation is so flexible and mobile in its high-tech feats of generating temporary-contract cyborgian labour that the transnational police forces of these nation and city states cannot prohibit (or even locate) them. If agency of production has been globally mystified, as in *Blade Runner*, the colonial dynamics of global capital remain intact and rising: 'Legally, the manufacturers of the Nexus-6 brain unit operated under colonial law, their parent autofactory being on Mars'.[5]

Rick Deckard's romance-quest in Dick's novel, to find and police the very boundary between the human and the high technological, depends upon his prior *film noir*-like search to locate the agents, corporations, and instruments of global capital in its latest transnational and supra-legal mode. These biocustom-engineered cyborgs of the Asia/Pacific that Deckard searches for within the neo-colonizing heart of late-capitalist desire would serve, as the TV ads for Rosen Inc. announce, to duplicate those 'halcyon days of the pre-Civil War Southern states' as 'body servants or tireless field hands'. Short of this racial humiliation, feminized cyborgs can be turned (like the 'Rachel Rosen' prototype) into pleasure machines for scopophilic desire like so many post-pastoral electric sheep chewing on the grasses in a transnational limbo.[6]

As John Naisbett and Patricia Aburdene hector the case for transnational prosperity in *megatrends 2000* (if somewhat belatedly preparing the US Cold War imaginary for 'the rise of the Pacific Rim' and new strategies of compulsory globalization) 'In the fast-paced Pacific Rim, the economic advantages belong to the swift.'[7] Given global capitalization of the Asian/Pacific local, power/knowledge still belongs to the conquest of space by time: that is, to the dematerialized movements of hypercapital and information highways across the Pacific as commodity chains diffuse across the region and reconfigure nation and globe into a cybernetic matrix of speed and profit.

Given this global restructuring of local spaces of identity and prior community, multiplex Pacific Basin cultures inside the Pacific Rim do not factor in as agents nor as locations of resistance so much as sites of tourist simulacrum and rest (or vacant spaces for weapons disposal) for Pacific Rim profit, tropological production, and pleasure. As post-national subject, Deckard moves from servomechanism of the American nation-state to become that lovable lackey, a Pacific Rim megatrend agent.

Later down the euphoric highway towards transnational postmodernity, and everywhere 'jacking' into the disembodied rush of space-become-information-matrix, Rick Deckard is soon superseded by the cyborg cowboy, Case, in William Gibson's *Neuromancer*, for whom the whole world has become a 'Chiba City' of global instantaneity. Turning the Pacific into sublime cyberspace, Gibson's heroes of transnational euphoria can leap across the orientalist dangers of cybernetic infinitude, always in the hire of an ever-more dematerializing corporation: 'With his deck, he [Case] could reach the Freeside decks as easily as he could reach Atlanta. Travel was a meat thing.'[8] Labour is a meat thing too, as feminist critics have shown of the transnational exploitation that now goes on in 'peasant Asia' and the maquiladoras of Mexico. From Tokyo to the trans-American Sprawl, the dynamics of the Pacific Rim (from one view in Vancouver) has all but dissolved into what William Gibson has lyricized as 'the bodiless exultation of cyberspace', as the doped-up cyborg promises to redeem the local Pacific from global isolation, if not the race and class contradictions of material history, in a new transnational sublime.[9]

The rampant neo-eclecticism of postmodern philosophies and tastes to consume, create, and mimic cultural difference and nomadic flux – what James Clifford *et al* would now theorize and embrace as so many 'discrepant cosmopolitanisms' routing and re-rooting across spaces of local globality[10] – cannot be dissociated from this by-now-advanced 'eclecticism in labor practices' and an international redivisioning of labour such that sweat-shops and family

6. *Ibid.*, p14.

7. John Naisbitt and Patricia Aburdene, *Megatrends 2000: Ten New Directions For the 1990s*, Avon, Avon 1990, p198.

8. William Gibson, *Neuromancer*, Ace, New York 1984, p77. On Japan as panic site of reconfigured subjectivity (the sublime cyborg), exotic Othering, and western dismantlement in the New Pacific, see David Morley and Kevin Robins, 'Techno-Orientalism: Futures, Foreigners and Phobias', *New Formations* 16, 1992 pp136-156.

9. *Ibid.*, p6.

10. James Clifford, 'Borders and Diasporas', unpublished lecture for 'Borders/ Diasporas' Conference, The Center for Cultural Studies, UC Sant Cruz, April 3-4, 1992.

11. David Harvey, *The Condition of Postmodernity: An Inquiry Into the Origins of Cultural Change*, Blackwell, Oxford 1990, p187.

labour systems can co-exist in the same urban space with spectacular telecommunication networks that would dematerialize local earth and sweat-shop into the capitalogic of time-as-money.[11] Clifford's invocation of a 'hybridity' discourse, which has all but achieved normative status in postcolonial studies, aims to articulate a third or in-between space of 'borders/diasporas', such that modernist binary oppositions of global capital posed against local culture are resisted and textualized even as to-and-fro transcultural flows (as in the scholarship of *Public Culture*) are foregrounded: 'Too often we are left with an awkward gap between levels of analysis: generic global forces/specific local responses', as Clifford stages the opposition.

Riding if not celebrating the diasporic global/local interface of an ever-creolizing transnational-cum-local poetics emanating from the 'black Atlantic' to the frontier US/Mexican border, Clifford would resist both a totalizing 'globalism' that is self-defined as progressive and historically dynamic as well as any 'localism' that remains too ' "rooted" (not routed) in place tradition, culture, or ethnicity conceived in an absolutist model'. This latter warning against local entrenchment and in praise of global hybridity should give us regional pause, however, especially in the Pacific Basin region where 'micropolitics' and not just 'megatrends' would trouble the 'postcolonial' horizon with alternative spaces and claims: aboriginal claims at the local level (resurgent in Hawaii, Australia, Taiwan and New Zealand) can become subordinated, in such a 'transcultural' euphoric analysis of the by-now-transnationalized ethnoscape, to more flexible/impure/creolized articulations of syncretic transformation at the border. The local needs to be worried into existence as the site of critical regionalism and what Raymond Williams called 'the bond to place' as ground of resistance to transnational capitalism (see Rob Wilson, 1993).

12. See Karl Marx and Frederick Engels, *The Communist Manifesto*, (London: Penguin, 1967), pp83-84. 'In place of local and national seclusion and self-sufficiency, we have intercourse in every direction, universal interdependence of nations. And as in material, so in intellectual productions.'

13. Takayuki Tatsumi, 'The Japanese Reflection of Mirrorshades', *Storming the Reality Studio: A Casebook of Cyberpunk and Postmodern Fiction*, Duke University Press, Durham, N.C. 1991), pp367-72.

The very dynamism of capitalism as a global system has been tied to the telos of a technoeuphoric poetics of what David Harvey has called 'creative destruction' in which, as Karl Marx noted at the outset of technological modernity, 'all that is solid melts into air'; and those Chinese walls of tradition, region, and local identity are relentlessly battered down by commodity exchange, cultural interchange, and forces of technological innovation.[12] This bashing of the 'Asiatic mode of production' has reached such an advanced state of Deleuzian sublimity, within cultures of Pacific Rim postmodernity, that Takayuki Tatsumi, reflecting on the spread of cyberpunk culture across the region during the hyper-capitalist 1980s, can claim that, in science fiction visions of globalized space in *Neuromancer* (1984) and *Mona Lisa Overdrive* (1988), William Gibson had circulated 'the signifier of Japanese language – like "Chiba City" or "Gomi no Sensei" – as its "semiotic ghost" ' without ever having visited Japan itself.[13] Gibson's 'semio-tech' misperception of an over-technologized matrix of cybernetic sublimity from a trans-Pacific Apple PC in Vancouver, Canada has already fed back into formations of 'Japanese postmodernism' itself to refashion local style, techno-identity, and to prefigure everyday Japanese custom. ('Japan's Ainu, needless to say, do not figure in technoeuphoric visions of Japanese postmodern identity as cyborgian 'technoscape', as the feminist fiction of Tsushima Yukio has worried.)

Pacific Rim visions of flexible labour production and the global mishmash of styles spreading across the Asian/Pacific reach an epiphanic level of new world intensity and global spectacle in Ridley Scott's *Blade Runner*, where the Babel-like Tyrell Corporation pyramid rises up out of the filthy third world heteroglossia of Los Angeles' streets to dominate all prior modes of production ('I just make eyes' says old Chun in his refrigerated sweat-shop in Late Capitalist Chinatown) and to intimidate urban subaltern agents ('He knows everything, he big genius'). Like some postmodernist version of Blake's anti-God, Irizen, Tyrell seemingly reigns over space, time, capital, and body and panoptically enchains worker-subjects from a Tower of Babel zigurrat over the cityspeak. Although, as Roy Baty, the Blakean-liberation cyborg confesses to Tyrell, before bashing out the corporate head's eyes with de-oedipalizing glee, 'You're a hard man to see'. Today's grimy-chic 'bladerunner look' of postindustrial ruin and multicultural sublimity now rises, as in Los Angeles and Vancouver – fusing with Tokyo and Hong Kong into 'the capital of capital in the Pacific Rim' – and threatens to turn into the cultural dominant of contemporary urban design. It resurfaces in Ridley Scott's *Black Rain* (1989) as the trademark post-industrial skies over Osaka.[14] Given global technologies of representation and image-exchange, Hollywood can generate and control, in such blockbusters, the emerging spaces and subjects of this Asian/Pacific transnational sublime as a space of sheer cultural immensity (the multicultural city gone offshore if not 'offworld') and of labour domination (the cyborg-human now starring as transnational subject).

Given these brave new worlds and emergent regimes of global production flowing into older spaces of local culture, as well as more hybrid fusions of technology and organic agent into 'buddah-nature', then, the difficulty facing postmodern cultural production at present is the contemporary problematic of 'TimeSpace' unrepresentability: that is, the inability to map, cognize, or aesthetically represent at a local level what Fredric Jameson clunkily calls our 'whole world system of present-day multinational capitalism' as this everyday totality impinges upon disparate locales.[15]

Because the local, increasingly refigured in various disciplines from cultural geography to ethnography to urban studies as some innovative and mobile global/local interface, has to think and feel the power of global capitalism in its full spatiality, the aesthetics of region, place, and location are very much back on the postmodern agenda: 'In clinging, often of necessity, to a place-bound identity, however,' as David Harvey warns within contexts of global-local marketing propagated by Kenichi Ohmae, Robert Reich *et al*, 'such oppositional movements become a part of the very fragmentation which a mobile capitalism and flexible accumulation can feed upon.'[16] The re-assertion and coalitional construction of 'place-bound identity', as I will detail through a focus upon the Bamboo Ridge culture in Hawaii, nonetheless has become

14. Edward Soja, *Postmodern Geographies: The Reassertion of Space in Critical Social Theory*, Verso, London, p192. On the 'bladerunner look', see Norman M. Klein, 'Building Blade Runner', *Social Text* 28, 1991 pp147-152. 'The film *Blade Runner* has achieved something rare in the history of cinema. It has become a paradigm for the future of cities, for artists across the disciplines.'

15. On this *sublime* problematic confronting the postmodern subject as the inability to grasp the 'whole world system of present-day multinational capitalism', articulated through Jameson's 'cognitive mapping' of cultural objects and the matrix-quests of cyberpunk science fiction, see Peter Fitting, 'The Lessons of Cyberpunk', *Technoculture*, Constance Penley and Andrew Ross (eds), Minnesota University Press, Minneapolis 1991, pp310-311.

16. David Harvey, *op.cit.*, p303.

crucial to the preservation of cultural difference for many locals given the spread of cyborgs across the Asia-Pacific zone. In the case of indigenous Hawaiians, this transnationalization of local space and identity threatens cultural survival itself.

'PARADISE' IN THE PACIFIC

17. Noel Kent, 'To Challenge Colonial Structures and Preserve the Integrity of Place: The Unique Potential Role of the University', in *Restructuring For Ethnic Peace: A Public Debate at the University of Hawai'i*, Majid Tehranian (ed), Spark M. Matsunaga Institute for Peace, Honolulu 1991, p119. For a related analysis, see Eric Yamamoto, 'The Significance of Local', *Social Process in Hawai'i* 27, 1990 pp12-19.

18. Eric Chock, 'On Local Literature', *The Best of Bamboo Ridge*, Eric Chock and Darrell H.Y. Lum (ed), Bamboo Ridge Press, Honolulu 1986, p8. See also Rob Wilson, 'Blue Hawaii: Bamboo Ridge as "Critical Regionalism",' in Arif Dirlik (ed), *What's In a Rim?: Critical Perspectives on the Pacific Region Idea*, Westview, Boulder, Colorado 1993, pp281-304.

19. See Philip Damon's review, 'Appealing "Paradise" goes far beyond its Island home', *The Honolulu Advertiser*, May 29, 1992. 'Peripherilization' implies the ongoing global process of uneven geographical development.

Against the image-thick onslaught of transnational forces of late-capitalist spectacle, localistic orientations have re-asserted themselves in the face of overwhelming modernization at least since the mid-1970s in Hawaii, despite the fact (as Noel Kent has observed) that any ' "localism" is all too easily equated with parochialism in this metropolitan age'.[17] Paradoxically, the most local works of postmodern cultural production in Hawaii are already affected if not *invaded* (to use the novelist Albert Wendt's polemicizing verb from *Towards a New Oceania*, to resist the culturally disruptive affect of modern architecture upon the 'faa Samoa' in Western Samoa) by this geoimaginary problematic, such that the global/local interface is a pre-given predicament Pacific authors have to work through in order to affirm and defend some enclave of 'local culture'.

This has been the case with the emergence of the 'local literature' movement at *Bamboo Ridge* journal and press which, since its founding in Honolulu in 1978, has resisted the metropolitan assumption that writers in Hawaii 'are subordinate to the mainland' or the national belief that 'we [in Hawaii] are really no different here and can even be *like* the mainland if we try hard enough', as the local poet Eric Chock remarked.[18] It is within the context of what has been called 'global localism' that I shall discuss the localistic culture articulated in the movie *Goodbye Paradise* (1991), which, not surprisingly given Hawaii's peripheralization to the Pacific Rim economy of California since the 1850s and on into the era of post-war tourist simulacrum, is the first feature-length movie ever to be produced entirely in Hawaii.[19] Kayo Hada's *Picture Bride*, set in the ethnic plantation culture of Waialua Sugar Company in 1915, is only the second locally produced independent feature film to be made in Hawaii: due out in 1994 and combining the work of Asian-American artists with transnational superstars like Toshiro Mifune from *Black Rain*, *Picture Bride* will also explore the ethnic makings, discrepancies, and tensions of local culture in Hawaii.

Goodbye Paradise, if only in its tropologically over-determined title, recalls earlier tropes and Edenic master-narratives of Hawaii as a lingering Asian/Pacific paradise in the South Seas. These tropes of garden-like embodiment in the out-of-history (actually North) Pacific retain some material legitimacy in the postmodern American imagination even while prior master-narratives of the United States as 'utopia achieved' bite the deregulated dust of late capitalist Reagonomics.[20] Paul Theroux, wandering as voraciously as Malinowski or Henry Adams across the vast Pacific ('happy isles of Oceania') in an inflatable kayak with a stack of Euro-American intertexts, a broken male heart and a dog-eared copy of the *Sexual Life of Savages*, does not really find 'the happy isles of Oceania' he craves until he is back in his multicultural Asian/Pacific home in Honolulu. 'It often seemed to me that calling the Hawaiian Islands "paradise" was not an exaggeration, though saying it out loud, advertising it, seemed to be tempting fate', Theroux confesses, just before ending his transnational tourist romance-quest for Pacific paradise in the $2,500-a-night Orchid Bungalow at the Mauna Lani.[21] Perhaps Hawaiian novelist Armine von Tempski put this claim for paradise in the American Pacific most ostentatiously, as befits the granddaughter of Polish nobility and heir to a sixty-thousand acre Haleakala Ranch on Maui; as she writes in her 1940 autobiography, *Born in Paradise*, 'Attaining Paradise in the hereafter does not concern me greatly. I was born in Paradise.'[22]

Not to be outdone by Armine von Tempski's sweetly Nietzschean literalization of the literary-Biblical trope of paradise as the Americanized Pacific, the team of legal, social, and economic policy theorists charting the material costs of inhabiting the contemporary state of Hawaii in the recent cost-benefit collective analysis, *The Price of Paradise: Lucky We Live in Hawaii?*, do answer a qualified 'yes' to affirming life in this tax-ridden Eden, along with Sumner J. La Croix (in Chapter 21, 'Cost of Housing'). The latter, a Professor of Economics at the University of Hawaii at Manoa in Honolulu, assesses in this local best-seller that, despite the highest housing and cost of living expenses in the USA, Honolulu has clean air, clean water, warm winters and moderate summers, beautiful forests and mountains, spectacular views, a culturally diverse ethnic population tied into Asian and Pacific culture, good food, and a varied night life, and proudly concludes: 'No place is right for everyone but, aside from the high cost of living, Hawaii is most people's idea of paradise.'[23] *Most people's idea of paradise*, unless, for example, you are a native Hawaiian whose culture is being transformed into tourist simulacra or whose land has been alienated into military and state profit and for whom the struggle for national sovereignty is gathering juro-political force.

Can 'Paradise' be forever recuperated and pacified in the ecotourism of the American Pacific, even within a cost-benefit analysis? Yes, claims the tourist-knowledge apparatus of *The Price of Paradise*, 'as long as Honolulu retains its unique beauty, environment and cultural attractions'[24] and local citizens can endure a tourist-driven economy in which 'we get less for more', as runs the general refrain in *The Price of Paradise*.[25] 'Paradise', despite threats of over-government and international flux and tourist stagnation, is here – if only as hegemonic regional trope – to stay. Eric Chock, to the local contrary, has titled his recent Bamboo Ridge Press collection *Last Days Here* to suggest the imminent phasing out of local Hawaiian culture, language, and customary difference in and around Honolulu's Chinatown. If cultural ties to place-bound identity and community are strong, as in mixed-ethnic poems like 'Tutu on Da Curb' ('Her hair all pin up in one bun,/one huge red hibiscus

20. Jean Baudrillard traverses the huge freeways, empty deserts, and Disneyesque simulacra of American-sublime space as some neo-primitive 'utopia achieved' in *America*, Trans. Chris Turner, Verso, London 1988.

21. Paul Theroux, *The Happy Isles of Oceania: Paddling the Pacific*, G.P. Putnam, New York 1992, p482. For a polemic against Theroux's neo-imperial attitudes towards Pacific peoples, see Rob Wilson, 'Paul Theroux's Venomous Views', *Honolulu Advertiser*, January 8, 1994.

22. Quoted in Stephen H. Sumida, *And the View from the Shore: Literary Traditions of Hawai'i*, University of Washington Press, Seattle 1991, p91.

23. Sumner J. La Croix, 'Cost of Housing', *The Price of Paradise*, p136.

24. *Ibid.*, p138.

25. Michael A. Sklarz, 'High Rents', *The Price of Paradise*, p144.

hanging out/over her right ear') or 'Chinese Fireworks Banned in Hawaii' ('cousins eat jook from the huge vat/in the kitchen'), Chock's title poem to his Pacific-local oriented collection more ominously shows a fished-out and polluted river near Honolulu Chinatown, where an old Chinese man fishes, if only to keep his old customs and preserve his ghostly memories of place, and keep local identity intact:

> The empty bucket stares a moment
> toward his brain, so he closes
> the closet door, hums
> the ashes off his cigar,
> and goes in to dinner.
> He will never forget his days here
> In the dirt under the mango tree
> prints of chicken feet
> go every which way.[26]

26. Eric Chock, 'Last Days Here', *Last Days Here*, Bamboo Ridge Press, Honolulu 1989, p71.

Given human costs of displacement and deskilling, 'Paradise' (minus the chicken prints, ethnic smells, rotting talapia, and sulking Hawaiian natives to be sure) remains a white-mythological trope by which to structure and integrate Hawaii into the mainland and transnational tourist flow. Paradise tropes project a vacation space of Pacific culture that, despite much evidence to the contrary (such as the American-backed overthrow of the Hawaiian monarchy in 1893), remains outside the workaday labours of EuroAmerican history. Can 'paradise' ever write back to challenge the Edenic fantasies of this American empire? One of cultural critic Stephen Sumida's strongest claims about the local literature movement in Hawaii that has flourished since the late Talk Story conferences of 1978 and 1979 is that, by resisting the sway of hegemonic national culture,

27. Stephen H. Sumida, *And the View from the Shore*, p38. On the complex plantation vision in Murayama's novel, see Rob Wilson, 'The Languages of Confinement and Liberation in Milton Murayama's *All I Asking For Is My Body*', in *Writers of Hawaii: A Focus on Our Literary Heritage*, Eric Chock and Jody Manabe (eds) Bamboo Ridge Press, Honolulu 1981, pp62-65.

the facile image of Hawai'i as paradise, everywhere associated with pop literature, music, film, and travel poster-graphics of Hawai'i, is contradicted by nonfictional and fictional works [of local literature such as Milton Murayama's *All I Asking For Is My Body* (1975)] that may serve as prototypes in the development of Hawaii's literature beyond the simple pastoral.[27]

As circulated through the pastoral discourse of authors like Mark Twain, Robert Louis Stevenson and James Michener, and rehashed as popular culture, 'the facile image of Hawai'i as paradise' has been challenged as the de-historicizing fantasy of a dominant culture expanding its terrain, and telos of development-driven material prosperity – at whatever cost to indigenous or local culture – into the Asian/Pacific.

During this moment of euphoric transnationalization and self-orientali-zation, Maui risks becoming suburb for Hollywood scriptwriters, post-hurricane Kauai is doing everything it can to attract more Stephen Spielbergs to come over from the Rim, film more *Jurassic Parks*, and turn the wilderness and eco-history of Hawaii into a theme park, and the backside of Diamond Head on Oahu is being reconstructed by the Waihee administration into a state-funded film studio even as I write. In short, this production of Hawaii into a 'paradise of the Pacific' needs to be placed in politicized italics and undermined as a trope of the dominant discourse helping to naturalize the American idea of the Pacific as a dreamy space both within but outside (exotic oriental other) to the dynamic workings of national/transnational capital in its global reach.

Absolutely crucial to the entry of the state of California, if not the Pacific Northwest, into the dynamism of the world system as recentred in the Pacific Rim in 1848 was communication with, labour from, and representation of Hawaii. In brief, Hawaii served as the intermediating space in the creation of an 'American Pacific', transmitting the cheap labour and abundant resources of the Asian Pacific region to mainland America via the west coast. As mediating link to the markets of Canton, the whaling waters off Japan and the furs of Alaska, Hawaii was linked and appropriated within seventy years, from the arrival of New England Calvinist missionaries in 1820 to the overthrow of the Hawaiian monarchy in 1893. American national self-interests were served by the twin strategies of (a) commercialization via the imposition of the plantation economy and all but total alienation of native lands by 1848, and, (b) pastoralization which turned Hawaii into a Pacific 'paradise' forever outside of Euro-American time and space, that is, outside the dynamism of Hegelian history.

The space of Hawaii would forever lead displaced American patriots, in James Jones's novelistic metaphor, *from here* (plantations, racial troubles, military battles) *to eternity* (paradise rephrased as a multicultural fusion in the Asian/Pacific little bars and dance clubs of River Street).[28] As the key American outpost into the Asia-Pacific at Pearl Harbor (what the Hawaiians knew as 'Pearl Lake') since the early 1880s, the space of Hawaii could be irrevocably linked to economic domination and military surveillance and yet paradoxically preserved, by sublimating body tropes of heaven-on-oceanic-earth as a region of Oceanic fantasy – at the Royal Hawaiian – forever immune to capitalist destruction and ecological damage; as Twain rhetorically boasted (in a key line for the tourist industry) they were 'the loveliest fleet of islands that lies anchored in any ocean.'[29]

GOODBYE PARADISE AS GLOBAL/LOCAL COMMUNITY

The Dennis Christianson and Tim Swage produced and directed movie, *Goodbye Paradise* (released by Pacific Focus Inc./Axelia Pictures International, 1991), which made its world première at the International Film Festival at the East West Center in Hawaii, portrays the upscale gentrification of Honolulu Chinatown through the closing of an old bar, called the Paradise Inn, and its abrupt transformation by Pacific Rim management into 'Katrina's In

28. James Jones's World War Two novel, *From Here to Eternity*, became an Academy Award-winning movie in 1953, with outdoor shots of Schofield Barracks, Kuhio Beach, Halona Cave, and Waialae Golf Course, though the multiculturalism of Hotel and River Streets was filmed in Hollywood and 'faked': see Robert C. Schmitt, *Hawaii In the Movies, 1898-1959*, Hawaiian Historical Society, Honolulu 1988, pp60-62. A remarkable number of movies about Hawaii 'took place aboard aircraft, ships, boats, or submarines', suggesting a cold war view of Paradise spatialized from the military shore (6).

29. Mark Twain, *Letters from Hawaii*, A. Grove Day (ed), University of Hawaii Press, Honolulu 1975, pvi. See Sumida, *And the View From the Shore*, pp38-56, on Twain's vision of a race- and class-divided 'Pacific paradise'.

Chinatown'. Focusing on the last Saturday in the business life of this multi-ethnic bar and a small upstairs business complex operating since the 1930s, the film traces the commodified conversion into a site for the consumption of 'California Cuisine' and an upscale art gallery. The half-million dollar movie thus traces, on a small and contradictory scale of place-bound sentimentality to be sure, the threatened fate of Hawaii's local culture/literature/film within a global context of cultural reinvention and economic displacement.

As *Goodbye Paradise* problematizes through the suavely cynical yuppie gaze of the Chinese-American owner of the Paradise Inn bar, John Young, for whom 'public opinion is a commodity you buy and sell like anything else', the Hawaiian locale must put itself on the pathways of transnational capital to prosper. This is painfully clear in a tourist-driven economy where more visitors mean surplus value for everybody from university professors to hotel busboys since the 'jumbo jet age and mass tourism' came to Hawaii in 1970 and boomed into a global/local necessity even as the poetics of place began to be reconstituted into an 'ex-primitive' or user-friendly tourist landscape.[30]

This process of global modernization has, in many respects, already become a recognizably postmodern process of mimicking, simulating and, in effect, imagistically displacing local style and indigenous customs, as in the commercially recontextualized hula of the Kodak Hula Show or the Mormon-sponsored performance of South Pacific cultures as Hawaiian at the Polynesian Cultural Center: 'See all of Polynesia! All in one place!' proclaims one of their 1993 ecotourist Center advertisements. Inputs from global culture, technologies of the video image from Betamax to IMAX and commodity forms would thus disrupt the ethnically mixed community of locals who once took care of one another during the post-war era (over-sentimentalized in the film through the pidgin-speaking pathos of Pat Morita, playing Ben, a former pineapple cannery worker turned street person and drunk). Such locals, in and around Chinatown (or in more staunchly Hawaiian communities like Waianae on the Leeward cost of Oahu) are increasingly confronting the transformation of the American/Pacific region into the site of a highly simulated transnational ethnicity that goes under the user-friendly rubrics, 'ecotourism' or 'cultural tourism'. Haunani-Kay Trask describes this postcolonial scenario, while defending the resurgent claims of the Hawaiian sovereignty struggle one hundred years after the McKinley-endorsed American annexation of the native kingdom and land: 'Burdened with commodification of their culture and exploitation of their people, Hawaiians exist in an occupied country where hostage people are forced to witness (and, for many, to participate in) their own collective humiliation as tourist artifacts for the First world.'[31]

Most indigenous Hawaiians (20 per cent of Hawaii's population by the most expansive count of mixed-blood quantum) do not necessarily want to be absorbed into the great American multiculture, as Trask has relentlessly argued of the *kanaka maoli*, and are forging a Pacific version of cultural nationalism tied to the preserving of language, custom, and land. But Big

30. James Mak and Marcia Sakai, 'Tourism in Hawai'i: Economic Issues for the 1990s and Beyond', in *Politics and Public Policy in Hawai'i*, Zachary A. Smith and Richard C. Pratt (eds), State University of New York Press, Albany 1992, p187. On any day, there are some 170,000 tourists in Hawaii.

31. Haunani Kay-Trask, '*Kupa'a 'Aina* [Hold Fast to the Land]: Native Hawaiian Nationalism in Hawai'i', in *Politics and Public Policy in Hawai'i*, p246.

Sharon, the big-hearted Hawaiian waitress in *Goodbye Paradise*, nostalgically dances with Joe and Tiny to the awesome Gabby Pahanui's slack-key 'Moonlight Lady' to signify the threat of global foreclosure, from the Pacific Rim, to the multi-ethnic proletarian culture in Hawaii of those 'who work in the fields by day' and would still party in the Paradise Inn at night.

As social text, *Goodbye Paradise* warns that the ethos of contemporary tourist-driven Hawaii has seemingly become one (as the hospital warns Joe, who gets behind on his payments for Ben) of 'just doing business' and following the economistic mandates of turning place into space and both into accumulated powers of time and money. (As Hawaii property-law expert David Callies rather preposterously claims of the resort takeover of local landscapes, 'Golf courses tend to be good neighbors', whatever the shape or size of the neighbourhood that is left.)[32] As the movie rather unphotogenically intimates – the constrained image-scheme recalling in a lesser key Nagisa Oshima's refusal of the colour green and 'characters sitting and talking on *tatami*' – 'paradise' seen as a distinctive Pacific space and unique location of Hawaiian culture may be phased out piece by piece and neighbourhood by neighbourhood in the name of Californian cuisine and the rise of transPacific profits.

In the movie's most contentious narrative twist, the agent of the cultural change in *Goodbye Paradise* is no global outsider from Japan or Hong Kong, however (as in the reiterative orientalism of TV's new *Raven* series, with its endless supply of inscrutable *yakuza*, Samoan bouncers, and slimy Japanese businessmen invading a calmly photogenic Hawaii), but the yuppie architect son of the original owner, Mr Waichee Young, who as a second-generation Chinese had worked his way up from his father's plantation life on Maui to owning business and real estate in Honolulu. This older Mr. Young hovers over the movie like a *genius loci*, his calming voiceover of decency and paternalistic good cheer recalling the *haole* (White) bar manager, Joe Martin, to the ethic of care, compassion, and humour that his architect son is helping to phase out. This new Asian-American MBA-wielding son has married a vulgar capitalist *haole* from California (who, in true postmodern intertextual fashion, looks and acts like the Ivana Trump of Chinatown) who embodies a cool blonde style of selfishness and profit, local indifference, and feels no ties to the old compassionate ethic his father kept towards his workers and tenants: a local multiculture comprised of Cook, the thrifty and scurrilous Chinese who plans to open his own Thai restaurant ('it's just Chinese food with peanut sauce and curry'), Tiny, the huge Hawaiian with heart of gold and scraps of Hawaiian wisdom about *mahus* and the moon, Big Sharon, Little Sharon, Billy, even Lieutenant Nomura, Evelyn and Elmira Lymon, the old Catholic sisters who are coldly being evicted.

The Chinatown neighbourhood around the Paradise Inn bar, personifying the mix and scrappy endurance of local identity, 'has survived disease, fire, war, and even tourism', as old Mr Young quips, but the attack of Californian cuisine upon local favourites like Spam *masubi* seems ever more dangerous to the fate of Hawaiian hybrid/indigenous identity. The movie is thus riddled with

32. David L. Callies, 'Development Fees', *The Price of Paradise*, p170.

a recognizably postmodern nostalgia for what David Harvey calls (after the affirmative rearguard 'critical regionality' theorized by British architect, Kenneth Frampton) cultivating and amassing the oppositional force or a 'place-bound identity'.[33] Tiny's unironic affirmation of Hawaiian local identity as the upbeat (essentialist) claim that 'Chinatown is always going to be Chinatown, Joe' does not match the global/local circumstances, nor does Joe's one-man charity organization to radiate a thousand points of socialist-Christian light on Hotel Street.

Given Hawaii's state economy that costs 34 percent more to live in than on the mainland[34] and in which state and local government collects 30 per cent more taxes per person than the US national average,[35] the movie is correct to suggest that one tends by economic necessity (as much as by local tradition) to build an *ohana* (extended family) of mothers, fathers, uncles, aunts, grandparents, friends, 'or other reluctant but co-operative souls' in order to survive.[36] This results in a watered-down parody of residual Hawaiian values in *Goodbye Paradise*, here captured through the hearts of gold in Tiny (the huge Hawaiian bouncer) and Billy (the half-Hawaiian, half-Chinese bartender) who finally, with saintly Joe, decides to 'stay in the neighborhood' for food and bonds of local affection after the bar is closed.

By now, transnational tourism has already become the 'primary export' of Hawaii (like the casino economy of Nevada)[37] and, in this process of consensual displacement, the state's natural beauty and landscape sublimity has been seemingly instrumentalized into its primary 'asset'.[38] The language of Pacific Rim economism can always conclude that supply-and-demand dynamics will keep the cost of living in Hawaii very high but the standard of living 'admirable'. Still, the claustrophobic and residually impoverished spaces of Honolulu Chinatown cannot compete with the scenic and sensual allure of hotel-heaven Waikiki or the 'fearful beauty' of the wilderness in Volcano National Park: to invoke the 'tourist gaze' of Paul Theroux, in its full orientalist and exotic splendour, 'The two most obvious facts of Hawaii are the huge sluttish pleasures of its Nipponized beachfront hotels and, in great contrast, its rugged landscape of craggy volcanoes and its coastal headlands.'[39] Hawaiian nationalism, in such a calculus, is never even mentioned as real or emergent threat to tourist pipedreams of a native-emptied resort or volcano. Cultural nationalism in the new Pacific cannot be marketed as ex-primitive tourist delight – at least not yet.

In a theme that resonates with the complex social dynamics driving the contemporary 'local literature' movement in Hawaii, *Goodbye Paradise* helps to show (through the synecdochal allegory of the bar as space of local culture) that a once-pastoral ethic of mutual care and multicultural unity in Hawaii is fast giving way in contemporary Honolulu to an ethic of profiteering and a fluidly delocalizing style of image- and self-promotion. In the imaginary polity of *Goodbye Paradise*, this restructuring most hurts the old residents and scrappy citizens like old Ben and the white Christian ladies who have dwelled over the bar, although the costs to indigenous Hawaiians are barely even measured.

33. See Kenneth Frampton, 'Towards a Critical Regionalism: Six Points for an Architecture of Resistance', in *The Anti-Aesthetic*, Hal Foster (ed), Bay Press, Port Townsend, Washington 1983, pp16-30.

34. Leroy O. Laney, 'Cost of Living', *The Price of Paradise*, p29.

35. Jack P. Suyderhoud, 'Government Size', *ibid.*, p53.

36. Leroy O. Laney, 'Cost of Living', *ibid.*, p27.

37. James Mak, 'Tourist Taxes', *The Price of Paradise*, p97.

38. David McClain, 'Hawaii's Competitiveness', *The Price of Paradise*, p10.

39. Paul Theroux, *The Happy Isles of Oceania*, p473. On the British lineage of Theroux's 'tourist gaze' that prefers wilderness scenery to the turmoil of history, see John Urry, *The Tourist Gaze: Leisure and Travel in Contemporary Societies*, Sage, London 1990.

Local TV news celebrity, Joe Moore, plays (and saint-like, overplays) bar manager, Joe Martin, who holds on to a virtually Christian socialist ethic of neighbourhood care and concern (*aloha* spirit affirmed as local core) like the old Mr Young's who had years ago taken him in as a stepson after his dog soldier days in Vietnam had landed him across the Pacific in Hawaii – feeding stray cats, putting drunks in taxi-cabs home, caring for street people and the older people. While *Goodbye Paradise* gets excessively sentimental through Moore's unselfish unconcern for money, and waxes nostalgic for the multi-ethnic *all-in-the-ohana* Hawaiian way of life in old Honolulu that is now being phased out from the inside by transnational capitalist transformations of the inner city into upscale real estate, it does show the process and cost of cultural displacement at work in downtown Honolulu.

Goodbye Paradise does, if humourously and tenderly by turns, reveal the creolized multicultural community that had come about and been forged over years of co-existing on the plantation as in the bar, mixing Chinese cook, Hawaiian bouncer, Chinese owner, Japanese cop, white manager, and half-Chinese, half-Hawaiian bar hostess with newcoming *haole* waitress from the American south, even as this local community is now being disrupted, phased out, molested from local space. Threatened is that very complex of Hawaiian values, still much touted at the core of local culture, called *aloha 'aina* (love of the land) which, even transformed from its agricultural origins in *taro* farming, implies (in Sumida's multicultural rephrasing) 'symbols and metaphors integral to the Hawaiian language [and which] bind love of the land (i.e., if you love and cultivate the land, the land will return by feeding you), family, sustenance, and culture itself into a rich complex of values – values involving reciprocity among people and between people and nature.'[40]

Like the starry-eyed localist hero, Ben Knox, who squats on the Scottish beach in Bill Forsyth's *Local Hero* (1983) to resist the transnational encroachment of an oil refinery upon the pastoral community at Furness Bay, Joe Moore, local news anchor, plays a *local hero* of the scrappy resistant multiculture and agent of this uncanny *aloha* spirit of 'reciprocity among people'. Martin labours to uphold and preserve local charms and local mores from the damages of historical molestation and that American common sense master-narrative called 'progress'. That this localized and working-class *haole* who came to Hawaii by way of Vietnam, across Asian/Pacific space, loses spatially and politically but gains a moral-sentimental victory of love over time and money offers little consolation. Two capitalist ethics compete, a residually paternal and a more brutally transnational one, and the former wins only at the symbolic level as the bar gets closed and redone into California cuisine art. Both ethics all too easily repress the presence of the Hawaiian sovereignty movement, that is presently refusing such accommodations to state-driven future planners and economistic knowledge-workers from the University of Hawaii calculating their own 'price of paradise'.

At least since 1988, it has become apparent that the majority of Hawaii's multicultural citizens have opposed the influx of over-blown foreign

40. Stephen H. Sumida, *And the View from the Shore*, p108. For a more place-bound treatment of Asian-Pacific American identity in Hawaii, see Stephen H. Sumida, 'Sense of Place, History, and the Concept of the "Local" in Hawaii's Asian/ Pacific Literatures', in Shirley Geok-lin Lim and Amy Ling, (eds), *Reading the Literatures of Asian America*, Temple University Press, Philadelphia 1992, pp215-237.

41. James Mak and
Marcia Y. Sakai,
'Foreign Investment',
The Price of Paradise,
p33.

investment in general, and Japanese investment in particular.[41] Almost two thirds of the hotel rooms in the state are owned by foreign investors, especially Japanese, so this retrenchment in the local economy and place can be read as a defensive reaction to the makings of a borderless transnational economy that peaked across the decade of the 1980s and is dismantling place and culture of the very distinctiveness which makes Hawaii attractive. This new Pacific of hotel resorts and microchip factories is the dream of the Pacific Rim, the paradise of APEC. But the loss of land and property imparts a sense of lost control and cultural displacement, from Honolulu to Vancouver, and works to dismantle dreams of individual homeownership, as even the governor of Hawaii (a Hawaiian by blood) recognizes. Yet the postmodern context of hyper-capital is such that the local is increasingly effected by the invasion and retreat of global capital, in this instance the very mobility of the Japanese yen in foreign real estate markets like upscale Kahala, or Indonesian capital from the notorious transnational big spender, Sukarman Sukamto, at 'Landmark

42. *Ibid.*, p36.
Throughout 1993,
Sukarman Sukamto
served as the focus of
controversy
concerning the site,
form, and funding of a
Hawaiian Convention
Center which he
wanted to place on the
Aloha Motors site
along with an array of
resort hotels and shops
to be owned and run
by his Indonesian
conglomerate.

Waikiki'.[42] The local is driven up, down, and out by fluctuations in the global financial system, as neighbourhoods like Kahala in Honolulu experience the influx and out-flight of Tokyo yen, given the dynamics of repatriated capital that burst in 1991.

Local assets, in what seems to be the makings of a deregulated global economy from NAFTA to APEC, are palpably threatened by capital from Japan, Australia, Taiwan, Canada, or California. Much like a country or a company, the local economy of Hawaii is instantly effected by global events (in economics and politics) such as the 1985 United Airlines strike, Operation Desert Storm in 1991, and the national recession as it effects the tourist flow from Pacific Coast states like California.

As what some would call a tourist microeconomy, the state of Hawaii must compete with countries and city-states like Bermuda, Fiji, Hong Kong, Las Vegas, and the Bahamas for tourist capital and market its local soul as the stuff of global fascination and redemption. Also, given the global and national dynamics of knowledge flow and productive employment, 'Hawaii may very well have a brain drain problem [of out migration] like that commonly found in

43. Walter Miklius,
'Out Migration', *The
Price of Paradise*, p243.

third-world countries.'[43] This is especially so, in post-industrial terms, given the global shift towards developing a tourist-driven local economy that is riddled by low-wage and low-skill service industries. In Hawaii, this means that pineapple production and sugar plantations are being phased out and tourist resorts and golf courses are phased in as is happening with Hamakua Sugar on the Big Island or, on a near-total scale, to the Dole-run island of Lanai. Given the rise and spread of tourism into the major global industry, cultural criticism must now stand and measure the costs and claims of this transcultural flow upon local place-bound identity, in Hawaii as in England.

According to David McClain, Walker Distinguished Professor of Business Enterprise and Financial Economics & Institutions at the University of Hawaii at Manoa, the local market of 1.1 million people is quite 'unsophisticated' compared to Asian citizens and those of the West, since 'related and supporting industries for anything but travel and tourism are not world class' and cannot compete with Pacific Rim countries which manage and evaporate the interior Pacific with their APEC-like gaze from Hong Kong to Los Angeles.[44] In social science ways, this economistic discourse establishes that, with an entrenched élite who benefit from restricted competition, the state of Hawaii resembles a 'one-export-commodity developing country model, with an overdeveloped public sector that adversely affects entrepreneurial activity and an entrenched élite trying to maintain its privileges': such factors prevent Hawaii's long-delayed emergence into the 'Capital of the Pacific'.[45]

The Pacific Basin is bypassed, suppressed, if not ignored in most Pacific Rim mapping of capital's megatrends: this Pacific 'finanscape' centre can be better located in Hong Kong, Tokyo, Los Angeles, Vancouver or Sydney.[46] With an acute sense of Pacific Rim decentring, Meaghan Morris has described the metamorphosis of the Sydney Tower in Australia into technological icon of Pacific Rim domination from downunder, as if for once undoing the tyranny of northern space and Atlantic time: 'Inside the Tower, electronic communications were repeatedly invoked as enabling Australia's integration into the age of global simultaneity: no more time lag, no more "isolation" by vast space from the rest of the world and from each other.'[47] With canny cultural politics, Morris is again thinking through the sway of EuroAmerican cultural technologies over Pacific cultures and remote spaces in her uncanny reading of the Australian film, *Crocodile Dundee* (1986), as an '*export-drive* allegory' in which a Pacific wilderness space and alien clture on the outback 'manages to export its crocodile-poacher and, with a little help from the American media, market him brilliantly in New York.'[48]

If the transnational 'cyborg of buddha-nature' promises to redeem the ancient Pacific and Asian locals from any lingering sense of global isolation, meanwhile local space is being reconstituted (as in Sydney or Honolulu) into a tourist landscape (as outback/as Eden) on the transcultural flow from Tokyo and Indonesia. An *aloha* to local culture, *Goodbye Paradise* was barely shown in Honolulu, never mind Sydney or Los Angeles: pastoral politics do not circulate in cyberspace. But a micropolitics of place and identity, from Bamboo Ridge to Suva to Papua New Guinea, surges up elsewhere and otherwise to challenge the global flow of representations and the glut of cargo-cult culture.

According to the multicultural politics and affirmative idealism that drives the plot of *Goodbye Paradise*, then, to return to that ill-fated local bar and small-scale movie circulating in its praises, racial and ethnic jokes can abound in an economy of mutual exchange, in which 'the rules down here' specify that you 'make one joke and take one joke.' Despite the multicultural mix and mixed-blood match (Joe quits as Young's manager and goes off with the Asian local, Billy), the movie does, like *Hawaii Five O*, preserve a racial hierarchy, with Hawaiians kept in lowly physical service positions (Big Sharon, Tiny), Japanese in middle-management positions (Lieutenant Nomura), the charitable white as paternal luna managing the plantation (Joe Martin), and the Chinese scrapping to rise from farmer rags and stigmatized pidgin (like Ben's) to yuppie riches

44. David McClain, 'Hawaii's Competitiveness', p10. All of APEC's (Asian Pacific Economic Convention) 14 countries are located on the Pacific Rim from South Korea to New Zealand to Canada to Indonesia. 'Pacific Basin' island states, sites, and countries are viewed only as tourist sites, not as global agents.

45. *Ibid.*

46. See Arjun Appadurai, 'Disjuncture and Difference in the Global Economy' on 'the five dimensions of global cultural flows' which he terms (a) ethnoscapes, (b) mediascapes, (c) technoscapes, (d) finanscapes, and (e) ideoscapes.

47. Meaghan Morris, 'Metamorphoses at Sydney Tower', *New Formations* 11, 1990, p9.

48. Meaghan Morris, 'Tooth and Claw: Tales of Survival, and *Crocodile Dundee*', *The Pirate's Fiancée: Feminism, Reading, Postmodernism*, Verso, London 1988, p248.

(like John 'Junior' Young's) in two generations.

Despite the contradiction-ridden nature of local culture, ethnic customs and ways of life do linger on and would collage and endure across time and memory. Of each local character in *Goodbye Paradise*, with the crucial exception of John Young, it could be said, as Juliet Kono Lee claims in 'Yonsei' of her American-pop fourth generation son moved so far from prior generations of Japanese who worked the sugar plantations on the Big Island,

> Your blood runs free
> From the redness of soil.
> But you are mired
> Into this locality.[49]

49. Juliet S. Kono, 'Yonsei', *The Best of Bamboo Ridge*, p52.

50. Rodney Morales, 'The Speed of Darkness', *The Speed of Darkness*, Bamboo Ridge Press, Honolulu 1988, p127. For Morales's devotion to the Hawaiian cause, see the collection he edited in support of de-militarizing the island of Kahoolawe, *Ho'Iho'Ihou: A Tribute to George Helm & Kimo Mitchell*, Bamboo Ridge Press, Honolulu 1984.

51. Joseph P. Balaz, 'Da Mainland To Me', *Chaminade Literary Review* 2, 1989, p109. On the formation of a distinctly Hawaiian localism in the decolonizing American Pacific, see Richard Hamasaki, 'Mountains in the Sea: Emerging Literatures of Hawai'i', in Paul Sharrad (ed), *Readings in Pacific Literature*, University of Wollongong Press, Wollongong, NSW 1994.

52. June Watanabe, 'Dig turns up best look yet at old Hawaii', *Honolulu Star-Bulletin*, November 5, 1992. Watanabe quotes from Joseph Kennedy, head of Archaeological Consultants of Hawaii.

As Rodney Morales announces his Pacific claim for place-bound identity, in a short story about a surfer with a mystical attachment to the Pacific Ocean and Hawaiian/local culture, '*Me and the Pacific have this thing, see?*'[50] Or to invoke the localist claim of Joe Balaz, enunciated in his beloved Hawaiian Creole English (pidgin), 'Eh, like I told you,/dats da continent—? Hawai'i/is da mainland to me.'[51]

DIGGING DOWN INTO 'PARADISE'

During a recent excavation in Honolulu's downtown Chinatown, where the old Wong Building was being demolished to make way for a new housing project, material archaeologists for the city were again astonished to find layers of local and Hawaiian culture reaching back to a seventeenth century Hawaiian settlement. Just ten feet of soil provided a chronological history of Honolulu Chinatown from the mid-1600s through the eighteenth and nineteenth centuries. The 87-year old Wong Building was the last wooden structure in Hawaii and had housed the old Cebu Pool Hall, a local Filipino hangout fallen into decrepitude in the 1970s. Uncannily, beneath the Wong Building were three burn layers pointing to three separate Chinatown fires. Radiocarbon dating further suggested a pre-contact Hawaiian settlement called *Kikihale* (supposedly named after a daughter of Kou, a former chief on Oahu) where Kamehameha the Great had later quartered his lieutenants and retainers after the conquest of Honolulu on his way to the uniting of Hawaii into a new nation comparable to the states of Cook, Vancouver, and missionaries from Boston. Other findings included objects of indigenous Hawaiian material culture that ranged from a drilled shark's tooth to bits of shell necklaces, Chinese porcelain from the 1700s, ale bottles from Glasgow, champagne bottles from Paris, and samples of English creamware.[52]

By the international traffic of Honolulu Harbor, buried beneath the ethnic community of the Paradise Inn, *local* culture was already *global* in a complex Asian/Pacific/European mix that expresses the vernacular history of Hawaii as a place ever-amalgamating the debris of an Asian/Pacific future. No android's limb was found.

KIPLING, A 'PRIMITIVE' NATIONAL IDENTITY AND THE 'COLONIAL CONDITION' AT HOME

C.J.W.-L. Wee

I

Modernity is generally the entrenched concept we associate with western nationalism and cultural identity. Indeed, as the Australian critic Simon During notes, 'The peculiar force of the modern is such that ... one can qualify that clumsy spatializing metonymy ["the West"] only by the adjective "modern" itself.'[1] In speaking of 'modernity' and 'nationalism', I refer to nationalism as the attempt to actualise in socio-political and cultural terms a presumed universal desire for liberty and progress: this is the 'normal' type of nationalism, best represented by the early emergence of France and Great Britain as nation-states, and it shares the same intellectual and material bases with the Enlightenment, and is thus also connected with the emergence of industrialised societies. Within this particular teleology, science and modern education function to gradually eliminate archaic socio-political and religious structures – 'tradition' – and create cultural homogeneity.

1. Simon During, 'Waiting for the Last Post: Some Relations Between Modernity, Colonization, and Writing', in Ian Adam and Helen Tiffin (eds), *Past the Last Post: Theorizing Post-Colonialism and Post-Modernism*, University of Calgary Press, Calgary 1990, p23.

Of course, nationalism has not always been received in the West itself as a uniformly blessed instrument of rationality: the Second World War saw to that, as has recent 'ethnic cleansing' in Eastern Europe. Still, as the political philosopher Partha Chatterjee observes in his *Nationalist Thought in the Colonial World*, many western liberals and Marxists seem to believe that the West maintains a stranglehold on the power of reason in the activity of nation-building, and that it is Asian or African nationalisms – the very idea of nationalism itself being imperfectly borrowed from their colonial masters – which are ambivalent or disturbed. For instance, India with its Muslim 'problem' is still seen as the failure of Enlightenment nationalism's presence overseas, given an apparent inability to overcome irrational, pre-modern difference in its constitution of the nation.

I will attempt a look at a disidentificatory moment within English cultural history, when a progressive image of the nation and its empire was rejected for a more romantic, sometimes magical, anti-modern image. My chosen representative figure is Rudyard Kipling, a champion of the late-Victorian 'New Imperialism', who firmly rejected what might be called an older free-trade conception of the nation-empire. Through looking at one rebellion against the process of cultural homogenisation *within* the very homeland of industrial modernity, I suggest that the 'irrationality' which English nationalism uses to constitute its own modern/rational identity is not only to be found in the colonial periphery, but *inside* the imperial homeland itself; and that a kinship exists between the creation of a primitive or traditional, rural identity at home and – very oddly – an ambivalent admiration of primitive peoples and landscapes abroad: the empire and the (ongoing post-) 'colonial condition' of pre- or non-modernity, one might say, also dwells within England. For Kipling, pre-modern vitality must not only be appropriated but surreptitiously *imported* into the homeland. There is a fascinating story still to be fully told of the encounter between 'a world-conquering western thought and the ["traditional"] intellectual modes of non-western cultures.'[2] This will help give us a clearer understanding of the historical affectivity of what might be called (with Edward Said in mind) a form of 'Occidentalism', the imaginative and intellectual creation and representation of the western Self for itself and for others.[3] I shall return to these general issues at the end of the essay.

Given the above focus, I will discuss some of Kipling's less-studied English stories of an elemental and magical East Sussex in the fairy stories of *Puck of Pook's Hill* (1906). Both texts and contexts are important to me for I am concerned with a historical moment in the English history of modernity. Kipling displaces overly-refined concepts of 'feminine', over-aestheticised, bookish culture (as perhaps typified by the anti-imperial Schlegel sisters in *Howards End*) and inserts, in its place, a more 'fundamental' notion of culture first formulated in his Indian tales, and based upon his preference for the most manly of Indian men – war-like tribesmen like the Pathans rather than 'effeminate' Bengalis – and the pre-modern landscapes they inhabit.[4] His Indian frontier is both a literal and romantically imaginative site for the re-making of English vigour, the core value in *Puck*. Kipling then tries to blend what he values with a historic English character (a 'primitive peasantry', as he calls it in a 22 December 1902 letter to H. Rider Haggard) and landscape.[5]

The exchange sought is an odd one: modern man, here to spread civility, wants to acquire barbarism; in return, he offers to bring the energy he so much wants from the native under harness. The exploitation involved is clear. By the publication of *Stalky & Co* (1899), though, Kipling shows in the way the three boy heroes can drum up the presence of the primitive that such energy can also be found *within* England.

Puck of Pook's Hill is the end result: here, Kipling finds a native English vigour which more than matches anything from the imperial frontier, and the Indian-to-English link becomes obscured; the virtue of manly energy, however, remains as a sign that the colonised other is not altogether erased in this text.

Kipling's invocation of an organic culture thus includes the recreation of England as a land of rugged warriors living amidst an agrarian society removed from any urban setting. A 'primitive' society is envisioned as a *counter*-civilisation to effete and supposedly advanced metropolitan life.[6] Kipling is the outsider – the overseas-born Englishman – who defines Englishness by initially conceiving that the 'true' English spirit is at its best overseas. He only later looks 'inside' England to wonder how English identity was 'originally' formed in an imperial centre he sees as blighted by a weakly liberal high culture. What sort of

2. Partha Chatterjee, *Nationalist Thought in the Colonial World: A Derivative Discourse?*, Zed Books, London 1986, p41.

3. This is as opposed to the representation of the 'West' by the 'non-West'; for instance, the economically successful nation-states on the Pacific Rim currently depict a monolithic West as a site of moral and economic decline because of its 'obsession' with individual identity and freedom. This seems to be a new form of muscle-flexing, anti-colonial discourse based upon the idea of an emerging Asian (and not just 'Asianised') modernity – witness Malaysian prime minister Dr Mahathir Mohamad's clashes with the UK.

4. The work which most clearly states and itself represents the principle of masculinist realism is his only novel, the misogynist *The Light That Failed* (1891).

5. Morton Cohen (ed), *Rudyard Kipling to Rider Haggard*, Hutchinson, London 1965, p50.

'centre' is England if Englishmen need to be overseas to even vaguely recall England's own adventure-filled frontier past? Kipling's subsequent work after going 'home' to England attempts to deal with this question. Given his public stature in Edwardian national-imperial politics, it would be wrong to dismiss or ignore the substantial body of his English work as being anomalous, as being less central than the Indian material.

II

By the end of the nineteenth century, as is well-known, it had become a commonplace among imperial spokesmen that frontier-living could alleviate the problem of metropolitan 'softness', inculcating toughness or manliness, a practical intelligence and group loyalty to other men and to the nation. The intellectual historian John Burrow reminds us that the idea of adventure found 'a ready audience around the turn of the century, among a people ... who began increasingly to worry about their international position ... and the poor physique of recruits ... [and were hence] generations which also listened to Dilke and Seeley, recited Kipling and Sir Henry Newbolt, admired Baden Powell and excused Jameson'.[7]

By 1907, the idea of the revitalising barbarous frontier was entrenched enough that the Chancellor of Oxford and former Viceroy of India, Lord Curzon, was able to tell the University in his Romanes Lecture that

Outside the English Universities no school of character exists to compare with the Frontier... The Frontier officer takes his life in his hands; for there may await him either the knife of the Pathan fanatic, or the more deadly fevers of the African swamp. But the risk is the last thing he takes into account... I am one of those who hold that in this larger atmosphere, on the outskirts of Empire, where the machine [of civilisation] is relatively impotent and the individual is strong, is to be found the ennobling and invigorating stimulus for our youth, saving them alike from the corroding ease and the morbid excitements of Western civilization.[8]

The frontier was therefore both a literal and imaginative site for the building of English manliness and vigour. Curzon's imperial version of nation-building indicates that there is a re-staging of the later-eighteenth century primitivist enthusiasm, though this enthusiasm is treated with more caution that it had been previously.

The attempts to formulate what can be called an anti-modern national-imperial culture had its origins in the radical re-assessment in the mid-nineteenth century of a national culture which, in the first half of the Victorian age, had advocated 'industry' (in both senses of that term) and mercantile values as the key to international survival, by (among others) Thomas Carlyle, the novelist and broad churchman Charles Kingsley, and his brother-in-law, the historian J.A. Froude.[9] Industrial life produced politically

6. This parallels the larger 'history of colonialism', which is 'a *counter-history* of the normative, traditional [and progressive] history of the West' (Homi K. Bhabha, 'The Third Space: An Interview with Homi Bhabha', in Jonathan Rutherford (ed), *Identity: Community, Culture, Difference*, Lawrence & Wishart, London 1990, p218.

7. J.W. Burrow, *A Liberal Descent: Victorian Historians and the Past*, Cambridge University Press, Cambridge 1981, p282.

8. Lord Curzon, *Frontiers*, 2nd edn. Clarendon Press, Oxford 1908, p56, 57.

9. Patrick Brantlinger calls the period from about the 1850s to 1880 the 'noon' of English imperialism. See *Rule of Darkness: British Literature and Imperialism, 1830-1914*, Cornell University Press, Ithaca 1988, p14.

restless, unhealthy and weak men.

Froude's studies, such as his extensive *History of England from the Fall of Wolsey to the Defeat of the Spanish Armada* (1856-70) and *Oceana, or England and Her Colonies* (1886), especially sanctioned a nationalist view of England which took to task irresponsible plutocracy and progressive commercialism. He recuperated the energetic glories of the bold, Protestant and sea-faring Elizabethan England he thought he saw in Hakluyt's *The Principal Navigations of the English Nation* (1599).[10] In the colonies, Froude says,

10. See Burrow's chapter on Froude, *op.cit.*

> children grow who seem once more to understand what was meant by 'merry England.' Amidst the uncertainties ... gathering around us at home ... it is something to have seen that there are other Englands beside the old one, where the race is thriving with all its ancient characteristics.[11]

11. J.A. Froude, *Oceana, or England and Her Colonies*, Charles Scribner's Sons, New York 1887, p17.

A nostalgic reactionism is balanced by a belief that History was about to unleash the potentialities of a Greater Britain.

In more specifically literary-cultural terms, there is a movement which Martin Green has tried to trace from Defoesque modern adventure,[12] with its connexion with 'free trade imperialism' (an expression following the 1953 Robinson-Gallagher thesis on informal imperialism) towards what he calls 'the saga or Viking adventure'; this is a more 'savage, and more atavistic kind of adventure ... [represented] in England by, for instance, Rider Haggard'.[13] This 'atavism', I believe, gets translated in mid-century into a more anti-modern (and territorially-based) conception of nation and empire. If previous (often Evangelical) Christian heroes brought civilisation to imperial outposts and freed slaves, Charles Kingsley's popular *Western Ho!* (1855) revealed an ambivalence towards contemporary English civilisation.[14]

12. See his important *Dreams of Adventure, Deeds of Empire*, Routledge and Kegan Paul, London 1980.

13. Martin Green, 'Adventurers Stake Their Claim: The Adventure Tale's Bid for Status, 1876-1914', in Karen R. Lawrence, (ed), *Decolonizing Tradition: New Views of Twentieth-Century 'British' Literary Canons*, University of Illinois Press, Urbana 1992, p80. My focus, in contrast to Green's, is to try to locate the historically shifting relationship between 'atavism' in the frontier *as well as at home* in 'sheltered' England. Further, I am not concerned with adventure per se, but only in the way the imperial nationalist 'finds' in the primitive realm an alternative source of knowledge of the West.

The post-Mutiny India that Kipling was born in and subsequently returned to as a sixteen-year-old in 1882 had shifted its attention away from the major urban centres, the foci of the previous policy of creating a native middle-class who were now becoming critical of imperial rule, to the northwest. Kipling's stories in the 1880s and 1890s reflect a complicated fascination with the noble savage, who is admired even while being denigrated as war-like and revengeful.[15] Despite the civilising mission of modernity of the white man – endeavours Kipling records in 'The Bridge-Builders' and 'William and Conqueror' in *The Day's Work* (1898) – there is a strong sense that the project of imperial modernity loses its teleological trajectory when confronted by primitive vigour, though the rhetoric of law and progress for the natives is kept up. Whatever else the fascination with the primitive may have been in the Age of Empire, it was not 'rational'.

'The Tomb of his Ancestors' from *The Day's Work* is a clear example of the emergence of 'good' English values in negotiation with the non-urban native. While this story can partially be read as propaganda justifying the Indian occupation, it simultaneously shows the mutuality of the white/black relationship from Kipling's perspective.

The regional site in this story is not north but central India. However, the natives in the regiment, the Bhils, are 'wild men'[16] similar in type to Pathan tribesmen. The regiment had 'fewer English officers than any other native regiment' and were 'the most *pukka shikarries* (out-and-out hunters) in all India' (86). Part of the shared culture between native and master is a penchant for killing animals as sport, as the upper classes – Matthew Arnold's 'Barbarians' – and their middle-class imitators were wont to do.

There is no doubt, however, of the Bhils' subordinate status. At the end of his first day in the regiment, John Chinn goes 'to dinner like a prince who has newly inherited his father's crown' (92). However, Chinn does not enter the regiment with his character fully developed for the needs of kingship: Bukta, the chief Bhil, has to help Chinn attain his destiny. For Chinn to truly take his place as his father and grandfather had before him, he must shoot a tiger in the Wuddar style – on foot and in a calm, nonchalant manner, which sounds remarkably like the stereotype of the unruffled Englishmen with the stiff upper-lip.[17]

The shooting itself is an elaborately staged event. The entire officers' mess is aware, even if Chinn is not, of Bukta's labours. A suitable tiger is tracked down, and the surrounding bush is filled with Bukta's men, just in case Chinn endangers his own life. Naturally, that does not happen. However, it takes a loyal or, depending on your point of view, colluding native to orchestrate this charade so that an 'inborn' talent for leadership can be manifested.

A full circle has been completed. The original John Chinn brought English civilisation to the wild men and now the Bhils in turn help develop the virile qualities of the grandson fresh from the civilised world. The Bhils also believe Chinn to be a reincarnation of his paternalistic grandfather. Chinn is therefore able to practise *noblesse oblige* on a scale unimaginable in his native Devonshire; feudal England lives on – outside England. Kipling's later role as a squire in a rural East Sussex is not surprising.

A cultural miscegenation thus occurs within a homosocial grouping of a white man and his 'people', in which of course literal miscegenation cannot transpire. The imperial text does not merely use the native to reflect fixed 'master' qualities, but, instead, the very image of the white man is a space for (an unequal if mutual) negotiation between the colonised and the coloniser. Various dichotomies are hardly kept separate: Chinn's grandfather tamed the wild men, but it is the very virtue of primitive energy that confirms his grandson's manhood; Chinn, as with his ancestors, is the harbinger of progress, yet he will not scruple to play on native superstitions to bring about imperial modernity in the form of law and order. The political address of the imperial text is scarcely consistent.

By 1899, with the publication of *Stalky & Co*, a displacement of the frontier towards home begins in Kipling's work. He demonstrates in the adventures of Stalky, Beetle and M'turk that the vitality located in non-white territories could be called up *in* England as well.

Stalky & Co provocatively asks what ideals of authority and education best

14. Regarding Kingsley, see C.J.W.-L. Wee, 'Christian Manliness and National Identity: The Problematic Construction of a Racially "Pure" Nation', along with the other essays in Donald E. Hall (ed), *Muscular Christianity: Embodying the Victorian Age*, Cambridge University Press, Cambridge 1994.

15. See Lewis Wurgaft, *The Imperial Imagination: Magic and Myth in Kipling's India*, Wesleyan University Press, Middletown 1983, pp13, 46–49, 139-44.

16. Rudyard Kipling, *The Day's Work*, Macmillan, London 1964, p87; all page numbers will hereafter be given in the main text.

17. An obvious comparison can be made between Chinn and Dravot from 'The Man who would be King' in *Wee Willie Winkie* (1888); Dravot, however, has a much lower social background – he is a *lumpen* version of Chinn – and has to go through a great deal of regeneration before he attains the 'awareness' which momentarily allows him, before his death, to be a 'true' king.

prepare a boy for the world of imperial administration in the army. *Stalky* is important within the established genre of schoolboy training manuals, for it attacks and subverts the 'Tom Brown' games ethic of fairness and co-operation with public school masters as a civilising process in prepation for life, and puts forth, as Robin Gilmour says, 'an older code, at once more anarchic in relation to constituted authority and more primitively "tribal" '.[18] Fairness disappears, and a plethora of guerrilla tactics are advocated in the battle against priggish masters who do not know how life works. The book encountered a storm of protest, the best known being Robert Buchanan's 'The Voice of the Hooligan': 'The vulgarity, the brutality, the savagery, reeks on every page... And the moral of the book – for, of course, like all such banalities, it professes to have a moral – is that out of material like these [boys] is fashioned the humanity which is to ennoble and preserve our Anglo-Saxon empire.'[19]

The epithets which Buchanan uses – brutality, savagery – help reveal the nature of the code the trio live by. In 'Slaves of the Lamp, Part I', they prepare to go on the warpath against their arch-enemy, the master King. As a preliminary ritual, an African drum which decorates their study wall is taken down:

> Now that West-African war drum had been made to signal across estuaries and deltas. Number Five [study] was forbidden to wake the engine within the earshot of the school. But a deep devastating drone filled the passages as M'Turk and Beetle scientifically rubbed its top. Anon it changed to the blare of trumpets – of savage pursuing trumpets. Then, as M'Turk slapped one side, smooth with the blood of ancient sacrifice, the roar broke into short coughing howls such as the wounded gorilla throws in his native forest.[20]

Martin Green comments on this passage: 'And as Kipling evokes behind the boys this somewhat fanciful picture of primitive man, he evokes before them the more realistic image of the people they will be ruling and fighting in their adult careers.'[21] Green is correct; but I wonder how 'fanciful' the passage is. A comic effect is intended, but that does not suggest that a serious identification between the primal and the schoolboys is not also intended.

A larger world exists beyond the narrow pale of Balliol College, where King was educated, and the minor public school he teaches in. This is the world being conjured up in the playing of the drum, a world in which savages are related to white men. The evocation of this world invigorates the trio in their struggle against false authority. Yet, despite the blood-lust, the boys are able to exploit the drum's 'engine' capacity 'scientifically': the mastery implied in the modernity of the White Sahib is not eradicated in the contact with the primitive. (However, the boys' control over the primitive can only be taken as 'mastery' if the drumming up of dark forces constitutes a 'rational' control of things.) The key difference between *Stalky* and 'The Tomb of his Ancestors' is that primitive forces may now be conjured up at home as a preparatory step to travelling to the edge of civilisation.

18. Robin Gilmour, 'Stalky & Co.': Revising the Code', in Phillip Mallet (ed), *Kipling Reconsidered*, St Martin's Press, New York 1989, p27.

19. Robert Buchanan, 'The Voice of the Hooligan', *Contemporary Review* 76, December 1899; reprinted in Roger Lancelyn Green (ed), *Kipling: The Critical Heritage*, Routledge and Kegan Paul, London, pp245-46.

20. Rudyard Kipling, *Stalky & Co*, Isabel Quigley (ed), Oxford University Press, Oxford 1987, p64; all page numbers will hereafter be given in the main text.

21. Martin Green, *The English Novel in the Twentieth Century: The Doom of Empire*, Routledge and Kegan Paul, London 1984, p41.

In the last story in *Stalky*, 'Slaves of the Lamp, Part II', Kipling shows Stalky getting out of a tight spot in the Indian northwest frontier by directly drawing upon his previous experiences. At a gathering of old school chums, Tertius gives testimony to Stalky's brilliant leadership among Sikhs and Pathans: 'None of our Pathans believed that [Stalky's accomplishment] was [due] to luck... They swore Stalky ought to have been born a Pathan, and – 'remember we nearly had a row in the fort when Rutton Singh said Stalky was a Sikh? Gad, how furious the old chap was with my Pathan Jemadar! But Stalky just waggled his finger and they shut up' (287). Like Kim, Kipling's famous Irish spy, Stalky is able to identify with the primitive mind; unlike Kim, he not need play at cultural cross-dressing to display his ability to control the locals.

Stalky is a maverick: he does what is necessary rather than maintain correct boundaries. Officials in Simla find his independent behaviour insupportable. Abanazar, another of Stalky's class-mates, says, 'Von Lennaert ... gasped "Who the dooce is this unknown Warren Hastings? He must be slain. He must be slain officially!"' (294). Like Conrad's Kurtz, Stalky has angered the bureaucracy and looked in the abyss; unlike Kurtz, Stalky has restraint. He has been better primed for kingship: already in his youth and in his homeland, he has looked into the heart of darkness, and has harnessed the power within. The question that will next need to be addressed is: can a specifically *English* vitality, as opposed to an evocation of frontier energy, be found at home? This question increasingly becomes one of Kipling's main concerns as the Edwardian period begins.

The political context at the end of the Victorian era was clearly different from mid-century. As historians point out, the pre-war right became increasingly apprehensive about empire and the United Kingdom's own security. Kipling believed Conservative pig-headedness to be part of the problem. In the fable 'Below the Mill Dam', from *Traffics and Discoveries* (1904), he attacks Tory old guard snobbery and complacency as embodied in Salisbury's successor, Arthur Balfour, in the name of a more efficient England. As is often the case with Kipling, he will without any sense of the contradictoriness involved hark back to a pre-modern England only two years later in *Puck of Pook's Hill*. However, it is not the case that Kipling rejects modernity per se – only the 'deracinating' urban aspects of it. For him, modern vigour – the 'cooked' state of civilisation – could only be genuinely vigorous if it retained its connexion with its 'raw' origins. In Kipling's literary-cultural discourse, modernity and its opposite, 'tradition' or 'the primitive', are both required.

The Boer War had especially shown up the limitations of late-Victorian imperialism: 'If it took ... so long to beat a tiny rabble of untrained peasants (the description was misleading, but widely believed), what chance would Britain have against any of the more efficient rivals.'[22] There were thus pressing reasons for Kipling's more homeward search for the 'roots' of English strength. In this context, social-psychological questions took on national-imperial dimensions – and not only for Kipling: the Inter-Departmental

22. Bernard Porter, 'The Edwardians and Their Empire', in Donald Read (ed), *Edwardian England*, Rutgers University Press, New Brunswick, New Jersey 1982, p129.

Committee convened to investigate the causes of the South African debacle had found evidence of 'physical deterioration' in the physique of Englishmen. This revelation provided part of the desire for social reforms even on the part of the Liberal government (which Kipling so despised) in 1906.[23]

23. See Porter, *ibid.*, p130-31.

If the above represents a standard historiography of turn-of-the-century Britain, what I wish to specifically examine is how Kipling thought a primitive manliness could be reproduced in rural England – this was in fact one of the solutions touted in response to this late 'Condition of England' question.

The late 1870s to the early 1900s saw the transformation of English culture: England was seen less as an urban and industrial nation created through self-made men in the north, but instead as a rural nation, with a southern centre.[24] A contributing reason for the change to a rural idyll was the racial 'degeneration' already mentioned. The prominence of the City brought to attention the 'unnatural' breeding grounds of the Cockney, inner London, which had already received prior attention in the earlier works of Charles Dickens and Charles Kingsley.[25] The perception of growing urban, industrial and racial blight led to various proposals. One set of alternatives proffered were urban ones; another set were composed of rural alternatives.[26]

24. See Alun Howkins, 'The Discovery of Rural England', in Robert Colls and Philip Dodd (eds), *Englishness: Politics and Culture 1880-1920*, Croom Helm, London 1986; and *Reshaping England: A Social History 1850-1925*, HarperCollins Academic, London 1991.

25. Kingsley himself was a cultural precursor of Kipling; his *Westward Ho!* was a significant literary rebellion against modernist notions of society, economics and empire (see Wee, *op.cit.*; and Green, *Dreams*). Kingsley, however, tended to appropriate non-English vigour and keep it at the frontier rather than try to displace it home, as Kipling attempts.

26. See Gareth Stedman Jones, *Outcast London*, Oxford University Press, Oxford 1970.

It must be stressed that the shift in cultural self-representation was quite widespread by the 1900s: Conservatives, Liberals and Socialists – the last under William Morris's and Edward Carpenter's influence – all issued plans regarding the re-animation of rural life.[27] The need for racial regeneration was not a 'loony' hobby horse of the Radical Right, any more than the creation of rural England was. It is with the extreme right, however, that the connexions between urban and non-urban, empire and nation are most clear. The parallel with the earlier relocation of the imperial frontier in India from city to wilder, harsher areas is very telling.

H. Rider Haggard's reflections after his return to England in 1881 are instructive. The Boer Republic which had arisen had sullied his vision of Englishness in Africa. England's failure in her African mission as represented by Gladstone's South Africa policy and the later Boer war had been due to a limp moral fibre ennervated, Haggard later believed, through the (literally) emasculating corruption of city life and materialistic decadence:

> I am convinced – and this is a very important national aspect of the question – that most of our reverses during the recent war were due to the pitting of town-bred bodies and intelligences, both of officers and men, against country-bred bodies and intelligences. We laugh at the Boer for his rude manners and rusticity, but therein lies a strength which if he and his people are wise they will not exchange for all the gold and gems in Africa and all the most exquisite refinements of Europe.[28]

Haggard's non-fiction such as *A Farmer's Year* (1899) and *Rural England* (1902) call for racial regeneration through a return to the land. Uncorrupted man, as Haggard felt he had seen in Africa, had a rural nature. Hence, what he had seen had also been the inner core of European man: in *King Solomon's Mines*, Sir Henry Curtis puts on skins and feathers in KuKuanaland and becomes a Viking.

Kipling's response to Haggard's ideas in a letter of 27 December 1902 is revealing:

> I entirely agree with you about the town-bred person. He has to spend half his time keeping fit outside his employment which ought to be making him fit while he works. If there is any way in which my Agricultural Muse may be of service later, why then as Virgil says, 'come on, oh (young) husbandman' and command me.[29]

Strange words from a professional writer with bad eysight. In a 1901 letter to Charles Eliot Norton, Kipling's assessment of the English performance in the Boer War had been thus: 'the experience has been wholesome... Now we are slowly coming back to the primitives, and realising that a lot of what we call "civilisation" was another name for shirking.'[30]

Kipling puts his 'Agricultural Muse' to 'service'. We get stories pertaining to the discovery of a traditional England possessing an organic unity between man and nature such as 'An Habitation Enforced' (1905) and 'My Son's Wife' (1913), in which imperial manliness is reproduced.

The English fiction also explores the importance of the motherland and those 'irrational' required beings for the cultural and physical reproduction of vigorous men, women and children. The masculine imperial frontier may give glory, but glory without the continuity of racial line and masculine ideals leads to the imperilling of nation and empire. Kipling comes to these conclusions in *Puck of Pook's Hill*, in 'The Children's Song':

> Land of our Birth, our faith, our pride,
> For whose dear sake our fathers died;
> O Motherland, we pledge to thee,
> Head, heart, and hand through the year to be![31]

A larger community than the homosocial grouping of white men and noble primitives is envisioned; children pledge spiritual allegiance to a homeland in which, as 'men and women with our race' (210), they will one day take their rightful place; the motherland has been joined to the frontier of fathers, and imperial man can now belong to a national-imperial community and family.

Two children, Dan and Una, take centre stage in *Puck* and see the spectacular panorama of English history arise from the Sussex earth they will inherit. To spiritually as well as legally possess the land, they must recover the dormant memories in rural and true England, in the Motherland herself.[32] In the fairy stories, Kipling gives in detail what he believes to be entailed in rural Englishness and history, details only hinted at elsewhere.

The fairy Puck is first 'accidentally' conjured up by the children during a

27. See Howkins, 'Discovery', 67-69; *Reshaping England*, chap. 9; and Martin Wiener, *English Culture and the Decline of the Industrial Spirit, 1850–1980*, Cambridge University Press, Cambridge 1981, Chapter 4.

28. H. Rider Haggard, 'Conclusion', *Rural England*, volume 2, new edition, Longmans, Green and Co., London 1906, pp568-69.

29. Cohen (ed), *op.cit.*, pp51-52.

30. Cited by Lord Birkenhead, *Rudyard Kipling*, Weidenfeld and Nicolson, London 1978, p235.

31. Rudyard Kipling, *Puck of Pook's Hill*, Sarah Wintle (ed), Penguin, Harmondsworth 1987, p210; all page numbers will hereafter be given in the main text.

32. As Sarah Wintle says in her excellent introduction to the Penguin *Puck*, 'The plot is the story of the forging of a race and its imperial destiny, a process which is both learned about and in part re-enactd by the children' (18).

rehearsal of a classic text of Englishness, *A Midsummer Night's Dream*. As the custodian of English memories, Puck puts them through a ceremony so that they may claim their destiny: 'Now are you two lawfully seized and possessed of Old England ... Fast! Hold fast all I give you!' (48). Taking over a homeland requires the in-depth knowledge that Kim has of native territories, though at home a further historical dimension is required. The children are led to be a part of the Great Game and participate in a dream of omnipotent historical knowledge in the pursuit of the control of England. Access to a native vigour can be found by looking under the surface of a tame England to England's origins.

England when she herself was an imperial frontier territory, claimed first by the Romans, then the Saxons in the face of Roman weakness, and later by the Normans as the Saxons in their turn declined, is magicked up by Puck. Like India, England was once the site where a dynamic exchange between civilised coloniser and primitive colonised occurred. The history of present-day imperial England contains the combined histories of both colonised territories in which more advanced groups subjugate weaker groups, with the invaders themselves finally becoming assimilated into an elastic identity of Englishness, and a society slowly evolving from a peripheral land into a 'centre', able to provide a metropolitan narrative of freedom, progress and order. It is a history at once 'white' and 'native', so to speak. English history is therefore the history of how a mixture of peripheral cultures becomes a centre of civilisation which at the moment of enunciating its narrative of national arrival simultaneously rejects its attained modernity and progress for the pleasures of the past. *Puck* is Kipling's most ambitious, contradictory and complex monument of national historicist memory.

The major part of *Puck* is composed of three stories set in early Norman England and three stories set in late Roman Britain. Una and Dan discover that familiar landmarks stretch back to a time when England was young and at the edge of civilisation. A different perspective on English landscape is opened to the children. In 'On the Great Wall', the centurion Parnesius describes his journey to Hadrian's Wall; we do not see a 'garden' England:

> Of course, the farther North you go the emptier are the roads. At last you fetch clear of the forests and climb bare hills, where wolves howl in the ruins of our cities that have been... The houses change from gardened villas to shut forts with watch-towers of grey stone, and great stone-walled sheepfolds, guarded by armed Britons of the North Shore (135).

Parnesius paints a picture of an insecure world that needs to be protected always and at all costs – he and his friend Pertinax expended their youth at the Wall keeping first the 'Picts' (Celtic people) out and, later, the Saxon 'Winged Hats'. At the same time, dangers on the home front must not be ignored, for internal dissension affects the frontier's maintenance. In 'A British-Roman Song', the speaker says,

Strong heart with triple armour bound,
Beat strongly, for thy life-blood runs,
Age after Age, the Empire round –
  In us thy Sons,

Who, distant from the Seven Hills,
Loving and serving much, require
Thee – thee to guard 'gainst home-born ills,
  The Imperial Fire! (132)

The direct reference is to the Roman Maximus's attempt to become Emperor, an admirable if flawed hero who siphons men from Britain for his own purposes. Home weakness means imperial weakness. The note of warning is clear. The other stories in *Puck* give weight to the need to love the land and guard it from threats within and without. The past literally speaks lessons to us.

If the landscape of England is hybrid – both modern and magically ancient at the same time – what we further find out is that the English race is also not pure; in fact, Englishness is not primarily a matter of race at all but a matter of being manly and having a national commitment. The universal value of manliness remains important in *Puck* as it does in the Indian tales. Amal, the Saxon Parnesius lets escape because he like Parnesius is a worshipper of Mithras, later sends a gift to Parnesius through the Pict Allo with the message, 'He says you are a Man' (154).[33] What is new and noteworthy in *Puck* is the portrayal of the diversity of True Men who are allowed to take membership in a trans-historical English community. Parnesius was born on the Isle of Wight, and though an imperial Roman still loyal to Rome, he is told by his father that his 'place is among men on the Wall' (125). The choice to remain in Roman Britain of course cannot be a 'national' choice – that would be anachronistic. It is, however, indicative of the basis upon which other choices are made in *Puck*.

The necessity of forging an identity out of disparate elements is clearest in the Norman stories. The Norman knight Engenulf de Aquila says to Sir Richard and the Saxon Sir Hugh, 'In fifty years there will be neither Norman nor Saxon, but all English ...' (103).[34] The mixing of Saxon and Norman is indicative of Kipling's distance from the Victorian debates over Anglo-Saxon Englishness, when the Normans stood for a weak, illiberal and probably dishonest metropolitanism.[35] In the moments which comprise English origins, we see a willingness to accept 'racial' heterogeneity. If the binarisms of self/other and us/them are negotiated at the imperial frontier, the homeland itself at its originary inception is not exempt from the complex negotiations which lead to a multi-layered Englishness held together by Kipling's idealisation of a manliness connected to the reinvigorating English earth. His ideal binds Pict to Roman to Saxon, and Saxon to Norman. The Indian to English connexion, however, remains hidden in *Puck*, perhaps no longer found to be essential now that an indigenous strength has been recovered. Kipling's England is a 'centre' which at the same time still feels compelled to treasure the

33. This does not mean that race is not an issue for Kipling. In the last story of *Puck*, 'The Treasure and the Law', the Spanish-born Jew Kadmiel never becomes fully part of England in spite of his manly actions, which stop King John from getting hold of the gold Sir Richard and Sir Hugh had earlier hidden in Pevensey in order to oppose the barons and not sign the Magna Carta. Kadmiel cannot fully participate in the freedom he helps create. Manliness is a value at its most 'universal' when applied to white men.

34. Cf. Kipling's 'William's Work' (in *Rudyard Kipling and C.R.L. Fletcher, A History of England*, Doubleday, Page and Co., Garden City, New York 1911): 'England's on the anvil! Heavy are the blows! ... Little bits of kingdoms cannot stand against their foes./England's being hammered, hammered, hammered into one!' (49).

35. See Clare A. Simmons, *Reversing the Conquest: History and Myth in Nineteenth-Century British Literature*, Rutgers University Press, New Brunswick, New Jersey 1990; and Hugh MacDougall, *Racial Myths in English History: Trojans, Teutons, and Anglo-Saxons*, Harvest House, Montreal 1982.

'peripheral' in its primitive self so that it may reassure itself it will not be an ennervated future imperial culture. Notwithstanding the heterogeneity of English identity which results, this is an oddly subversive idea: what, after all, does it imply for the English as imperialists and colonisers during Kipling's time?

Given the above, Kipling's own description of *Puck* and *Rewards and Fairies* (1910) in *Something of Myself* (1936) must be taken with a pinch of salt: 'they had to be a sort of balance to, as well as a seal upon, some aspects of my "Imperialistic" output in the past'.[36] Despite this assertion, he immediately goes on to tell his reader that the poem 'If –' was translated into twenty-seven languages and was based upon the character of Dr Leander Starr Jameson (1853-1917), who led a raid into the Transvaal to try to instigate a rising against Kruger in 1885. 'If –' is a paean to a stoic but idealistic manliness, a necessary virtue for imperial domination, and a virtue which undergirds *Puck* and *Rewards*: 'If you can dream – and not make dreams your master ... Yours is the Earth and everything that's in it/And – which is more – you'll be a Man, my son!'[37] *Puck* and *Rewards* depict the 'balance' to an 'imperialistic' output by showcasing the origins of an imperial nation, and warning that the danger of decline can recur. George Wyndham, man of letters and former government minister, wrote to Kipling indicating his enthusiasm for especially the Roman tales in *Puck*, and quoted Kipling's reply to him in an October 1906 letter: 'Yes – Gibbon was the fat heifer I ploughed with... I swear I didn't mean to write parables – much – but when situations are so ludicrously, or terribly, parallel, what can one do?'[38] The dangers of decline embodied in a cyclical, rise-and-fall historiography which frames *Puck* are weighed against the more hopeful individual stories which stress an England still possessing a regenerative potential.

Despite the flexibility of English identity we see in *Puck*, the limits of national self-representation are quickly reached in the attempt to conjoin rational to irrational. The importance of the feminine with its ability to facilitate regeneration and the magical are given full play in *Puck*. For instance, Una listens attentively to Parnesius's long discourse on his family life, his caring nurse, and how careful nurture at any historical moment is vital: 'Good families are very much alike' (121). Only the magical and the intuitive can give the frontier life. But despite all of this, the tension encountered between the modern and the intuitive is not eliminated.

In 'The Knights of Joyous Adventure', a proleptic tale of imperial adventure and exploitation in the territory later to become the Gold Coast, Sir Richard is bedazzled by the pirate Thorkild's compass and the African contact with gorillas, which he takes to be devils. Dan, however, bursts the bubble of wonder by explaining the enchantments in modern, scientific terms. As with the boys in *Stalky*, the White Sahib retains a progressive mastery of knowledge over both the native and his very own past. The primitive invigorates the modern, yet cannot be as good as it. Deflated, Sir Richard asks, 'Is there no sorcery left in the world?', only to be answered by Puck, 'I warned thee they were wise

36. Rudyard Kipling, *Something of Myself*, Robert Hampson (ed), Penguin, Harmondsworth 1977, p145.

37. Rudyard Kipling, *Rewards and Fairies*, Rogert Lewis (ed), Penguin, Harmondsworth 1987, p163.

38. George Wyndham, Letter to Mrs Drew, in *Life and Letters of George Wyndham*, volume 2, J.W. Mackail and Guy Wyndham (eds), Hutchinson and Co., London, n.d.), p555.

children. All people can be wise by reading books' (96). The Voice of Enchantment himself momentarily elevates a sceptical modern attitude and subverts his own self and mission.

Kipling's strategy as an Englishman born in the primitive frontier has been to explore English identity first at the frontier, in which it seemed at its very best, and then later to displace this frontier to England and re-imagine effete England especially through using the historical moments when the country herself was an imperial frontier, fuelled by the dynamic interchange between the civilised and the barbarous. However, to the very end, rationality and irrationality, the modern and the primitive, the realistic and the intuitive clash in Kipling's national-imperialist discourse. The normative history of the English civilising mission is disrupted by the counter-history of colonialism which threatens to displace the progressive, and to do so not only at the literal frontiers of empire but in the recovered frontiers of England's own past.

III

How are we to react to the binarisms of civilised/primitive or rational/irrational within which Kipling's thought oscillates, and which never seems to find a resting ground? One response would be to see the binarisms in his national-imperialist discourse as instruments of imperial or nationalist self-identification and legitimation – as they indeed are, to a large extent. The primitive, the primal, English rural traditions: they all then would be the contents of an imperial fantasy, a fantasy Kipling shared with the like-minded of the Radical Right, such as Rider Haggard.[39]

And yet, Kipling's alternative view of the West, or at least England, is more than simple national-imperial legitimation, even when we take into account the elements of fantasy involved. (The 'primitive' or the 'primal' as sought in the imperial frontier for hidden home consumption obviously cannot designate actual energies.) The *desires* Kipling expressed cannot be dismissed so easily: he was striving for a different or alternative knowledge of the English national self, a 'knowledge' which admittedly could possibly be used for national mobilisation. Kipling wanted an England still 'modern', but which rejected the industrial and urban components of modernity. This is not so different, in many respects, from the contemporary western interest in 'traditional' (for lack of a better term) Asian medicine, such as Chinese acupuncture; and this in turn has helped rekindle interest in western traditional or alternative medicine, such as homoeopathy.

Kipling's resulting image of rural England is not so different from that projected in the USA, for example, by the British Tourist Authority: that of 'traditional' England – castles and southern thatched cottages. Kipling fits in well with – and, I believe, needs to be considered as part of – the 'high' tradition of English culture with its concern for wholeness and continuity which Raymond Williams so well described for us in his *Culture and Society* (1958). To Williams, this had been a *native* tradition which could be appropriated for a

39. Kipling and Haggard also connected the occult with the primitive. In fact, quite a number of late nineteenth-century English literary works dealt with the paranormal in native territories.

40. This 'old New Left' approach to socialism has been sharply criticised, the best-known of these critics being Terry Eagleton. See his *Criticism and Ideology: A Study in Marxist Literary Ideology*, Verso, London 1978.

socialist humanism.[40] If Kipling's rural vision of England was entirely trumped up, he is in good company. The creation of 'irrational' tradition, in response to the various manifestations of 'modern' society, as is well-known, has a major role in nineteenth-century English cultural history.

To return to my opening point, the question of the supposed inherent connexion between western modernity and nationalism: this, I think, cannot be taken for granted. Kipling (and, for that matter, Haggard) in his colonising discourse of ideology was unable to see 'England' as a fixed, modern subject, and refracted this subject through his conception of the values of other cultures, though this process was hidden when it came to displaying England proper. In trying to trace the hidden role of what can be called imperial primitivity in *Puck of Pook's Hill*, I have tried, as Homi Bhabha has put it, to rethink 'through the resistances of moments that will not be spoken within its [that is, western modernity's] logic and within its rationality'.[41] This leads me to another, and larger, question.

41. Homi K. Bhabha, 'Location, Intervention, Incommensurability: A Conversation with Homi Bhabha', *Emergency* 1, number 1, 1989, p75.

Some recent anthropological and literary work has emphasised the difficulties inherent within the orthodox conception of 'culture', in which individual countries, peoples or nations maintain distinctive cultures.[42] Arjun Appadurai, for instance, argues that 'the modern world ... is now an interactive system in a sense which is strikingly new'; thus, the 'new global economy has to be seen as a complex, overlapping, disjunctive order, which cannot any longer be understood in terms of existing center-periphery models (even those which might account for multiple centers and peripheries)'.[43]

42. For an example of the anthropological work, see Arjun Appadurai, 'Disjuncture and Difference in the Global Cultural Economy', *Public Culture* 2, number 2, Spring 1990. For an example of the literary work, see Homi K. Bhabha, 'DissemiNation', in Homi K. Bhabha (ed), *Nation and Narration*, Routledge, London 1990.

In the context of this work, pertinent questions have been raised by Akhil Gupta and James Ferguson: 'To which places do the hybrid cultures of postcoloniality belong? Does the colonial encounter create a "new culture" in both the colonized and colonizing country, or does it destabilize the notion that nations and cultures are isomorphic?'[44] My concern lies with the second question, specifically in relation to the 'colonizing country'. While of course Victorian and early twentieth century England did not experience today's intense, global cultural interactiveness and flows, the same question can be asked of far-flung empires of an earlier moment. The fact of interaction – of a relationship – between coloniser and colonised is obviously necessitated by the governance of empire, if by nothing else; and if so, then cultural interaction and negotiation (either willing or unwilling) should take place between the centre and the periphery.

43. Appadurai, *op.cit.*: 1, p6.

44. Gupta and Ferguson, *op.cit.*: pp8-9.

The proponents of what is now called 'historical anthropology' (for example, Bernard Cohn, Jean and John Comaroff, Nicholas Dirks) may also be said to be pursuing Gupta and Ferguson's questions, taking, as they do, 'the domain of culture as the locus of influence and change ... [as opposed to earlier social scientific interest in] the economic and political impact of colonialism'.[45] Among their interests are the cultures of response and resistance of both the colonised and the colonisers. Such an approach to anthropology has benefitted from the identification and the examination of 'colonial discourse' by critics such as Homi Bhabha, Gayatri Chakravorty Spivak and, of course, Edward Said.

45. Nicholas B. Dirks, 'Introduction' to Nicholas B. Dirks (ed), *Colonialism and Culture*, University of Michigan Press, Ann Arbor, 1992, p10.

Literary criticism, like anthropology, has become a more interdisciplinary field of study, and a dialogue with anthropological concerns occurs in journals such as *Social Text*. Nevertheless, literary criticism, with notable exceptions, generally seems less interested in the interactive aspects of colonial cultural formations. Mary Louise Pratt, whose own work has an historical anthropological slant, and whose preferred term for cultural interaction is 'transculturation', asks the following questions, questions which also make a comment: 'How are metropolitan modes of representation received and appropriated on the periphery? That question engenders another more *heretical* one: with respect to representation, how does one speak of transculturation from the colonies to the metropolis? [emphasis mine][46] To answer those questions, we shall have to undertake what Satya Mohanty has called for, a 'colonial cultural studies ... including both metropolitan Britain and the colonial "outposts", in which centre and periphery, inside and outside, can be seen as implicating and potentially redefining one another'.[47]

The overall literary-critical situation is probably not surprising given the pressing demands to 'rescue' and 'free' subject subaltern voices among the colonised; with these demands in sight, it might seem superfluous to give attention to the dominating coloniser. However, it strikes me that the danger here is that we may dehistoricise the colonising society (oddly enough, given that History and progress always seem to be on the European side), making imperialism/colonialism an unchanging and monolithic object.[48] And while we do not want to erase the historical violence of colonialism, we also do not want to forget, as Ashis Nandy vehemently reminds us, that the oppressor is

a self-destructive co-victim with a reified life and a parochial culture, caught in the hinges of history he swears by... All theories of salvation, secular or non-secular, which fail to understand this degradation of the colonizer are theories which indirectly admit the superiority of the oppressors and collaborate with them.[49]

I wish to thank Elizabeth Helsinger, Norman Vance, Jean Comaroff, Walter L. Reed and Ronald Inden for reading and commenting upon earlier versions of this essay. Thanks also go to members of the Centre for the Study of Developing Societies, Delhi, for their support during the revision of this essay. Special thanks to Ashis Nandy and Suresh Sharma.

46. Mary Louise Pratt, *Imperial Eyes: Travel Writing and Transculturation*, Routledge, London 1992, p6.

47. S.P. Mohanty, 'Kipling's Children and the Colour Line', *Race and Class* 31, number 1, July-September 1989, p38.

48. See Dirks, *op.cit.*, pp7-10.

49. Ashis Nandy, *The Intimate Enemy: Loss and Recovery of Self Under Colonialism*, Oxford University Press, Delhi 1983, pxv.

This paper was written
during a postdoctoral
fellowship at the
Society for the
Humanities, Cornell
University, 1992-93. I
benefited enormously
from discussions with
and presentations by
my colleagues and
especially the helpful
commentaries and
suggestions in the
course of writing this
essay from Jay Tribby,
Meaghan Morris,
Anna Marie Smith,
Mark Seltzer and
Patrick Hagopian.
Many thanks to Peter
Kulchyski, as always,
for sharing his wealth
of knowledge about
northern native
politics.
   Permission to
publish the images
from Lynx has been
granted by the anti-fur
organization *Respect for
Animals*. Jill Posener's
photograph has been
reproduced with her
permission. I owe a
special debt of thanks
to Dorothy Chocolate
for permission to print
her unpublished
photographic series of
her mother's camp.

SIMULATED POLITICS:
ANIMAL BODIES, FUR-BEARING WOMEN, INDIGENOUS SURVIVAL

Julia Emberley

Millions of animals are trapped each year in steel-jawed traps, then cruelly killed, like this North American coyote dying slowly beneath the boots of a hunter. And millions more are incarcerated for brief lives in tiny, squalid cages on fur farms, before being gassed, electrocuted or lethally injected and stripped of their pelts. All this waste and misery to serve the whims of the fashion trade. It's a cruel, despicable business. Because no-one needs a fur coat. They are simply status symbols – luxury garments bought at a heavy price in animal pain and suffering.

No civilised country should tolerate the cruelties of the fur trade. And people who wear fur coats should be shamed out of the belief that fur is glamorous. Furs are beautiful – but only on their rightful owners, the fur-bearing animals.

Join the moral majority. Oppose the fur trade.

Leaflet produced by Lynx, an anti-fur campaign group.

Blasphemy protects one from the moral majority within, while still insisting on the need for community.

Donna Haraway, 'A Cyborg Manifesto'

During the 1980s, the fur industry and its profit margins were challenged by increasing pressures from animal liberation activists. Throughout the last two decades, spectacles of human indifference to the suffering of animals for economic gain occasionally dominated the mass media, especially in the event of the annual harvesting of infant seal-furs off the coast of Labrador in Canada, a media event supported by another no less noteworthy media spectacle, Brigitte Bardot. On another side of the political field we can locate the struggle of northern indigenous peoples, for whom fur-trapping represents one means of material support, as well as a symbolic tie to traditional ways of life, in an otherwise poverty-inducing economic system. Nowhere has the conflict over the significance attributed to fur became more apparent than in the recent debate between animal liberationists, such as the British animal welfare organization Lynx, and northern Inuit and Dene claims for self-determination which include the collective right to live off the land, to hunt animals and to engage in various cultural and economic activities involving the selling and treating of animal fur. Out of this global tension spirals a productivity of imaginary spaces, textual and visual, from which to begin to tell a story of fur.[1]

The contradictory interests in the contemporary arena of fur-trapping cultural politics signal a certain tension in both textual and visual fields of political and aesthetic modes of representation. This tension is obviously marked by a struggle among different political, economic, and cultural values: for native hunters on the one hand and animal rights and welfare organizations such as Lynx, on the other hand. What is not so obvious is the degree to which the values and meanings ascribed to the fur-object in particular and the fur-trade in general are inflected by libidinal investments. In these various discursive fields fur as an object is constituted by divergent and at times competing meanings and values. Not only are the stories this written object relates constitutive of palaeonomic[2] narratives of European expansion into North America, the effects of the early fur-trade between England, France, and North America and the globalization of the fur industry in general in the twentieth century, fur also circulates within a libidinized economy. The sexualized status of fur as an object of desire and as an object which creates the meaning of desire reaches its textual zenith as sexual fetish in Leopold von Sacher-Masoch's late nineteenth-century novel *Venus in Furs*. In contemporary fashion advertisements, the sexual fetishism of fur contributes to a fetishistic voyeurism as fur's commoditization as an image of symbolic status becomes imbued with sexual desires.[3] When fur is constructed as a desirable object, sustaining or rejecting that desirability can only be accomplished for capitalist patriarchy through the mediation of sexual difference. How sexual difference is figured within the competing texts and images of the pro-fur/anti-fur lobbies will of course differ within these respective discursive fields. In Lynx's use of mass media to disseminate politically charged messages, fashion photographic images of a psychical fantasy of woman are recoded through a provocative, and I would stress, disturbing set of depictions in which the uneven gendered and racially orientated relations among the figures of the human, animal, and woman, are recontained and reproduced in all their sumptuous and fetishistic appeal. From a feminist perspective, the discourse on northern hunters is also problematic as it excludes the specificity of native women as gatherers and their work in the treatment and selling of furs. Although I am critical of both sides of the debate, this feminist intervention concentrates primarily on Lynx while taking the discourse on northern hunters as an occasion to address an important debate within feminist theory on the epistemological characterization of egalitarian gendered relations in gatherer/hunter cultures.

1. How an object, such as fur, is constituted by these conflicting, if not competing conceptions depends, as Chantal Mouffe and Ernesto Laclau argue, on its discursive conditions of emergence. See Ernesto Laclau and Chantal Mouffe, *Hegemony and Socialist Strategy*, Verso, London 1988, p108.

2. Paleonomy captures the complex weaving of meanings that comprise a text. Spivak elaborates its meaning as the 'the charge which words carry on their shoulders.' Like a postmodern nomad's pack, textual meanings and values are carried on the backs of the makers and unmakers of words. See 'The Post-modern Condition: The End of Politics?' interview with Gayatri Spivak, Geoffrey Hawthorn, Ron Aronson, and John Dunn, in *The Post-Colonial Critic: Interviews, Strategies, Dialogues*, Sarah Harasym (ed), Routledge, London 1990, pp17-34.

3. See Laura Mulvey, 'Visual Pleasure and Narrative Cinema', in *Visual and Other Pleasures*, Indiana University Press, Bloomington 1989, pp14-26.

SELLING POLITICS TO THE MASSES: THE CASE OF LYNX

> Reality is assured, insured, by the image, and there is no limit to the amount of money that can be made.

> Donna Haraway, 'Teddy Bear Patriarchy'

> And it just seemed to me that, given our general unpreparedness for knowing what is and is not radical, that beleaguered position is seen today as the white ideological subject-position of reactive welfare-state radicalism.

> Gayatri Spivak, 'In Praise of *Sammy and Rosie Get Laid*'

In September 1984 Greenpeace International announced in England that it would launch a campaign against the fur-trade with the intention of 'sham[ing] the wearers of fur coats off the streets'.[4] With the aid of bad boy of 1960s fashion photography, David Bailey and a 'celebrities charter' of forty signatories supporting the campaign, Greenpeace geared up for a massive media assault on the cruel sensibilities of the rich and glamorous. When Greenpeace withdrew its support over a controversy involving the potential effects of this campaign on the already tenuous economic stability of indigenous trappers in northern Canada, the media based animal welfare organization Lynx consolidated its existence.[5]

The Lynx campaigners outline their media strategy in the following terms:

> Our aim is to create a new climate of opinion which ensures that wearing fur garments is no longer acceptable. In this way we will strike at the heart of the fur industry depriving it of customers for fur products and so dramatically reducing the number of animals killed for their fur. This is being achieved by a spectacular and innovative advertising campaign using billboard and bus-shelter posters and cinema commercials, which show the unpleasant reality behind the glamorous image portrayed by the fur industry. (Lynx promotional material)

Lynx also announced a commitment to parliamentary reform, although their resolutions, which include lobbying the government to legislate against fur factory farms in England and the EEC and prohibiting fur imports from countries which still use steel-jawed leg-hold traps (although they were banned in the UK over thirty years ago) appear far less at the forefront of their activities when compared to the energy and money put into their media campaign.

The use of various kinds of mass media including cinema commercials,

4. As announced in *The Times*, 'Campaign against furs', 8 August, 1984.

5. Lynx ceased to exist under its current name in early 1993. Another organization 'Respect for Animals' has been set up to resume the anti-fur campaigns. As they write in their newsletter: 'On November 5th, following a five week trial, Lynx, along with Mark Blover and Stefan Ormrod lost the libel action brought against it, ostensibly by Swalesmoor Mink Farm Ltd., and were ordered to pay £40,000 damages and the plaintiffs' legal fees. Unable and unwilling to pay over such money to the fur trade, Lynx became insolvent and thus ceased to operate.' See *Fur Campaign Review*, 1 January-March 1993, 1.

billboard signs, and made-for-in-house-viewing videos situate Lynx's strategy as belonging to a particularly prevalent mode of aestheticized politics in the late twentieth century. The advertising medium is one ideological apparatus of representation capable of disseminating political as well as commercial interests. As the Benetton fashion advertising campaign of the autumn and winter of 1992-93 demonstrated, with its use of documentary photographs of 'real-life' events previously published in news magazines and dealing with themes of 'immigration, AIDS, terrorism, violence, and the plight of political refugees', the aestheticization of political events is a highly profitable enterprise capitalizing as it does on the twin currencies of provocation and mystification. In the case of Lynx the distinction between the political and commercial would all but seem to disappear as the high production values of their proto-fashion images provide a protective gloss for the simulation of their political agenda.

Like astute semioticians of the political economy of the sign, the Lynx advertising campaigners convey their political message by utilizing the seductive power of the image, especially high production value, fashion images of sumptuously clad fur-bearing fashion models, albeit these images are turned to other purposes. Lynx purports to be engaged in a form of image critique when it announces its intention to 'show the unpleasant reality behind the glamorous image portrayed by the fur industry'. In several of their glossy posters, fashion photographs of women in fur appear in order to remind the spectator of these already symbolically invested signs of social distinction. Contrary to what one might expect, however, the symbolic recoding of the fur fashion images by the Lynx campaigners did little to challenge such images for their ideological effects in interpellating the female or feminine consumer; rather the fashion photo is reproduced precisely for the fetishistic voyeurism that dominates its spectral reception. In the poster entitled 'Fur coat with matching accessories' a model appears in a fur coat and hat wearing an expensive looking silver ear-ring made from the foot of an animal and dripping with blood. A thick silver chain with a miniature leg-hold trap, also stained with drops of blood, hangs around her neck like just another fine accessory, like just another fashion photograph.[6] In this 'anti-fashion' example, the written image is articulated through the primary text: 'Fur Coat with Matching Accessories'.[7] The supplementary text, contained in small letters in the bottom left-hand side of the image, alters the significance of this fashion photograph for its anti-fur spectatorship: 'The leg-hold trap. For animals that don't get strangled, beaten, gassed or electrocuted.' In this tainted fashion image the so-called referent − the real woman who wears the fur coat − is brought into the realm of individual accountability where she resembles more the social scapegoat than a model for ethico-political behaviour. The fur-bearing woman, as a class unto herself, collectively comes to figure as a cold and cruel monstrosity, an accessory to the crime, who would wear her capacity for terror and violence on her sleeve.

Raymond Williams has argued that to change the deepest habits and

6. For a discussion of blood-tones in the British fashion designer John Galliano's fashion spread, 'Visions of Afghanistan: Layers of Suiting, Shirting, and Dried-Blood Tones', see Julia Emberley, 'The Fashion Apparatus and the Deconstruction of Postmodern Subjectivity', in *Body Invaders: Sexuality and the Postmodern Condition*, Arthur and Marilouise Kroker (eds), MacMillan Education Ltd., London 1988, pp47-60.

7. In *The Fashion System*, Roland Barthes insists that 'without discourse there is no total Fashion, no essential Fashion'. Indeed for Barthes, no 'system of objects ... can dispense with articulated language', for it is the linguistic signifying order which constitutes fashion's meanings. See Roland Barthes. *The Fashion System*, trans. Matthew Ward and Richard Howard, Hill and Wang, New York 1983, xi.

8. See Raymond
Williams, 'Ecology and
Socialism', in *Resources
of Hope: Culture,
Democracy, Socialism*,
Robin Gable (ed),
Verso, London 1989,
pp210-226.

assumptions of a consumer society is a sound ecological approach to the problem of diminishing resources.[8] Lynx predicated its 'radicality' on this position by arguing that consumer habits must change in a world of not unlimited resources of wild animals. One way to effect such a change has been to offer alternative consumer markets. Underlying Lynx's usage of various media and ideological apparatuses to change public opinion exists an extensive commercial enterprise. And Lynx was very much in the business of fighting the fur-trade through a competitive commercial strategy which ranged from selling T-shirts, coffee mugs, and glossy posters to distributing a mail order catalogue which sells these and other commodities representing commercially invested signs of cultural rebellion such as Dr. Martens' boots and shoes, made from 'the finest non-leather material available'. Lynx's mass media advertising campaign not only sells an anti-fur morality, it also sells commodities; indeed all of these libidinally and ideologically invested images are deployed for the purposes of developing, as ironic as it seems, a commercially viable political constituency: or is it a politically viable commercial constituency? In either case the aestheticization of commodities 'as a dimension of the semiotic, celebrates the transformation of the material by the abstract': as Susan Stewart elaborates, '[t]he capacity of all play and fictions to reframe context is a transformation performed by means of signifying practices, the transformation of use value into exchange value by means of signification. It is not surprising that the age of late capitalism is marked by the aestheticization of commodities and the commercial exploitation of sexuality'.[9]

9. See Susan Stewart,
*On Longing: Narratives
of the Miniature, the
Gigantic, the Souvenir,
the Collection*, Duke
University Press,
Durham 1993, p32.

Although Williams may have anticipated, however much he may have disagreed with, the opening of new consumer markets as one strategy to effect consumer habits, I doubt he could have foreshadowed the ideological twists and turns which would be manufactured in order to bring about such shifts. Lynx's making of a social referent to blame for the continuation of the fur-trade in the late twentieth century, by casting as enemies the women who wear fur coats, not only abstracts consumption from the real processes of the world's economy in trade,[10] this scapegoating mechanism represents one important means by which the radicality of Lynx was ideologically engineered as a leading voice within the politicized field of ecological struggles.[11]

10. Raymond
Williams discusses the
effects of 'uneven
development' in
ecological strategies in
'Ecology and
Socialism' in *Resources
of Hope*. See especially,
pp223-25.

11. See Gayatri
Chakravorty Spivak,
'In Praise of *Sammy and
Rosie Get Laid*', *Critical
Quarterly* 31:2' 1989,
pp80-88.

Some of the questions to emerge from this study of Lynx include: What are the political ramifications of the politics of this animal liberation agenda? What kinds of gendered and racially oriented myths are subject to aestheticization for the purposes of deploying their political message? And what interests did their commercial enterprise hold for the advertisement of a politics of cruelty to animals? The particular combination of media advertising, a fragmentary focus on a singular aspect of ecological struggle, and commercial investments, gives way to what I call a simulated politics. In one sense I use the term 'simulation' to draw attention to the technological mediums of photography, film, and video used as they were in the case of Lynx to simulate a relatively closed world in which a tragic drama is enacted between animal victims and glamorous women whose complicity as consumers of fur coats is taken as lending support to the perpetuation of this cruel and barbarous enterprise. I also use the term in its vernacular sense: the notion of a simulated politics designated Lynx's political agenda as one that pretended to be a popular political struggle even when there existed no political constituencies whose voices were being represented, supported or advocated. On the contrary the moralistic and aggressively self-righteous political voice expressed by Lynx was designed, like its American moral majority counterpart, the Pro-Life campaign, to represent those who cannot represent themselves and, therefore, must be represented: animals and foetuses. Is it accidental that Lynx and other moralistic and self-righteous organizations developed in the 1980s as new social movements asserted their right to speak for themselves? The simulated politics of Lynx does not only effect a silencing of the voices of these new social movements, this postmodern aestheticization of political representation also points to a problem of political agency for those liberal-minded individuals who participated in and supported the Lynx enterprise; the need to represent an especially problematic animal-constituency which cannot represent itself signals an attempt on Lynx's part to reinstate hegemonic equilibrium where the established voices of a post-World War Two regime of power are being openly challenged.[12]

While Lynx's simulated politics did not represent a social group, and their agenda did not consider the social relations between human and animal or the human/animal organism and technology, the material and ideological effects on such social groups as European bourgeois women, fur factory workers in South Korea, and Inuit and Dene hunters and trappers, are very real. The following three sections explore the simulated politics of Lynx through some examples of the images they deployed.

NATURAL AUTOMATA AND FUR-BEARING WOMEN

For next to the error of those who deny God, which I think I have already sufficiently refuted, there is none which is more effectual in leading feeble spirits from the straight path of virtue, than to imagine that the soul of the brute is of the same nature as our own, and that in consequence, after this life we have nothing to fear or to hope for, any more than the flies and ants.

Descartes, *Discourse on Method*

When animals are killed for fur, two kinds of scavengers move in. The difference is the flies don't know any better.

Lynx, 'The Scavengers'

The notion of the 'dumb animal', devoid of both speech and reason, not to mention a soul, is at the basis of an anthropocentric modern philosophical tradition which uses the animal/human opposition in order to produce a

12. See John Solomos, Bob Findlay, Simon Jones and Paul Gilroy, 'The Organic Crisis of British Capitalism and Race: the Experience of the Seventies', in *The Empire Strikes Back: Race and Racism in 70s Britain*, Solomos et al. (eds), Hutchinson with the Centre for Contemporary Cultural Studies, University of Birmingham, London 1982, pp9-46, see especially, p20.

hierarchical equation between the inferior faculties of the animal and those superior to the human (that is, Man). Descartes, for example, reasoned in his *Discourse on Method* that animals differ from humans.[13] In a somewhat ironic anticipation of the cybernetic realities of postmodern life, Descartes deploys a cyborg figure in order to dramatize this human/animal distinction: in mobilizing a comparison between the machine animal or 'natural automata' and the human, Descartes attempts to ratify the human/animal distinction:

13. See René Descartes, *Discourse on Method*, in *Philosophical Works of Descartes*, trans. E.S. Haldane and G.R.T. Ross, London, Cambridge University Press, volume I, pp115-118.

> And this will not seem strange to those, who knowing how many different *automata* or moving machines can be made by the industry of man, without employing in so doing more than a very few parts in comparison with the great multitude of bones, muscles, nerves, arteries, veins, or other parts that are found in the body of each animal. From this aspect the body is regarded as a machine which, having been made by the hands of God, is incomparably better arranged, and possesses in itself movements which are much more admirable, than any of those which can be invented by man. Here I specially stopped to show that if there had been such machines, possessing the organs and outward form of a monkey or some other animal without reason, we should not have had any means of ascertaining that they were not of the same nature as those animals. On the other hand, if there were machines which bore a resemblance to our body and imitated our actions as far as it was morally possible to do so, we should always have two very certain tests by which to recognise that, for all that, they were not real men.[14]

14. Descartes, *Discourse on Method*, pp115-16. For further excerpts taken from various philosophical accounts of the human/animal opposition see Tom Reagan and Peter Singer (eds), *Animal Rights and Human Obligations*, Prentice Hall, Engelwood Cliffs, New Jersey 1976, 1989.

15. Descartes, *Discourse on Method*, p116.

16. *Ibid*, p117.

What are those two tests? Animals differ from humans firstly, because 'they could never use speech or other signs as we do when placing our thoughts on record for the benefit of others' and secondly, because they 'do not act from knowledge, but only from the disposition of their organs'.[15] Note that it is not simply the ability to speak which is being underlined here but to speak in a rational manner such that speech can be recorded, that is 'written' (video taped? photographed?) for the benefit of others and hence, constitutive to the production of cultural memory.[16]

From Descartes we learn that animals are truly dumb, they do not speak nor do they reason with the capability of a rational soul. The dumb animal, then, serves as the anthropocentric other to the rational and belief bound human, a human that is also always already 'Man'.

The implications of this Cartesian logic are strikingly apparent in a Lynx advertising poster which includes an image of a woman shown from the waist down in a short black skirt and stiletto heels dragging a fur coat while leaving a trail of blood behind her. The poster reads 'It takes up to 40 dumb animals to make a fur coat. But only one to wear it.' While representing the rights of fur-bearing animals that 'lack speech', the image of the dumb woman, cut off at the waist, effectively renders her speechless. But the attribution of dumbness to women evokes yet another, perhaps more spurious, meaning: women are also, it would appear, stupid. But how are they stupid and what form of stupidity is being called to the spectators' attention? Clearly a fur coat is not in and of itself a stupid thing to desire. The lack of intelligence on the part of women would seem to lie elsewhere.

Constitutive to the making of the female consumer is an individual-subject interpellated as passive when confronted by advertisers' persuasive marketing tactics. Lynx represents the primary consumer for the fur market in the figure of the white, bourgeois woman whose purchasing power is deemed unstable and subject to relatively easy manipulation. For Cathy Griggers women figure 'as splintered as the markets which women comprise.'[17] In other words, women are susceptible within the social discourse of consumption to competing changes in the meanings and values ascribed to commodities. In keeping with this feminized logic of consumption, Griggers writes: '[Women] represented a major market to be divided and redivided, and the dark continent of their desire meant new terrain, unmapped territories of objects for satisfaction as they entered consumer markets either newly opened to them or newly created in the name of their desire.'[18] If we were to apply Griggers's logic of passive commodity acquisition to the Lynx mandate we would conclude that the fur coat which once represented an object to be consumed by white, bourgeois women in order to exhibit their materially superior social status now represents an object to be rejected in order to exhibit a morally superior social status. I want to pause here and reflect on the use of advertising by Lynx and note the contradictory assumptions constitutive to the psychical fantasy of woman at work in their campaign concerning the female consumer-cum-politicized subject.

The stupidity of the female consumer manifests in her susceptibility to a value system which privileges the fur coat as a mark of social distinction. She has been duped by the fashion advertising system which is held responsible for producing the desires needed to maintain the values of a hierarchical class society. And yet, while Lynx implicitly critiques the fashion advertisements for promoting fur coats, they use the advertisement format to promote an anti-fur morality. In theory, then, the logic of female passivity which pervades the advertising genre will condition women's consumer habits whether the fashion advertisers promote furs or Lynx's advertisers promote anti-fur morality. In either case, the construction of women as dumb, silent and stupid, is essential to the success of Lynx's media campaign.

But while for Lynx it could be said that every advertising viewer is equally dumb, it could also be said that Lynx interpellates the viewer as intelligent where other advertisements do not. The latter position is equally essential to Lynx's mandate to provoke the necessary critical response which would shift consumer registers from wanting desirable commodities to amassing intelligent ideas.[19] Their cinema commercial, entitled 'The Scavengers', is representative of Lynx's attempt to interpellate an intelligent female spectator, although a particularly circumscribed intelligent female spectator. The commercial depicts a rather conventional bourgeois *fabula* in which Sugar Daddy purchases fur coat for Mistress Woman. The commercial is shot using avant-garde filmic

17. Cathy Griggers, 'A Certain Tension in the Visual/Cultural Field: Helmut Newton, Deborah Turbeville, and the *Vogue* Fashion Layout', *Differences: A Journal of Feminist Cultural Studies* 2:2 Summer 1990 pp76-104, especially p96.

18. Cathy Griggers, 'A Certain Tension in the Visual/Cultural Field', p96.

19. Cathy Griggers's notes that '[c]onsumption functions now, and has since the early decades of this century, as a form of social discourse, a means of communication and of differentiating consumer communities, and also as a means of perpetually constructing and reconstructing that first and most important product of advanced consumer culture – the ideal (if no longer unified) social self'. *Ibid*, p98.

techniques of distortion and fragmentation to create an effect of moral degeneracy. At the conclusion to the commercial the woman pulls away the front of a fur coat hanging on what appears to be a seamstress dress form, only to be confronted by an inside that is full of rotting flesh teeming with maggots and flies. This scene is followed by a black background on which the words appear: 'When animals are killed for fur, two kinds of scavengers move in. The difference is the flies don't know any better.' Whereas in the 'dumb animal' poster women are passively positioned as lacking in the capacity to reason or voice intelligent choices, in the cinema commercial women are positioned in a paternalistic manner as intelligent enough to know better, or, at least more intelligent than the flies. The problem with the intelligent woman, however, is the way she would compromise herself by trafficking both her intelligence and her sexuality merely for the sake of possessing a fur coat. Not surprisingly, the critical response Lynx might have hoped to provoke has backfired. Lesbian-identified graffiti artists voiced their own particular brand of criticism by writing over a billboard sign which exhibited the 'dumb animal' image/text with the following words: 'MEN kill animals ... MEN make the profits ... and MEN make sexist ads! with friends like Greenpeace, who needs enemies?' (See figure 1).[20] Contrast this graffiti commentary with the spray-painted anarchist symbol on the back of a luxurious fur coat in Stephen Frears' film *Sammy and Rosie Get Laid* (1987) screenplay written by Hanif Kureishi. Women who wear fur coats have reacted, according to one major fashion magazine, by 'refusing to be intimidated' and insisting on their right to wear their precious and expensive possessions.[21]

In a poster designed by Linda McCartney, who along with her famous husband Paul McCartney, supports the Lynx campaign, a picture of a woman in a fur coat below which are written the words 'Rich Bitch' is placed above a picture of a dead fox below which is written 'Poor Bitch' (See figure 2). If women are intelligent enough to know better than to wear a fur coat, then for the woman who does wear fur, the implication is that she must be a cruel sort of person. This S/M motif of the cold and cruel woman justifies Lynx's use of the derogatory and demeaning curse, Bitch! The contradictory dichotomies that make up the psychical fantasy of woman – the classic opposition being the virgin/whore – also operates in this poster to divide the good female consumer – Linda McCartney as the good bitch who would disown her class-based gender privilege – from the bad female consumer – the rich bitch who would flaunt her class privilege at the expense of exploiting animals, but not workers, of course. The discontinuous relationship between the real women who wear furs and the fashion images which promote the wearing of fur, not only constitutes the 'specular logic' of Lynx's anti-fur-trapping media campaign, this collapsing of the imaginary into the real is what gives Lynx's images, in part, their rhetorical force.[22]

The dramatization of a moral justice, on the part of Lynx, in the form of a spectacular media campaign, becomes a substitute for the voicing of political constituencies of disenfranchised groups, such as women. Lynx's aestheticized

20. This image has been recorded by Jill Posener, *Louder Than Words*, Pandora, London 1986.

21. See '*Are Fur Coats Becoming Extinct?*' *Glamour*, December 1992, pp183-184. Of course we should note that the fashion magazine has a vested interest in promoting the fur fashion industry.

22. Gail Faurschou, 'Obsolescence and Desire: Fashion and The Commodity Form', in *Postmodernism: Philosophy and the Arts, Continental Philosophy III*, Hugh J. Silverman (ed) Routledge, New York 1990, pp234-259. In her discussion of fashion and Baudrillard, Faurschou notes a ' "specular logic" of abstraction' at work in the fashion system, 'in which the concrete dimensions of social life and the symbolic world are increasingly reduced, recoded, and smoothly reprocessed into the one-dimensional, glossy (or increasingly fluorescent) signifying surfaces of their photographic (or televisual) equivalent' p257.

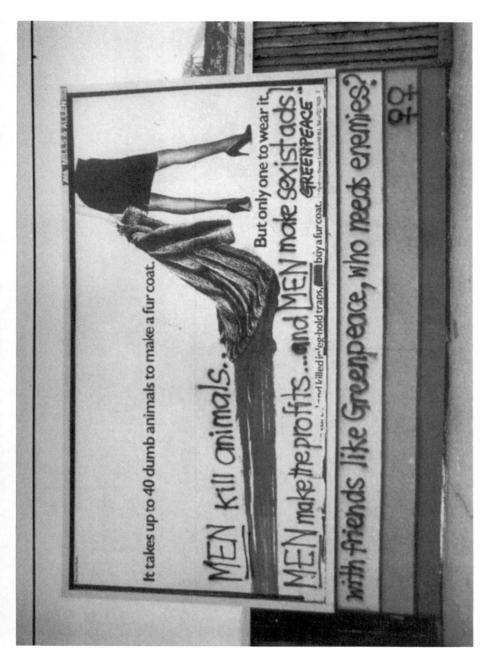

Figure 1: Courtesy of Jill Posener.

Rich bitch.

Poor bitch.

If you don't want millions of animals tortured and killed in leg-hold traps don't buy a fur coat.

Visit the Lynx Shop at 79 Long Acre, London WC2.
Or write to: PO Box 509, Dunmow, Essex.

Figure 2: Courtesy of Respect for Animals.

politics constitutes a simulation of political struggle, while other political struggles and politicized constituencies are agitating elsewhere. Through its presence on the media landscape in the urban environment Lynx's simulated politics could be said to render mute the voices of those new social movements who represent the complex articulations among the categories and political realities incorporating gender, race, class, sexuality, and decolonialism: including the women's movement, anti-racist and anti-imperialist struggles, new forms of socialism, gay and lesbian liberation movements, and, the ecological movement, or as it has also come to be known, the 'green' revolution.[23]

Bailey and McCartney's use of the stereotypical image of the dumb blonde woman should alert us to the powerlessness of bourgeois women within their own relatively privileged class and imperial positions: for in this media campaign such women are quite literally 'fair game'.[24] However, the racial privileging of the wealthy white women in this campaign, both as targets – those who are being 'shamed into not wearing fur coats' – and as advocates – those who are its greatest supporters, such as Linda McCartney – signals another, more insidious, politico-economic border which is being sharply policed by the ideological effects of the Lynx campaign. All non-European peoples are rendered invisible and non-existent in their media campaign, only to surface in their educational videos as part of their condemnation of the practice of fur farming, or, as Lynx puts it, fur factories, in so-called Third World countries such as Korea.

23. See Donna Landry and Gerald MacLean, *Materialist Feminisms: An Introduction*, Blackwell, Oxford 1993.

24. Middle- to upper-class women do, of course, have a choice as to whether they do or do not wear fur coats, nevertheless, their 'complicity' is, to some extent, overdetermined by the libidinal investments of capitalism.

OF WILD DOGS AND DOMESTICATED SPECTACLES

Once domination is complete, conservation is urgent. But perhaps preservation comes too late.

Donna Haraway, 'Teddy Bear Patriarchy'

The first video, entitled *The Lynx Roar of Disapproval* (1989), sets out to 'show the fur trade as it really is.' The 'truth' about fur trading and trapping can be summed up with the descriptive terms, barbarous and cruel, usually applied to the use of steel-jawed leg-hold traps which are designed to trap an animal without killing it immediately. Bullets rank as an unacceptable method for obtaining fur pelts because they damage the fur. The video begins with several distressing shots of fur-bearing animals struggling to free themselves from traps. The narrative voice-over informs the viewer that animals often mutilate themselves by chewing off the caught limb in order to escape. The images of these trapped animals effectively render their powerlessness and their status as victim. As much to heighten the emotional response of the viewer as to underscore the experience of pain these animals suffer, the video also represents images of domestic animals, such as pet dogs, who have lost limbs from 'accidentally' encountering the leg-hold traps. Trapping is an indiscriminate activity, the viewer is told, which victimizes both wild and domestic animals. The difference between the wild and domesticated trapped animal is determined by the value of their skins; wild animals constitute a treasure whereas domesticated pets or other undesirable animals constitute 'trash', and are labelled as such.

The borderline between wild and domestic animal is further breached in the discussion of fur factory practices, which began in the US and then moved to the USSR and Scandinavia before they emerged in Korea. During this segment, which is reproduced in a second video directly focused on 'Fur Factories', images of mink and foxes caged in small and confining spaces are shown combined with an authoritative commentary by a zoologist and socio-biologist, Desmond Morris, who explains the erratic behaviour of the animals in the cages as a symptom of psycho-social distress caused by the animal's inability to exercise naturally wild instincts. Morris's commentary is compelling precisely because of the anthropocentric mimesis of human suffering that is projected onto the caged animals. The methods of 'execution' range from neck breaking, lethal injection, gassing and electrocution. The viewer is shown images of all methods of death, including a longer segment on electrocution in which the viewer witnesses the insertion of a prod into the anus of an animal. When the electric current is administered for a few seconds the body of the animal stiffens and dies immediately. The Korean-based fur factory, which produces pelts for the Jindo fur coat manufacturing corporation, kills animals through somewhat more 'primitive' and less efficient means. For example, a Korean man demonstrates a method – no animal is actually shown in this presentation – which uses two long planks of wood between which the neck of the animal is presumably inserted and then squeezed to death. This specific discussion of the Korean-based fur factory in the first video is supplemented with another seemingly related representation of cruelty. The viewer is shown a large dog being strung up by a noose and left to hang, writhing and struggling. In the following set of frames, presumably the same dog, now dead, is having its outer body hair burned off with a blow torch. These images have very little to do with fur factories and it is interesting to note that in the second video, exclusively focused on fur factories, they do not appear while the rest of the discussion in the first video on fur factories has been reproduced in its entirety. The images of the dog's death and subsequent cleansing of fur reproduce an ethnocentric contempt for the treatment of an animal the West holds sacred as a symbol of successful animal domestication. That Korean culture should treat a domesticated pet of the 'first world' as merely another animal without sentimental or emotional status – as just another piece of trash – contains the behaviour of the men depicted in these images as that of an essentially barbarous people, who not only administer such forms of inhumane torture on wild animals in the fur factories but, more importantly, do not understand a foundational neolithic distinction between the wild and the domesticated.[25]

In the Lynx mandate, quoted in the epigraph to this essay, a categorical imperative that 'no *civilized* country should tolerate the cruelties of the fur

25. The distinction between the edible and the inedible may be deployed in order to encode ethnic or racial differences, rendering the status of persons and cultures in terms of their general ordering within a schema of 'civilization'. See Marshall Sahlins, 'La Pensée Bourgeoise: Western Society as Culture', in *Critique of Practical Reason*, University of Chicago Press, Chicago 1976, pp166-204.

trade' (emphasis added), followed by another 'and people who wear fur coats should be shamed out of the belief that fur is glamorous', suggests that the demon of barbarity that exists in the figure of the white, wealthy, British female citizen – the Rich Bitch – can be exorcised through its projection on to Korean factory workers and their culturally specific, but represented as uncivilized, use of dogs – the Poor Bitch – for food rather than domestication. What the video sublimates for the 'first world' viewer is a vision of these men as wild, out of control, and in need of domestication. The subject of this process of domestication, however, is the First World viewer's gaze – domesticated into an unquestioning acceptance of these images as a comfortable and comforting affirmation of their already ingrained anthropocentric and ethnocentric imperial assumptions. Yes indeed, fur sells politics and the 'politics' it sells are culturally imperialist.

Lynx's images are at times all too reminiscent of other images that recall twentieth century human atrocities. Heaps of discarded, pink, dead mink carcases resemble images of mass graves. These images evoke a structure of experience for the generation of individuals who have constructed this media campaign and whose voices had a place during the contestation of German nationalism and the Holocaust. This suggests that the politics of post-World War Two have left them feeling disinherited from the political field of struggle and yet still sympathetic to a national cause that cannot conceive of democratic participation outside of an imperialist configuration which had hitherto given them their 'voices' – but at the cost of the global exploitation of non-European peoples. Writing in his essay 'Torture: A Discourse on Practice', Ñacuñán Sáez notes that 'in the United States, even among liberal observers, compassion for the victims of torture [in Argentina] is almost invariably accompanied by an ethnocentric contempt for the societies where torture is practised, which are thought to be imperfect, immature political systems, prone to fluctuate between anarchy and authoritarianism. Only Anglo-Saxon style democracy, the argument goes, can protect the Latin people from their own innate unruliness.'[26] It is worth noting that the Falklands War (1982), along with the existence of new political movements in Britain in the early 1980s, represents another instance of how the British dominant classes have been determined 'by the historical development of colonial societies which was central to the reproduction of British imperialism.'[27] Not least as an effect of this historical development is the shift in work forces and industries to the so-called Third World from major capital accumulating countries such as Britain. This shift takes place as a result of the expansion of transnational capitalist interests to extract ever increasing amounts of surplus labour and value. The Korean-based fur factory is one example of such a shift.

Both Korean factory workers and cultural practices and bourgeois European women emerge as the primary scapegoat figures in the Lynx media campaign and educational videos. Further to Lynx's reproduction of British cultural and economic imperialism is their equally problematic portrayal of northern indigenous hunters.

26. Ñacuñán Sáez, 'Torture: A Discourse on Practice', in *Tattoo, Torture, Mutilation, and Adornment: The Denaturalization of the Body in Culture and Text*, Frances E. Mascia-Lees and Patricia Sharpe (eds), State University of New York Press, New York 1992, pp126-170, especially p127.

27. See John Solomos et al., 'The Organic Crisis of British Capitalism and Race: the Experience of the Seventies,' p11.

THE DISCOURSE OF INDIGENOUS SURVIVAL

The original inhabitants of the Americas, Australasia and many other huge areas of the world have suffered an appalling and vicious colonialism. The surviving aboriginal societies, however, are not frozen in some archaic condition, but are our contemporaries. Their existences may be different, but they are modern; they live now, and – like us, like everyone – have to make accommodations between their pasts and their present. And if only we could break out of our political and imaginative constraints, if only we could shed the monopolistic belief in what might be called United Soviet Man, then we would see, hear and accept the peoples of the fourth world as modern societies with their own histories.

Hugh Brody, *Maps and Dreams*

The Lynx media campaign belongs to what Donna Haraway calls the 'informatics of domination', a rearrangement of global relations through science and technology.[28] According to Haraway: 'we are living through a movement from an organic, industrial society to a polymorphous, information system.'[29] Produced within the interstices of this world-wide shift, Lynx represents a contradictory formation, a commercial enterprise masking as a political movement, a simulation of political movement through micro-electronically produced images which rely on old-fashioned modernist tropes of 'depth', 'integrity', 'organic sex role specialization', and nature/culture hierarchies of difference in order to construct their message.[30] How surprising, then, that this simulated progressive movement is structured around the social residues of sexism and ethnocentrism. Its position on indigenous fur-trapping and trading among First Nations in North America is even more alarming.

Lynx is part of a general shift in the 1970s and 1980s towards a broadly based, international approach to animal liberation. A very successful lobby to prohibit the harvesting of harp seals off the Labrador peninsula in the early 1970s soon spread, as Hugh Brody notes, 'into a general campaign against sealing and trapping.'[31] Indigenous communities, such as the Inuit, which relied on seal harvesting to supplement their cash flow, were dramatically affected:

Sealskin prices tumbled and the International Whaling Commission was pressured to effect an international ban on all hunting of whale and dolphin species – though some special consideration was given to aboriginal subsistence hunters. Ringed sealskin prices fell from approximately $30 to as little as $2 or $3 each. The economic basis of hunting families and, in the eastern Arctic, whole communities collapsed.[32]

The devastating effects of this animal rights lobby, itself a major media event, cause Brody to conclude that 'in the grip of moral righteousness, animal rights

28. Donna J. Haraway, 'A Cyborg Manifesto: Science, Technology, and Socialist-Feminism in the Late Twentieth Century', in *Simians, Cyborgs, and Women: The Reinvention of Nature*, Routledge, New York 1991, pp149-82, 161.

29. Haraway, 'A Cyborg Manifesto,' p161.

30. In the section 'Informatics of Domination' in 'A Cyborg Manifesto,' Haraway sketches out two opposing columns to characterize the conceptual shifts that are part of this global restructuring.

31. Hugh Brody, *Living Arctic: Hunters of the Canadian North*, Douglas and McIntyre, Toronto 1987, p83.

32. Brody, *Living Arctic*, p83.

activists have been slow to recognize that their campaign had become a new example of southern imperialist intrusion.'[33]

33. Brody, *Living Arctic*, p85.

When Greenpeace withdrew its support from Lynx over the issue of aboriginal economic security, Lynx minimized the importance of aboriginal peoples in fur-trading and shifted the attention of its political spectatorship towards the 'enemy within', the largely white, middle- to upper-class women who wear fur coats. In response to Greenpeace's action and to anyone concerned about the effects of this anti-fur trapping campaign on indigenous cultures, Lynx assures them in their 'fact sheet' that the part played by native people in international fur markets is so negligible as to be insufficient to warrant any major concern for their economic well being:

> Most trapping by truly native people [as opposed to those non-native people who trap and hunt 'like' the native] is carried out in the Yukon and North West Territories (NWT) in Canada. During the 1982-83 season, 200,000 animals were taken (by all categories of trapper) in these two provinces [sic] compared with the 4 million trapped in all Canada and 25 million in N. America as a whole. That is less than 1% of North American trapped animals originate from native peoples. In other words, native people are responsible for around a quarter of 1% of furs produced worldwide. In the NWT trapping AND fishing represents 1% of the Territorial Gross Domestic Product as well as 1% of the labour force.
>
> In the NWT the cost of trapping with even a minimum amount of equipment exceeds the average fur income and only 5% of trappers claim that trapping is their occupation. The vast majority are part-time trappers.
>
> In a discussion document entitled 'Defence of the fur trade' (1985) the Canadian Department of External Affairs stated that, 'Defence of aboriginal cultures could be a good counterbalance to anti-fur or anti-trapping campaign.' (Fur Trade Fact Sheet)

What does this information connote? There are at least three points I wish to raise. Firstly, the well-educated and liberal-minded reader will pick up on the closing paragraph as a sign of how the Canadian state, due to its own vested interests, will readily exploit its indigenous population to ensure that the benefits it derives from the fur trading market, however marginal, will be maintained. In other words, if it speaks to us, it says 'Don't you, the educated, liberal reader, fall into the same trap of defending native fur trappers. You will only be supporting the Canadian state's economic interests.' And, of course, it is true that the Canadian state has actively qualified its continuing economic interests in the fur-trade. An article published in *The Times*, entitled 'Canada fur trade under fire', reports that the House of Commons Committee on Aboriginal Affairs and Northern Development 'produced a report which describes the [animal rights] activists as 'a wealthy growth industry'. It said the fur industry and the livelihood of about 100,000 trappers, the majority of them Eskimos [sic] and Indians, were in danger of destruction.' In defence of its

'$Can 600 million in direct earnings' and about '$Can 200 million a year for allied industries, such as transport' the Canadian government maintains that 'trapping' 'has always been and should remain' an essential part of Canada's 'cultural and economic mosaic.' Further to this point, the Fur Council of Canada enlisted the fashion designer D'Arcy Moses, a member of the Gitskan nation, located on the Pacific coast, to launch a fur collection in Europe in December of 1991. Commenting on his talents as a fashion designer, who 'works motifs from his native heritage into his designs', a representative of Industry, Trade and Technology Canada explains that Moses is 'exploring his own and native traditions and finding ways to fit that into fashion.'[34] Tailoring their cultural heritage to the needs of the Canadian fur-trade, as producers and more recently designers, aboriginal people are made to figure as a seamless authenticity with which to legitimate the continuing economic policies of the colonial government. That trappers and designers may be fitting these colonial industries into their own cultural strategies for survival remains a moot point.

34. 'Getting a Jump on Spring', *The Toronto Star*, October 3, 1991.

A second issue raised by the Lynx fact sheet is that the definition of fur-trapping as an occupation which can be measured by quantifiable categories such as full or part-time work misrepresents what has largely been characterized as an unquantifiable activity.[35] The Inuit in northern Canada hunt and trap to acquire a cash flow that enables them to live their gathering/hunting way of life. By 'way of life' I mean specifically that gatherers/hunters constitute a competing mode of production within a globally dominated multinational capitalism. The way in which postmodern gatherers/hunters acquire cash and make use of periodic wage labour does not conform to the neat capitalist model Lynx imposes on what could more accurately be described as a kind of 'mixed economy' or mixture of gatherer/hunter and capitalist economic strategies. A mixture, that as Hugh Brody points out, indicates the flexibility of hunting peoples, such as the Inuit, to incorporate wage employment opportunities into their system.[36] The need for money, which periodic wage labour satisfies, such as trapping, carving walrus ivory for the art market, and making moccasins, jackets and beadwork, reinforces, according to Brody, 'hunter's flexibility: if periodic wage labour can ensure that they, or some other member of their household, can hunt and trap with maximum effectiveness, then a wage labour job is part of what is wanted and needed.'[37] And this brings me to the third and final point I want to make about the so-called facts that appear in Lynx's information pamphlet. When Lynx writes that '1% of North American trapped animals originate from native peoples' and further, 'Native people are responsible for around a quarter of 1% of furs produced worldwide', what this foray into statistical authority does not tell us is that the minimal amount of cash that gathering/hunting peoples earned as trappers, until the recent fluctuations on fur prices due to the anti-fur trapping lobby changed it, represents their only source of cash income. In other words, that 1% contribution to the global economy of fur trading translates into approximately 100% of the total cash resources of a Dene trapper.

35. The labour of women in the domestic sphere and the labour of indigenous peoples are represented by the established order through a similar technique of exclusion. See Christine Delphy, 'For a Materialist Feminism', *Feminist Issues* 1:2, 1981 pp69-76.

36. Brody, *Living Arctic*, p221.

37. Brody, *Living Arctic*, p221.

Hugh Brody's *Living Arctic: Hunters of the Canadian North* not only emerged as one of the prominent counter-discourses to respond to the earlier animal rights' opposition to seal harvesting in the 1970s, as well as simultaneously with the anti-fur organization Lynx, it was commissioned as the official publication of a British Museum exhibit held during 1987 and 1988.[38] The exhibit and Brody's text were produced in collaboration with Indigenous Survival International (ISI), an aboriginal organization composed of indigenous peoples from Alaska, Greenland, and Canada. ISI formed in order to protest against anti-fur-trapping organizations such as Lynx and protect indigenous cultural values of fur-trapping and trading. The exhibit and the book *Living Arctic* were designed to aid their readership and museum spectators in unlearning the stereotypical conceptions of the hunting peoples of the far north, their cultural practices and strategies for economic and political survival. In the face of these educational efforts to influence animal welfare/rights organizations, Lynx have remained wilfully ignorant, maintaining a singularly misinformed representation of northern indigenous hunters. The mass media campaign launched by Lynx, in conjunction with the publication of Hugh Brody's book for the British Museum, and the formation of ISI, indicate that the discourse on anti-fur-trapping both inside and outside Britain is fractured along different lines of counter-hegemonic struggle. It would appear that what conditions the popularity of these different struggles depends on access to the ideological apparatuses of technological reproduction, in particular, the mass media.

CYBORG POLITICS

The question of technology is an important aspect of the debates in green cultural politics. In the arena of cultural productions, the technological mediations of television and the satellite have come to play a significant role in the lives of Inuit people.[39] In her ground-breaking essay, 'A Cyborg Manifesto: Science, Technology, and Socialist-Feminism in the Late Twentieth Century' Donna Haraway ironically reconfigures the 'cyborg', a half-human/animal organism and half-machine, as an exemplary postmodern figure of detotalization capable of projecting an ecologically blasphemous, and far from correct, fantasy for social transformation. Among the multiple articulations that can be made in the current political field of new social movements, Haraway is particularly interested in hingeing together feminist, Marxist, and environmentalist struggles. In keeping with the cyborg's irreverent disposition towards the idea of a coherent and unified human subject, Haraway's own political assemblage resists the conventional unifying origin myth at the heart of ecofeminist utopias. In critical opposition to the ecofeminist utopia which would have us return to an innocent, natural, organic past in the name of protecting mother earth, cyborgs represent a more flexible mediation capable of incorporating rather than repudiating science and its strong arm, technology. Thus, the cyborg is designed to incorporate the contradictory relationship technologies occupy in the nature-transforming societies of

38. For a description of the exhibit see 'On the Move in the Arctic', in *Bulletin*, British Museum Society official publication, Autumn, 1987, pp3-5.

39. See Peter Kulchyski, 'The Postmodern and the Palaeolithic: Notes on Technology and Native Community in the Far North', *Canadian Journal of Political and Social Theory*, 13:3, 1989, pp49-62.

40. See Raymond
Williams, 'Socialism
and Ecology', pp211-
12.

41. See, for example,
Irene Diamond and
Gloria Feman
Orenstein (eds),
*Reweaving the World:
The Emergency of
Ecofeminism*, Sierra
Club Books, San
Francisco 1990; and
Judith Plant (ed),
*Healing the Wounds:
The Promise of
Ecofeminism*, Between
the Lines, Toronto
1989.

42. Haraway, 'A
Cyborg Manifesto,'
p181.

43. Haraway, 'A
Cyborg Manifesto,'
p151.

industrial and post-industrial modes of production.[40] In a controversial move, Haraway situates her cyborg figure against the competing ecofeminist representative of political change: the mother-goddess reinvention that has become so fundamental to ecofeminism's self-representation.[41] Given a choice between the comforts of divine resolution and the contradictions of everyday material life, Haraway writes, 'I would rather be a cyborg than a goddess'.[42] It must be said, however, that the main trouble with cyborgs, as Haraway acknowledges, 'is that they are the illegitimate offspring of militarism and patriarchal capitalism.'[43] As both symptom and critique of the expansion of the 'military industrial complex' cyborg politics is, itself, tricky business.

Haraway's argument is relevant to an examination of the redemptive place gatherer/hunter peoples have come to occupy in the discourses of deep and social ecology, there to cure the ills of the West's deep-seated nature-destroying and pollution-causing pathologies. As an imaginary resolution to the contradictory place of an eco-politics of conservation in late-capitalist social life, gatherers/hunters represent a stable emblem of a 'traditional' and therefore more truly 'conservative' way of life. What presupposes this utopian investment in gatherer/hunter peoples is a fetishistic containment of gatherers/hunters as, indeed, stable, fixed, and traditional belonging to an (ab)original past from which European and Euro-American civilizations can trace their origins, development, and progress.

Gatherers/hunter peoples still exist in the world today venturing into various kinds of technological applications in order to survive the postmodern world. The postindustrial aspects of Inuit palaeolithic existence include, among other things, the use of snowmobiles and rifles, economic and somatic dependency on southern commodities and foodstuffs, and an active trade in craft goods and artifacts. The presence of industrial and postindustrial economic, military, and political forces in the Canadian north, especially in the period from the 1930s to 1950s, radically transformed Inuit cultural practices and activities. Nevertheless Inuit cultures, in the face of a southern Canadian government's wish fulfillment to vanish and vanquish them, and multinational desires for control of oil and gas resources, continue to fight back the frontiers of development and have engaged in a politics of survival I would call after Donna Haraway a 'cyborg politics'.

To the degree that Inuit culture is a product of such industrial technologies as the snowmobile and the rifle and such postindustrial technologies as the satellite, Lynx is also a product of such postindustrial technologies as microelectronics and a range of media outposts from made-for-home-viewing video to cinema advertisements. However, their respective incorporations of technologies into the political sphere would suggest that what for the Inuit and Dene is a need to survive politically in the postmodern world is for Lynx the need to maintain hegemony over the political field through simulating a radical political movement that effectively silences European and indigenous women.

This essay has situated the British animal welfare organization Lynx in a multiple frame of competing and contesting political narratives. The geo-political space in which these narratives emerge spans the historical distance between the British/New World colonial trade routes of the sixteenth and seventeenth centuries to their re-presentation through a dramatic sea change into the global communication networks of the late twentieth century. The use and exchange values inscribed on commodities, such as fur pelts, that once travelled on the surface of the ocean in human- and cargo-bearing vessels now travel, semiotically, through a vast network of micro-electronic mediated transmissions via satellite technology. The contradictions and clashes to emerge from the contemporary simulcast production of competing discourses are constitutive to the vicissitudes of cyborg politics; not least because of the communications technologies and ideological apparatuses deployed in order to imagine and bring into being both Lynx's anti-fur-trapping 'green' political constituency and Hugh Brody's anti-imperialist constituency in support of fur-trapping cultures such as the Inuit and Dene. In conclusion, I will consider another mode of cultural contestation through the intervention of native women's access to print and photographic mediums. Through the use of accessible media to shape political subjects, these storytelling technologies inscribe a veritable cartography of difference, a map with which to navigate the ebbs and flows of postmodern politics. Access to the technologies of representation and the place of micro-electronics, generally, in casting the paleonomic meanings and values attributed to the making of a resourceful network of subjectivities, are important considerations for any struggle interested in assembling the political affinities that are becoming and coming into being in and across the disparate worlds of postmodernism.[44]

44. See Terry Eagleton, *Literary Theory: An Introduction*, University of Minnesota Press, Minneapolis 1983, p216.

STORYTELLING TECHNOLOGIES

Jessica: I want to show you something [she opens her suitcase, pulling things from the mess inside]. We go to ceremonies, I have to change into a skirt ... I say, 'Why can't women wear pants?' Everyone looks at me like I'm crazy ... You see these jeans? They're a part of me. I sit in a room full of sweet grass and animal skins, with rattles and drums, as if I wasn't carrying a walkman and a computer the size of a briefcase. As if it was two hundred years ago. Vitaline, I like spike heels. I read Karl Marx and *People* magazine.

Maria Campbell and Linda Griffiths, 'Jessica' in *The Book of Jessica: A Theatrical Transformation*

This final intervention into another geo-political scene of representation is predicated on an important debate within feminist theory concerning minoritized versus universalized conceptions of women's oppression. Perhaps the most significant impact on the thesis of women's universal oppression stems from Eleanor Leacock's research into the sexual division of labour among the Naskapi and Montagnais peoples of the Eastern Labrador coast. Leacock's reading of the gender relations of precapitalist social formations challenges the conventional idea that a sexual division of labour is symmetrical to gendered divisions in the distribution of power. Leacock, along with Mona Etienne, explains that the division of labour in gatherer/hunter societies

> is by sex only, and relations between the sexes are based on the reciprocal exchange of goods and services ... in egalitarian society [i.e., that of the gatherer/hunter] a 'private', familial female domain is not defined and made secondary to a public, political male domain. Instead, authority is dispersed and decisions are by and large made by those who will be carrying them out. All manner of social arts are used by both women and men to influence people, resolve problems, and hold groups together.
>
> (9-10)

The egalitarian gender thesis put forth by Leacock and Etienne is adopted by Brody in order to support the kinds of rhetorical gestures of equivalency he evokes throughout *Living Arctic* in his repetitive usage of the phrase 'men and women'. However, his consistent assumption that hunting is an exclusively masculine activity points to an inequality elsewhere: Inuit and Dene women's work and experience is rarely specified beyond either the inclusive rhetorical gesture of equivalency or the exclusive presuppositions of Brody's privileging of hunting over other activities such as gathering and the treating of fur and hides. The absence of attention in Hugh Brody's *Living Arctic* to the specificity of indigenous women's labour as trappers and tanners of fur hides in contrast to the extraordinary images of European bourgeois women deployed by Lynx's anti-fur media campaign not only maintain a conventional gender hierarchy between the masculine and the feminine, this particular constellation of the denial of native women's specificity and the surplus of libidinal investment in the psychical fantasy of the European woman reinforces a different order of subordination between competing conceptions of female genders. On the one hand, the denial, or on a psychoanalytical register, disavowal of the specificity of the egalitarian experience of native women introjects a gender hierarchy into those egalitarian gender relations as it assumes that constitutive to a sexual division of labour is a hierarchical distribution of power according to gender among gatherers/hunters. To Brody's credit, he does not fall prey to this all too common assumption. And yet, on the other hand, to the degree that Inuit and Dene hunting practices are affected by the uneven forces of postindustrial technological interventions, it must be said that the effects of postindustrial ideologies can also be felt in the redistribution of gendered social relations. To retain the egalitarian gendered relations of Inuit culture, as Brody does, while at the same time acknowledging the uneven relations of postindustrial technological forms of exploitation on hunting culture is at best utopian and at worse mythic as it turns indigenous women into cultural 'equalizers' even as their confrontation with postindustrial society is clearly not equal.

The consequences of eclipsing native women as subjects in and for themselves, both for native decolonization and the feminist movement, are enormous; particularly as feminism's relationship to the struggle of native

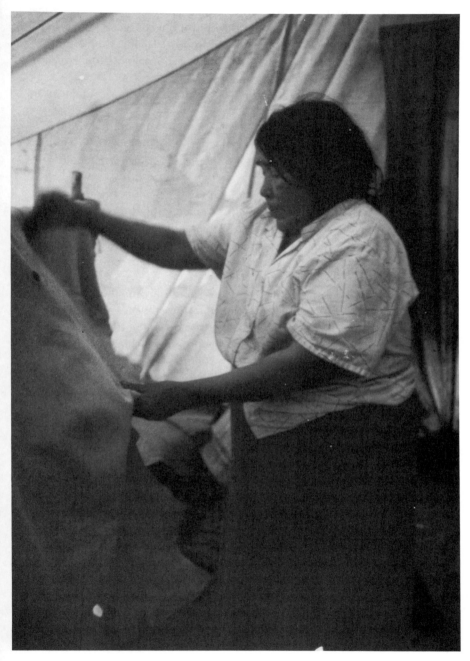

Figure 3: Courtesy of Dorothy Chocolate.

women in Canada is a subject of some ethical and political concern. For the uneven relationship that exists between an examination of the libidinal investments into the psychical fantasy of the European bourgeois woman and a recognition of the absence of Inuit and Dene women's labour in the competing ecological discourses of Lynx and *Living Arctic* mark a limit from which to rethink feminist theoretical inquiry.

I would begin to do some of this rethinking by turning to images and texts by native women.

Angela Sidney, the Tagish/Tlingit elder whose following words were recorded and transcribed by the ethnologist Julie Cruikshank, recounts a similar and yet different story about woman the gatherer/man the hunter:

> Sometimes I would hunt just for fun, I guess. Trap gophers with a snare.... All women worked on skins, those days: women trapped around while men hunted. Then they make fur – when a woman fixes skin, then it belongs to her and she can trade it. Most women don't hunt big animals – my mother did, though. One year when she was still well she got fourteen caribou![45]

45. Julie Cruikshank, in collaboration with Angela Sidney, Kitty Smith, and Annie Ned, *Life Lived Like a Story: Life Stories of Three Yukon Native Elders*, University of Nebraska Press, Lincoln, Nebraska 1990, pp84-85.

This figure of woman the hunter, or more specifically, mother the hunter, introduces another competing dimension into the current configuration of debates between animal rights and welfare advocates and northern indigenous struggles for self-determination. A critical approach which acknowledges the differences the cultural and gendered conceptions of sexual difference make, will in turn, I think, make or break the possibility of moving beyond the current impasse between the discourses of northern hunters and animal welfare or rights organizations such as Lynx.

I conclude with two photographs taken by Dorothy Chocolate, a well-known photographer in the North West Territories whose images of her mother working on an animal hide pose an interesting dialectical problem for the potentialities of *storytelling technologies* in these palaeolithic/postmodern times. The following photographs were taken at Dorothy Chocolate's mother's camp outside Yellowknife, NWT and are of her mother scraping a caribou hide to remove the fat. In part, I offer these images as a corrective to the exclusion of non-European women's role as gatherers and Brody's lack of attention to the specificity of Dene women's involvement in the fur trade (See Figures 3 and 4).

In her essay 'Teddy Bear Patriarchy: Taxidermy in the Garden of Eden, New York City, 1908-36', Donna Haraway tells a series of stories about the early twentieth century hunter, taxidermist, inventor of cameras and photographer, Carl Akeley, and the visual, specular, and sculptural productions of his life that inform the discourse of natural history at the beginnings of this century.[46] In her reflections on the construction of nature by Akeley and his stuffed animal dioramas, Haraway writes:

46. Donna J. Haraway, 'Teddy Bear Patriarchy: Taxidermy in the Garden of Eden, New York City, 1908-1936', reprinted in *Primate Visions: Gender, Race, and Nature in the World of Modern Science*, Routledge, New York 1989, pp26-58.

Akeley sees himself as an advocate for 'nature' in which 'man' is the enemy,

Figure 4: Courtesy of Dorothy Chocolate.

the intruder, the dealer of death. His own exploits in the hunt stand in ironic juxtaposition only if the reader evades their true meaning – the tales of a pure man whose danger in pursuit of a noble cause brings him into communion with nature through the beast he kills. This nature is a worthy brother of man, a worthy foil for his manhood.[47]

47. Haraway, 'Teddy Bear Patriarchy', p48.

Constitutive to the making of masculinity through this ennobling of man the hunter are Akeley's exploits into the field of photography. 'Now it was time to hunt with the camera.'[48] As the 'naked eye' of science came to dominate the ideological determinations motivating the collection and display of exoticized foreign animals in the American Museum of Natural History, the camera became more perfectly suited to this mode of containment, 'ultimately so superior to the gun for the possession, production, preservation, consumption, surveillance, appreciation, and control of nature' … 'to make an exact image is to insure against disappearance, to cannibalize life until it is safely and permanently a specular image, a ghost. The image arrests decay.'[49] By blaming or scapegoating 'Woman', the transparent woman of white, civilization, construction, man the hunter-turned-photographer preserves, or rather conserves, his moral and noble superiority as the true father and author of nature. The video camera and fashion photographer take off where the gun can no longer reasonably follow: 'When we are afraid, we shoot. But when we are nostalgic, we take pictures.'[50]

48. Haraway, 'Teddy Bear Patriarchy', p33. For a wonderful reading of 'men in fur' and the libidinal constructions of masculinity in the writings of Jack London, see Mark Seltzer, 'The Love-Master', in *Engendering Men: the Question of Male Feminist Criticism*, Joseph A. Boone and Michael Cadden (eds), Routledge, New York 1992, pp140-158.

49. Haraway, 'Teddy Bear Patriarchy', p45.

50. Susan Sontag, quoted in Haraway, 'Teddy Bear Patriarchy', p42.

In light of Dorothy Chocolate's photographs and Angela Sidney's recorded text how can we continue, as Haraway suggests, to circumscribe the technologies of visual and print media as necessary evils solely at the service of the expansion of the military industrial complex? What are we to make of Dorothy Chocolate 'hunting with a camera' and Angela Sidney's 'mother the hunter'? How as feminists, trained in the universalizing narratives of women's oppression, are we to understand these examples, which both delimit the sexual division of labour among native women and yet transgress the symmetrical relationship of that sexual division of labour to Eurocentric conceptions of the uneven gendered division of power? The contradictions raised by these questions are graphically contained by Dorothy Chocolate's photograph of her mother working an animal hide – a picture taken by a native woman, professional photographer, using state of the art photographic technology to 'capture' an image of her mother working here and now, and not in some nostalgic regime of the past, on an animal skin: as her mother does the work of a gatherer in her treatment of the caribou hide, Dorothy Chocolate gathers images of her people, the Dene. Since I am dealing here with the politics of images, I would like to imagine positioning these photographs against Lynx's representations – as against the cold and cruel depiction of the fantastical bourgeois woman; I would place these images of the labour of an indigenous women, the images themselves signs of labour: the activity of native women in their daily lives. This dialectical image shores up the contradictions of its modern technological form and its palaeolithic technologies of tanning hides. I read these images beside Walter Benjamin's demand for art, that it 'undo the alienation of the corporeal sensorium, to restore the instinctual power of the human bodily senses for the sake of humanity's self-preservation, and to do this, not by avoiding the new technologies, but by passing through them.'[51] Dorothy Chocolate's image of her mother restores the human senses to indigenous women's labour in preparing animal skins and hides; as a photograph this image simulates an experience, for the photographer and her subject, that transgresses and yet confirms the egalitarian gendered divisions of Native women's work in these palaeolithic (post)modern times.

51. As paraphrased by Susan Buck-Morss, 'Aesthetics and Anaesthetics: Walter Benjamin's Artwork Essay Reconsidered', *October 62*, Fall 1992.

HISTORY, THE BAROQUE AND THE JUDGEMENT OF THE ANGELS

Iain Chambers

There is no health; Physitians say that wee,
At best, enjoy but a neutralitie.
And can there bee worse sicknesse, then to know
That we are never well, nor can be so?

John Donne, *An Anatomie Of the World – The First Anniversary* (1611)

Donne's words echo with the 'fall into secular time', with the fall into a world that 'is fractured into a series of discrete entities, dissolved from some supposed transcendent state of primal and eternal unity.'[1] An anthropomorphic universe, whose ultimate and inaccessible truth was once secured in the revelation of God, is decentred by an indifferent heliocentrism. Humankind finds itself consigned to a permanent exile, exposed to the raging sickness of the world, where time, truth and the body are ravaged by history and the error of its ways.[2]

The Baroque 'is not as an art of abstraction, but an art of imitation.'[3] It resonates with its perceived place in the universe as the art of witnessing, as the art of testimony. Lost in space (Kepler, Pascal), decentred, the uniformity of logic and nature is punctuated by the accidental: the ornamental, the decorative and the monumental. The continuum of urban space is interrupted and deviated by the ephemeral and the surprise that threatens the persistence of its order.[4] As 'mere appearance', as a *facciata*, the ornamental reveals the essential 'structure of feeling' of the baroque. Here in the aesthetics of the embellishment, in the refusal to conclude and acknowledge a *natural* order, in the insistence of a temporal witness and the accidental provocation of the event, we behold the senses at work as they unfold, interrupt and deviate the predestined and the ordained.

Santa Maria del Giglio in Venice was unveiled in 1683. It presents us with a *facciata* in which religious referents have been completely substituted by a sculptured paen – 'strutting statues in the common stage postures of the day' (John Ruskin) – to Antonio Barbaro and his family.[5] The façade by Giuseppe Sardi is dominated by the statute of this Venetian admiral. Beneath his feet are scenes from six naval battles against the Turks, statues of his brothers, and maps of the six cities (Zara, Candia, Padova, Roma, Corfu, Spalato) that featured in the military and diplomatic life of this Venetian commander. The

1. Thomas Docherty, *John Donne, Undone,* Methuen, London & New York 1986, pp37-8.

2. On the baroque as a period of 'general crisis' which monarchical absolutism sought to control and direct, see José Antonio Maravall, *Culture of the Baroque,* Manchester University Press, Manchester 1986.

3. Suzanne Clercx, *Le Baroque et le Musique: Essai d'estethétique musicale,* Éditions de la Librairie Encyclopédique, Bruxelles 1948, p18.

4. Severo Sarduy, *Barroco,* Editions du Seuil, Paris 1975; I am using the Italian translation: *Barroco,* Il Saggiatore, Milano 1980, pp50-3.

whole affair is crowned with the statue of Glory flanked by the Cardinal Virtues, and accompanied by Honour, Virtue, Fame and Wisdom. In this public display of historical triumph an apparent transcendence is knowingly undermined by a pomp and vanity built on the transient emblems of mortality.[6] We view a façade, a spectacle, a canvas, a screen, in whose glance the baroque reflects upon itself. Caught in history, guaranteed by nothing but its own death, this sensibility extracts a sense of being from a continual dialogue with its limits. Its purpose lies within itself: the erotics of the gesture, the designed frustration of form and function that supplements and subverts the closure of *logos* and makes of language an event whose artificial, historical, truth echoes throughout the grammar of the baroque.

Between the melancholy melody and sombre chords of John Dowland's *Semper Dowland, semper dolens* (1604) and the echoing bass ostinato and haunting arpeggios of Silvius Leopold Weiss's *Tombeau Sur La Mort De Mr De Logy* (1721), between these two lute pieces, we traverse the musical arc of the baroque. The lute itself, delicate and intricate in its construction, tuning and the execution of its music, is an allegory of that fragile bridge of melancholia spanning the extremes of the rational and the unrepresentable that so characterises the age. Already by 1750, the year in which both Weiss and Bach died, it was destined for the antiquarian, its place taken by the altogether more robust, rational simplicity of the guitar.

The lute masters of England, France and Germany cast their sonorities in the shapes and tempos provided by existing dance patterns subsequently collected into suites: the galliard, the alman, the gigge, later the courante, the minuet, the gavotte, the bourée and the sarabande. But alongside the exploration of these ready-made structures, of equal importance were the musical freedoms of style and execution that were cultivated from Dowland to Weiss, from René Mésangeau to Denis Gaultier and Robert De Visée, in the fancies, preludes, fantasies, and their sombre culmination in the funeral oration of the *tombeau*. What pulls me to the lute, and to the latter group of compositions, is the insistent inscription of the melancholic in these scores. Dowland's titles are, as always, emblematic reminders of this sensibility: *Lachrimae antiquae, Forelorne Hope, Fancy, Farewell*; but it is with the seventeenth-century *tombeau* of the French and German lutenists that this tendency reaches its apotheosis. These compositions mark and name past time – Monsieur Bianrocher (Dufaut), Monsieur de Lenclos (Gaultier), Baron d'Hartig (Weiss) – in a perpetual dialogue with the dead. To inter-pret the past is also, as Michel de Certeau points out, to inter it: to honour and exorcise it by inscribing it in the possibilities of language.[7] To name and mark past time and recover it for the present is to produce a *tombeau*, a funeral commemoration that simultaneously celebrates life.[8] For it 'is to make a place for the dead, but also to redistribute the space of possibility, to determine negatively what must be done, and consequently to use the narrativity that buries the dead as a way of establishing a place for the living.'[9] It is, perhaps, from this encounter, along the borders of different worlds, of life and death, where certainties are transmuted into

5. John Ruskin, *The Stones of Venice*, quoted in Mary Laura Gibbs, *The Church of Santa Maria del Giglio*, Venice Committee, Venice & New York n.d. Ruskin considered the church 'so grossly debased that even the Italian critics … exhaust their terms of reproach …', *ibid*.

6. See Mario Perniola, 'L'essere-per-la-morte e il simulacro della morte', in Mario Perniola, *La Società dei Simulacri*, Bologna, Capelli 1983.

7. Michel de Certeau, *The Writing of History*, trans. Tom Conley, Columbia University Press, New York 1988, p101.

8. For the resonance of the idea of the *tombeau* in historical reasoning see Iain Chambers, *Migrancy, Culture, Identity*, Routledge, London & New York 1994.

9. Michel de Certeau, *op.cit.*, p100.

circumscribed limits, and the ego mocked, destabilised, and temporarily held in melancholy before being irreversibly undone by a mean mortality, that the poetics of the baroque draws its greatest resources.

In the ornamental the baroque reveals the corner-stone of its structure: 'Artefice, as sublime meaning for and on behalf of the underlying, implicit nonbeing, replaces the ephemeral.'[10] A sustained *appoggiatura* in the melody, rhythmic variations in the bass, a lingering dissonance hovering between notes (*acciaccatura*), a rapid trill or accidental note, the tremolo, the mordent or the bite, are all ornaments that register tonal uncertainties; shades of potential dissonance that conduct us into the folds in sound. Although seemingly auxiliary they reveal themselves to be obligatory.[11] As if a jewel, the ornament or 'grace note' is not an afterthought, a subsequent embellishment added to the finished work, but is rather the essential point towards which the work strives.[12] Like the small windows high up in the baroque *cupola* the ornamental notes cast light down into the interiors. They direct us into the creases in the body of sound. We traverse the melody and descend into the *basso continuo* of the world.[13] A sombre dissonance, hovering over the formless abyss that lies at the bottom of being, pulls us down through the sound to release a tragic vision of the world and a musical redemption of truth.[14] Over our heads the 'centre' continues to oscillate in the arabesque of an elaboration that is never an 'extra', but is essential to the execution, to the unfolding that disseminates the tonality.[15] As an opening in the sound, usually improvised, it surprises the form with the individual responsibility and freedom of the performance. It forcefully reminds us that the language of the baroque is elliptical. It neither pretends to be transparent nor presumes to be eternal. Sense is unfolded into a sensibility where language becomes the art of the interruption.

The Platonic idea of a perfect form, the circle which functions as the transcendental guarantee of a harmony to which the heavens were expected to correspond, is displaced by Kepler's discovery of the ellipse traversed by the planets. The circle is breached. The centre is duplicated and dispersed within the ellipse. The archetype fractures, the orbit vacillates, the mind migrates. The closed order of cosmology gives way to the infinity of astronomy.[16] Suspended between anterior and posterior certainties – the precedence of Renaissance humanism and the subsequent convictions of scientific logic and rationalism – the baroque involves a self-conscious act of throwing a construction over nothing. Alone, and responsible for our actions and the place of our making, we acknowledge Giordano Bruno's 'heresy' in Zarathrustra's joy.[17]

In the parable of the Nolan heresy lie the seeds of a dilemma that will cast its shadows over the century that opens with his public execution in Rome, February 1600. Alongside the popular mythology of the persecuted man of reason and science speaking out against Papal obscurantism, is the more significant claim to be made on his behalf against the Inquisition for a freedom that permits a highly erudite magician to speak his mind without being reduced to ashes at the stake. This, of course, is the argument so brilliantly sustained by

10. Julia Kristeva, *Black Sun: Depression and Melancholia*, trans, Leon S. Roudiez, Columbia University Press, New York 1989, p99.

11. Robert Donington, *A Performer's Guide to Baroque Music*, Faber & Faber, London 1978.

12. For a discussion of the origin of the term 'baroque' in the context of jewellery, and Portuguese (*barrucco* – an irregular shaped pearl), see Severo Sarduy, *op.cit.*

13. See the description of Leibniz's multi-storeyed 'house of resonance' in the opening pages of Gilles Deleuze, *Le Pli: Leibniz et la Baroque*, Editions de Minuit, Paris 1988; I am using the Italian translation, *La Piega, Lebniz e il Barocco*, Einaudi, Torino 1990, p17. The English edition is *The Fold: Leibniz and the Baroque*, trans. Tom Conley, University of Minnesota Press, Minneapolis, 1993. The ever-present, and ever evolving, *basso continuo* can be compared to the modern day 'rhythm section' of guitar, bass, keyboards and drums in both jazz and rock music, see Thurston Dart, *The Interpretation of Music*, Harper & Row, New York 1963, p78.

Frances Yates in her book *Giordano Bruno and the Hermetic Tradition*.[18] But where she sees in Bruno (and Campanella), for example, the public termination of an esoteric Renaissance discourse before its disappearance underground into more obscure settings (the Rosicrucians, the masons), and its inevitable replacement by the scientific, post-Copernican formation of the modern epoch, I prefer to think that Bruno's thought constitutes a perennial disturbance. The provocation of Bruno thinking the infinite draws our attention both into the ambiguous languages of the baroque and into the usually repressed shadows of rationalism. Giordano Bruno, after all, was condemned as a 'man of letters'. His 'errors' stemmed from textual hermeneutics, from his interpretation of certain gnostic texts, particularly those carrying the collective name of Hermes Trismegistus. He was a sixteenth century semiotician who proposed an erudite, however mystical, reading of a decentred infinity that happened to formally coincide with the emerging, scientific geometry of space.

Yet that form of reading the logic of the universe does not simply disappear, it haunts and shadows subsequent enquiry. Before his death, and well into another century, Isaac Newton consigned his manuscripts to a trunk. The trunk was discovered by Keynes in 1936. The writings in it are concerned with Biblical exegesis, and with works on alchemy and magic. They starkly illustrate how 'the primary physicist was also the ultimate magician'.[19] We are here dealing, as Loup Verlet points out in his recent book on the contents of that trunk, with the occlusion of an initial discontinuity, with the hiding of the fractured foundation of a discourse. We are presented with a version that excludes breaks and fissions, with a version in which the contents of the trunk are ignored and denied. Newton's years of study of 'mystical language' are invariably separated and subsequently cancelled from his scientific production. But, as Verlet points out, the mathematisation of reality with which Newton's model established the basis of modern science, perhaps finds its genetic moment within a religious problematic that is inspired by and continues to seek responses in other, 'non-scientific', forms of knowledge. Here, suspended between the co-ordinates of mathematics and magic, we are back with Bruno.

The sense of loss, the rude displacement, the fall from grace into the immense landscape of an incomprehensible and infinite (dis)order, in which humankind 'rolls away from the centre towards X' (Friedrich Nietzsche), surely inaugurates the geography of baroque melancholia, the installation of irony, and the modern sensibility of historical secularism. Trapped in the fragility of a desire for transcendence, for completion, for the homecoming of truth, the baroque acknowledges in the very fabric of its language, in its voluptuous accommodation of loss, a destiny of interminable peregrinations that reveal in every instance, in 'all the mornings of the world', the folly of such a presumption.[20] Every statement, gesture or expression is immediately doubled by doubt, every resolution by the uncertain shadows of an imminent dissolution. It is this realisation 'of a truly temporal predicament' that so profoundly animates the baroque dissemination of allegory and irony.[21]

14. Christine Buci-Glucksmann, *Tragique de l'ombre*, Éditions Galilée, Paris 1990, pp229-30. 'De la musique, comme art de l'emotion sans concept, comme Affect de tout affect.', *ibid*, p230.

15. *Ibid.*, p202.

16. For the detailed nuances of this 'cosmological break' in the making of the baroque sensibility, see in particular Severo Sarduy, *op.cit.*

17. See Thomas Docherty, *op.cit.*, pp17-29.

18. Frances Yates, *Giordano Bruno and the Hermetic Tradition*, Routledge & Kegan Paul, London 1964.

19. Loup Verlet, *La malle de Newton*, Gallimard, Paris 1993.

20. The reference is to Pascal Quignard's *Touts les matins du monde*, and its subsequent realisation as a film, with Quignard's screen-play, by Alain Courneau in 1992. On 'sad voluptuousness', see Julia Kristeva, *Black Sun: Depression and Melancholia*, trans, Leon S. Roudiez, Columbia University Press, New York 1989.

21. Paul de Man, 'The Rhetoric of Temporality' in Paul de Man, *Blindness and Insight*, Methuen, London 1983, p222.

In this doubling, where the subject refuses to stand unequivocally by his own statement, irony shows both the refusal to give up expository discourse and the impossibility of assuming it totally. The interplay between statements about objects and reflection about these statements as objects is ambiguous. The subject is placed in a transcendent position with respect to discourse, but only to deny the possibility of being the guarantor of transcendence.[22]

The empty sockets of a skull, fresh flowers between its teeth, gaze blankly upon the everyday street.[23] The world, words, women ... truth, have become fickle, unstable tokens of a destitute cosmology: falling stars, children begot with mandrake root, the sound of mermaids' singing – signs destined to reveal their falsehood 'ere I come, to two or three.[24] The temporary abeyance of transcendental guarantees, prior to an imperious rationalism once again claiming the universe of humankind, permits the recognition of the full autonomy of representations whose only reason lies within themselves. Fallen to earth, language, images and signs 'stunningly joined to nothing', can only respond to their passage and presence in this world.[25] The acknowledgement of the image in and for itself, of the temporal construct of the artefice, of the simulacrum, 'implies the closure of metaphysics and the complete acceptance of the historical world.'[26] Yet this is compounded, rather than contradicted, in a contemporary intolerance to loss. For the fierce consolation of Protestantism and the aggression of the Inquisition are only seemingly opposed symptoms of a deep reluctance to forgo: both institutionalise an intolerance to loss. In refusing to give up the lost object, the primal thing, the terrestrial signatures of signs and sounds continue to gesture across the abyss of time in a perpetual mourning that contributes directly to the baroque affect:

> Like a tense link between Thing and Meaning, the unnameable and the proliferation of signs, the silent affect and the ideality that designates and goes beyond it, the *imaginary* is neither the objective description that will reach its highest point in science nor theological idealism that will be satisfied with reaching the symbolic uniqueness of a beyond. The experience of nameable melancholia opens up the space of a necessarily heterogeneous subjectivity, torn between the two co-necessary and co-present centers of opacity and ideal. The opacity of things, like that of the body untenanted by meaning – a depressed body, bent on suicide – is conveyed to the work's meaning, which asserts itself at the same time absolute and corrupt, untenable, impossible, to be done all over again. A subtle alchemy of signs then compels recognition – musicalization of signifiers, polyphony of lexemes, dislocation of lexical, syntactic, and narrative units – this is *immediately* experienced as a psychic transformation of the speaking being between the two limits of nonmeaning and meaning, Satan and God, Fall and Resurrection.[27]

So, the world is not only decentred but also doubled by the coeval insistence on

22. Fernand Hallyn, *The Poetic Structure of the World: Copernicus and Kepler*, Zone Books, New York 1993, p22; translation modified.

23. The church of Santa Maria delle Anime del Purgatoria (1604), Via Tribunali, Naples. The flowers are changed daily.

24. John Donne, *Song*.

25. Hélène Cixous referring to Shakespeare, in Hélène Cixous and Catherine Clément, *The Newly Born Woman*, Manchester, Manchester University Press 1987, p98.

26. Mario Perniola, 'Icone, visioni, simulacri', in Mario Perniola, *op. cit.*, p122.

27. Julia Kristeva, *Black Sun: Depression and Melancholia*, trans, Leon S. Roudiez, Columbia University Press, New York 1989, pp100-1.

dogma and doubt in every discourse. Open to construction and determinism, the world is also susceptible to a poetics of ambiguity, to a cleft in reason where rational design can slip into the alliterative contours of a dream.[28] The straight lines employed in astronomy and architecture for the geometrical rationalisation of time and space are shadowed, mimicked and mocked by alchemy and necromancey, by magical equations, emblematic insignia and the terrestrial trappings of life, before it all evaporates in the deceptive order of music: the note hangs in the air, and then falls away. In the fall ... in that transient, dropping away, in that excess of representation, the functional and the rational are exposed as fragile faiths: logics, despite their declared neutrality, that are always circumscribed by human desire. Nowhere is there more starkly displayed than in the insistent application of 'science' to music found in the writings of Pierre Gassendi, Marin Mersenne and René Descartes. Seeking a universal harmony in the geometry of sound and an arithmetic of the passions, they employed mytho-mathematics of Greek and Byzantine provenance that invariably betrayed the alchemical, astrological and magical drives that continually shadowed baroque reason.[29]

If the shortest distance between two bodies is a straight line, it is the shock of the allegoric that provides the most rapid transport from the obvious into the hieroglyphic and the other, obscured centre of the ellipse.[30] Nicholas Dyer, architect, responsible for the building of seven new churches in the cities of London and Westminster in 1711, here reveals a logic that accords with an unsuspected design:

> And thus will I compleet the Figure: Spittle-Fields, Wapping and Lime-house have made the triangle; Bloomsbury and St Mary Woolnoth have next created the major Pentacle-starre; and, with Greenwich, all these will form the Sextuple abode of Baal-Berith or the Lord of the Covenant. Then, with the church of Little St Hugh, the Septilateral Figure will rise above about Black Step Lane and, in this Pattern, every straight line is enrich'd with a point at Infinity and every Plane with a line at Infinity. Let him that has Understanding count the Number: the seven Churches are built in conjunction with the seven Planets in the lower Orbs of Heaven, the seven Circles of the Heavens, the seven Starres in Ursa Minor and the seven Starres in the Pleiades. Little St Hugh was flung into the Pitte with the seven Marks upon his Hands, Feet, Sides and Breast which thus exhibit the seven Demons – Beydelus, Metucgayn, Adulec, Demeymes, Gadix, Uqizuz and Sol. I have built an everlasting Order, which I may run through laughing: no one can catch me now.[31]

In his classic account of the English intellectual thought of the period, *The Seventeenth Century Background* (1934), Basil Willey returns again and again to the deep seated ambiguity in its voice. He carefully tempers talk of the dawning of the age of reason and the triumph of science by insisting on the Janus-like quality of the epoch, with its ability to live 'in divided and distinguished worlds'

28. Kepler's *Dream*, published posthumously by his son in 1634, describes celestial phenomena as they would have appeared from the moon. Earlier versions had circulated in manuscript form and Kepler thought it was known to John Donne; see Fernand Hallyn, *op.cit.* 'A Dream' is also the title of a fine fantasy for the lute by John Dowland.

29. See Marin Mersenne, *Questions Inouyes*, Fayard, Paris 1985, and Pierre Gassendi, *Initiation à la théorie de la musique*, Aix-en-Provence, Edisud 1992. Descartes wrote a *Compendium Musicae* that was published posthumously in Utrecht in 1650. It is available in a French translation as *Abrégé de musique*, Press Universitaires de France, Paris 1987.

30. To Heidegger's proposal that we dwell in language is to be added Vico's on the metaphorical character of reality: Ernesto Grassi, 'Il dramma della metafora', in *Informazione Filosofica*, n.6, marzo 1992.

31. Peter Ackroyd, *Hawksmoor*, Abacus, London 1985, p186.

(Sir Thomas Browne). For what was new did not necessarily imply an irreversible cut in time, but rather a novel configuration of elements that simultaneously encouraged *and* deviated the possibility of an indivisible truth to be located in a mechanical rationalism 'which supposes that which is fluctuating to be fixed' (Bacon). Writing in an epoch in which uncertainty had become a principle within the paradigm of the natural sciences (Heisenberg), Willey justly queries a rationalist vision of the earlier period. He notes:

> The distinctions were only beginning to be made which for later ages shut off poetry from science, metaphor from fact, fancy from judgement. The point about these different worlds was not that they were divided, but that they were simultaneously available.[32]

32. Basil Willey, *The Seventeenth Century Background*, Doubleday, New York 1953, p50.

This framing of thought, and life, was suspended in a fluctuating and ambiguous balance between light and shadows, between the flat, tabular frame of reason and the infinite spread and inter-layered folds of explanation. Fernand Hallyn writes:

> ... we can consider the seventeenth and eighteenth centuries as the period of transition from the predominance of the vertical axis, linking several levels of reality, to the predominance of the horizontal axis, reducing everything to a single level.[33]

33. Fernand Hallyn, *op.cit.*, p20.

Between a *spiegare* (to explain, expound, unfold) and a *piegare* (to fold, wrap, crease), emerges the *spiegamento* (the explication, the spread, the unfolding). Contrary to the fixed point of the rationalist *a priori* sought by Descartes lies the mutable point of view found in the body, where to explain is to unfold a complexity and to trace the in-finite in the folds, creases and envelopment of the world; in the finitude of our physical frame, time and place, in the world of our possibilities.[34]

34. 'The point of view is found in the body': Leibniz, letter to Lady Masham, June 1704, cited in Deleuze *op.cit.*, p17.

> To explain does not simply imply to extend, expand and lay out an argument, but is rather to be involved and evolve with it. Although the organism defines itself through its capacity to endlessly bend and fold its parts, it explains them not by referring to infinity but with reference to the limits available to the species.[35]

35. Deleuze, *op.cit.*, p13.

Sometimes the construction, in architecture, the theatre, and thought, leaned more towards the light, sometimes more towards the shadows; invariably it recognised its hybrid provenance in both. The constraints of mortality were inscribed as much in its rational flights as in the vivid movement of bodies and light that are obliquely pictured in Caravaggio: temporarily caught but not centred, falling away, out of the frame.[36] Like the dying note on the lute or viol de gamba, the texture and tonality is decentred, transient, melancholic. This passionate view of things emerges from the events of

36. Sarduy, *op.cit.*, p50.

suffering history – 'bound upon a wheel of fire' – and not from the secluded security of logic. In its violent affirmation this temper also announces the precarious space of the emergence of the modern urban world, and anticipates what in later centuries will be referred to as 'mass culture'.[37]

Along with the systematic installation of centralised government and court life (Madrid, Versailles, London), and the public rationalisation of financial, juridicial, educational and military control, renewed imposition of seigniorial rights on the land induced, sometimes physically enforced, the rural migrations of peasants, sharecroppers and small landowners from the countryside towards the cities. It led to the growth of a landless and propertyless street dweller: the anonymous faces of the future urban 'mob', 'crowd' and 'masses', as well as the urban criminal underworld. To these violent dislocations are to be added interminable religious wars and persecution resulting in rural regions being scoured by bandits and roving armies of disbanded soldiers and ex-mercenaries. Added to this were regular outbreaks of witch hunts and the plague. In an 'age drunk with acts of cruelty both lived and imagined', these were all immediate exemplars of the 'baroque pedagogy of violence', terrifying reminders of a fragile world and a precarious mortality.[38]

In the first half of the seventeenth century London was ravaged by plague – 1603: 33,500 deaths; 1625: 35,500 deaths; 1636; 10,500 deaths; 1665-6: the Great Plague; 69,000 deaths, followed by the Fire.[39] Similarly, baroque Naples is studded with allegorical *guglie* or obelisks built to exorcise plagues, earthquakes and vulcanic eruptions: the eruption of Vesuvius in 1631, the plagues of 1656 and 1657, the earthquakes of 1688 and 1694.[40] What was once held at a distance through the promise of another world, life and salvation, is dramatically brought close; it is re-presented (*vor-stellen*) and re-membered, in-corporated and rendered flesh. It becomes some 'thing' (*res*) that concerns and disturbs us.[41] So the last things – death and judgement – become immediate things.[42] The Italian philosopher Mario Perniola associates this baroque acknowledgement of the historical and ontological import of death in life, as opposed to something separate and extraneous to terrestrial existence, with Loyola and the Jesuits. It is not a head full of reason, but a body inscribed with terrestrial constraints, dwelling in the perishable shelter of the Earth and destined for the worms of time, that provides the constant and tragic corpus of Baroque drama, of the epoch's aesthetics and ascetic sensibility.

Yet in this powerful proximity, in the marked inscription of mortality into truth, there existed a remarkable amnesia.[43] As though in compensation for a lost centrality the century of the baroque is also witness to the violent and extensive elaboration of a eurocentrism that seeks to model and mould the rest of the world in its image and imaginary. In the moment that European thought considers itself to be a prisoner of time and is cast into the unprotected vicissitudes of history it discovers a terrible freedom. For elsewhere, in the wide avenues, the giant *plaza* and imposing church façades that the baroque realised in urban Mexico and South America, there is mounted an architecture in which

37. See Maravall, *op.cit.*

38. The first phrase is Benjamin's: Walter Benjamin, *The Origin of German Tragic Drama*, Verso, London 1990, p185; the second is from Maravall, *op.cit.*, p163.

39. Figures from Christopher Hill, *The Century of Revolution, 1603-1714*, Sphere Books, London 1969, p278.

40. Gaetano Cantone, *Napoli barocca*, Laterza, Bari 1992.

41. Martin Heidegger, 'La cosa', in Martin Heidegger, *Saggi e discorsi*, Mursia, Milano 1976.

42. Martin Heidegger, 'The Origin of the Work of Art', in Martin Heidegger, *Basic Writings*, Harper & Row, New York 1977, p152.

43. I am extremely grateful to Kathy Biddick for directing me to this amnesia.

non-European bodies and histories were included only to be ruthlessly negated. Silence, the intractable and the untranslatable was forced to bear testimony to a European narcissism which sought 'to represent even those experiences that resist it with a stubborn opacity.'[44] This invisible presence was traced in the labour, slavery, blood, torture and death of those beings that colonial government, military repression and the Inquisition administered and occluded. Maintained on the colonial periphery by force, fear and terror, the limits of a European possession, and position, were simultaneously installed and repressed as the west brutally insisted on becoming synonymous with the world.

44. Rey Chow, *Writing Diaspora*, Indiana University Press, Bloomington 1993, p38.

* * *

The Talmudic legend assigns to each instance of time a specific angel, that is to say its specific quality, or, in other words, its irreplaceable messianic virtuality ... this figure of paradoxical thought, according to which the end can be realised *immediately* 'in the very heart of history', subverts the very foundations of historical Reason. It implies that time is no longer to be considered as a directive axis, where one thing inevitably follows another, or as a river that flows from its source towards its mouth, but rather as a juxtaposition of instances, each of them unique and irreducible to a totality, and which therefore do not follow one another as if they were stages in an irreversible process. Here the past, the present and the future no longer succeed each other along a direct line as though viewed externally, but coexist as three states of permanent consciousness ...

Stéphane Mosès[45]

45. Stéphane Mosès, *L'Ange De L'Histoire: Rosenzweig, Benjamin, Scholem*, Éditions du Seuil, Paris 1992, pp19-20.

... all manifest discourse is the repression of what is not said which, in turn, undermines all that is said.

Noreen O'Connor[46]

46. Noreen O'Connor 'The Personal is Political', in R. Bernasconi & D. Wood, *The Provocation of Levinas*, Routledge, London & New York 1988, p59.

The complex play of the lights and shadows of the baroque, its limits and interrogation, opens up a critical space that returns to inhabit our present. It raises a question, creates an opening in the construction of our understandings, a rent in the fabric of our knowledge. It draws us into the shadows of illumination, into the repressed zones that our sense of being seeks to avoid. For it forces us to confront and converse with what we most avidly seek to ignore: our limits and our mortality. The Baroque critique of permanency and essentialism, complemented by the re-centring of sixteenth-century Europe in colonial directives, this simultaneous decentring and recentring, returns as a ghost – 'Remember me' – to haunt the dusk of western modernism. It erupts in the heterotopic challenge to the rational, utopic design of the latter. It calls out for an ethical reply to the needs of another scene, another story, another possibility, reminding us that historical reason is itself to be judged. For behind the 'perverse absolutism' (Lévinas) of western knowledge, and its universal desire for an unfractured, unitary logic, a rational teleology of time and causality, there lies the evasion of that judgement. To refuse to register the enigmatic, the discontinuous, the regressive and the hungry shadows of oblivion, and to eradicate them in the violent insistence on coherence, is to flee from life and the anguish of death, and is to repudiate responsibility for that condition.[47]

When the earth is refused and violently reduced to an ethereal pact between thought and trancendental logic, when the world is abrogated and distilled into the pure spirit and transparency of the rational word, all those unresolved, mutant, incomplete, uncanny, cracked, silent and undone languages that contribute to the insistent 'worlding of the world' are denied.[48] As we draw back from that blinkered perspective, turn away from that narrow path, and reinvest ourselves with the responsibility for our lives and what sustains them, other lives, we catch the echoes of our baroque antecedents in the duplicity, disturbance, excess, folds and opacity of knowledge, while at the same time listening to the counter-point of cultural amnesia and european narcissism. We re-member in that mortal mess-age and its history of shadows, the questions that permit us to continue to question, that permit us to live.

It is why, for some of us, the ragged, unwoven and incomplete *chiaroscuro* patterns of the baroque are far closer to our present sensibilities and modalities of being than the subsequent faith in instrumental reason and confident subjectivity. To recall that earlier interruption is to remind ourselves of the complex, sometimes indifferent, contingency of the world before positivism stepped in to reassure us with the secular god of 'science'. The proximity of the allegorical landscapes of the baroque to the radical and disruptive experiences of modernity has been well caught by Christine Buci-Glucksmann:

Here one can see, well before *modern* art, allegory as the testimony of the domination of the fragment over everything, of the destructive principle over the constructive one, of passion, as the excavation of an absence, over the mastery of reason. Only the fragment is able to demonstrate that the logics of the body, of feeling, of life and death do not coincide with those of Power or the Idea. In the fragment there appears precisely that which is mute (hence music), that which is new (even if it is death), that which is unmastered and profoundly ungovernable: catastrophes that embody the very act of representation.

Reality is here consigned to a perennial antinomy, to the deceptive game of reality as an illusion, in which the world is simultaneously evaluated and devaluated. 'The profane world, considered from the point of allegory, is simultaneously evaluated and devaluated.' In it there lies the specific seduction of the baroque, in which the pre-eminence of the aesthetic – of play, of appearance – is united with metaphysical loss against a background of affliction and melancholy. The metaphor of the theatre – of the world as theatre and the theatre as world – portrays the particular temporality of the baroque ... Over this eternal displacement of appearances there lies the

47. E. Robberechts, 'Savoir et mort chez F. Rosenzweig' in *Revue Philosophique de Louvain*, volume 90, Mai 1992.

48. Martin Heidegger, 'La cosa', in Martin Heidegger, *op.cit.*, p119.

presence of an omniscient, but now distant, spectator: God. The abyss between reality and illusion, however, is insuperable: the theatre now *knows* itself to be theatre.[49]

49. Christine Buci-Glucksmann, *La Raison Baroque: De Baudelaire à Benjamin*, Éditions Galilée, Paris 1984, pp71-2; *Baroque Reason: The Aesthetics of Modernity*, Sage, London 1994. She is quoting Benjamin.

This exposes and advances the contemporary baroquisation of the world in which the rationalist drive, and a facile faith in the linear accumulation of 'progress', is now perhaps to be considered as an interruption, an interval. In an altogether wider constellation the seventeenth century baroque, with its fragile allegories of excess and mortality, with its melancholy acknowledgement of the limits of reason and life, is affinitively linked to the reappearance of neo-baroque styles in the late twentieth century, where 'style', like the earlier baroque ornament, is not a trivial extra but rather exemplifies the self-conscious pathos of the languages we inhabit.

It is in the insistence of our being captured in time, subjected to history and mortality, rendering sense from the crisis and fragility of human existence, that the baroque sensibility flares up into an image that projects light into our world. Like the illumination from dead stars, the baroque arrives to become part of our lives, as something that is simultaneously present and absent.[50] The palpable instability of what we are accustomed to refer to as 'knowledge' and 'truth' provides a telescopic link between two historical constellations. It leads us to the suggestion that historical specificity does not lie in the factual annotation of the passage of time, but in our receiving and acknowledging a discontinued moment by interpreting it and ourselves in its present light. That moment is both unique and repetitive, 'irreversible and recurrent'.[51] For its truth does not lie in a 'foreclosure through facts ...' but in the event and resonance of language.[52] Truth is not our personal property, restricted to the range and intention of our will.[53] It is something that both invests us and escapes us: it is discontinuous.[54] So the transient past, apparently lost forever, can and does return to activate another, even novel, sense of the present, and, with it, an opening towards the future.

50. Walter Banjamin, *Charles Baudelaire: A Lyric Poet in the Era of High Capitalism*, New Left Books, London 1973.

51. Stéphane Mosès, *op.cit.*, p139.

52. Dori Laub, in Shoshana Felman & Dori Laub, *Testimony: Crises of Witnessing in Literature, Psychoanalysis, and History*, Routledge, London 1992, p73.

53. Emmanuel Lévinas, *Totality and Infinity*, Duquesne University Press, Pittsburgh 1969.

54. Stéphane Mosès, *op.cit.*, p132.

55. *Ibid*, p127.

This is to suggest an ethical and involved, rather than a positivist and distanced, paradigm of knowledge.[55] In this mode, the past is never recaptured 'as it was', as though, in a reversal of time, we could simply retrace our steps back along the path of homogeneous evolution to an earlier moment. The past does not come down to us smoothly across the passage of time. It erupts and resonates in our time as a disconcerting and discrete event: as the voice and body of the other that challenges our own. The past becomes the scene of traces. As signs, silences and resonance, we are directed towards what is irredeemably lost to us yet which continues to haunt our language and thoughts, and thereby interrogate our sense of the present. To translate (and transform) the past in this manner may well be to betray how things 'actually were', but it is also to refuse to discard the body of the past. If we were to reduce the baroque to the uniform tread, and ultimate oblivion, of 'progress', we would be cancelling the possibility of its return: the possibility of past generations to continue to interrogate, disturb and challenge our time and our custody for their times.

To temper and test time in this manner is to punctuate it in order to hear the respiration of other ways of being in time. It is to acknowledge our own precariousness in which the past is not given and the future is not predictable: all is to be undone, inter-preted, contested, again and again and ...

To open up the body of history, and expose it to the vindications of the world, involves the adoption of a figure of time, of knowledge, that is also a figure of speech, of writing, able to hold in suspension the ambiguous 'truth' that language sustains in our continual rewriting of the past as we research the historical potential of the present. For style is the body, the physicality of language. So, we acknowledge in the gesture of a style – of thought, of writing, of speech – the co-presence and responsibility for past, present and future. There the intractable, rebus-like quality of baroque allegory, as the speech and writing of a sensibility, as epochal expression, suggests to us something more than merely a literary technique or archaic poetics. Walter Benjamin writes:

> ... in allegory the observer is confronted with the *facies hippocratica* of history as a petrified, primordial landscape. Everything about history that, from the very beginning, had been untimely, sorrowful, unsuccessful, is expressed in a face – or rather in a death's head. And although such a thing lacks all 'symbolic' freedom, all classical proportion, all humanity – nevertheless, this is the form in which man's subjection to nature is most obvious and it significantly gives rise not only to the enigmatic question of the nature of human existence as such, but also of the biographical historicity of the individual. This is the heart of the allegorical way of seeing, of the baroque, secular explanation of history as the Passion of the world; its importance resides solely in the stations of its decline.[56]

56. Walter Benjamin, *The origin of German Tragic Drama*, Verso, London 1990, p166.

In the interregnum between religious faith secured in the divine stability of the pre-Copernican universe and later consolation in the idolatry of science, the baroque exposed a naked, unprotected being, in which any 'person, any object, any relationship can mean absolutely anything else. With this possibility a destructive, but just verdict is passed on the profane world ...'[57] Stripped of an obvious symbolic function, caught in the fall of the world, in the profanity of decay and ruin, the baroque points elsewhere by tunnelling into the body, the physicality, of language. As Benjamin points out, the typographic extremes and charged metaphors of the baroque are only the most obvious examples of a language that tends towards the visual, towards the illumination that emanates from an independent and autonomous image. But it is a marked, a wounded autonomy, for:

57. *Ibid*, p.175.

> In the field of allegorical intuition the image is a fragment, a rune.[58]

58. *Ibid*, p176.

The image is both a fragment, a ruin, but also a rune, a hieroglyph.

The false appearance of totality is extinguished. For the *eidos* disappears, the simile ceases to exist, and the cosmos it contained shrivels up. The dry rebuses which remain contain an insight, which is still available to the confused investigator.[59]

59. *Ibid.*, p176.

Beneath its flourish of pomp, the baroque insists on the imperfection and incompleteness of the world, it insists on our physical and terrestrial enclosure, on the inevitability of decay and ruin, and so wins for itself, out of the depths of its language, an insight destined to endure: 'Where man is drawn towards the symbol, allegory emerges from the depths of being to intercept the intention, and to triumph over it.'[60] José Marvall also insists on the centrality of the interruption and the incomplete to the baroque, suggesting that it offers, for example, a key to the reading of Shakespeare's later 'unfinished' plays.[61]

60. *Ibid.*, p183.

61. Maravall, *op.cit.*

The idea that historical time might be multiple and discontinuous, that history is an allegorical construction exposing the ruins of time, is not only what links Benjamin to the excessive and poetic underside of modernism (Baudelaire, Kafka), but it is also what links the German Jewish thinker to the baroque and his own marvellous and deeply allegorical reading of modernity. The key texts here are the volume on the mourning theatre (*Trauerspiel*) of the German baroque published in 1928, the only book that Benjamin actually completed, the massive and incomplete project on the Parisian arcades that he worked on in the last years of his life in exile, and the 'Theses on the philosophy of history' (1940).

To subvert and discard the links in the temporal chain of irreversible causality, in order to turn time back against itself and release another story, and another way of telling, is what animates Benjamin's continual engagement with the languages of time and being, with the writing of history. It is to give a name to the defeated and deceased, to return again to the overlooked and the shadows, and there to reveal in a diverse scansion of time the detailed instances that make up the eternal pathos of terrestrial existence in the repetitive discontinuities of mortality. In the ambiguous gesture of the collector – simultaneously salvaging and reifying the past – Benjamin seeks to actively re-member, rather than merely recall, such traces and fragments.[62] Like the baroque *tombeau*, he seeks to open up a space in language and time in which another history can appear and, with it, an alternative future in which each historical moment can be sundered to reveal an opening towards paths and possibilities not yet taken. Hence historical time, as opposed to the linear tyranny of physical time, becomes reversible. It permits a re-membering, a return, that produces the 'open' time of writing, of politics, of aesthetics and ethics, ready for judgement in every instance (Emmanuel Lévinas).[63] For it is the history of the 'untimely, sorrowful, unsuccessful', that is, in the discontinued, discarded and dispersed histories of the vanquished, that Benjamin continually sought to snatch from the hands of the victors, from the oppression of the continuity of *their* time and 'progress'. For this 'progress' is founded upon the continuity of catastrophe, on the defeat of the denied bodies

62. On the political ambiguities of collecting, and its place in the articulation and disarticulation of modernity, see Chow, *op.cit.*, pp43-4.

63. I have borrowed the concept of 'open time' from Stéphane Mosès, *op.cit.*, p177.

and stories of those excluded: the ruins of history.

This is to establish a new type of historical intelligibility that binds us to the time of the other, that binds us to a response and a response-ability (Shoshana Felman) for the excluded, for oblivion. In the transient act of writing under the eternal sign of ethical redemption, Benjamin, like Franz Rosenzweig, but the Heideggerian echoes here should also not be overlooked, sought an intelligibility that was not closed, 'scientific', or metaphysical, but was rather consigned to the custody of language; to the vital unfolding of my being in language and my language in being in which the breath of the living fans the ashes of the past that flare up to cast light on our future.

*　*　*

A passing note. In the centrality of music to the black Atlantic experiences of modernity we encounter not simply a historical and cultural archive, a vital storehouse of memories, but also a constellation of perpetual redemption.[64] Here past, present and future fuse in an abrupt interruption – the blue note on the bent guitar string, the shout, the saxophone growl, the bass story, the rap – that challenges immediate circumstance to reveal the presence of other histories. For rap invokes an interruption of language, a cut which folds language in upon itself, and then unfolds it across the fields of English rock music and urban style. It constitutes the act of testimony, of bearing witness, that reveals a diverse scansion of historical time, a different cultural inscription and musical signature. Unchaining such languages from their presumed referents, the supplement of rap proposes another centre. Usually considered to be an addition, an ornament, to the centrality of rock music, viewed from elsewhere rap registers an essential relocation and resiting of the musical (and cultural) score.[65] In this separation of sound from the earlier signified, we enter the 'topos of Unsayability'.[66] Like the baroque insistence on the ornament that permits us to glance into the interior and bear witness to the 'underground of language', rap's decoration and decentring of readily available languages and styles suggests that music reflects more than is accessible to the categories of reflection, and invokes the 'effort to say that of which one cannot speak.'[67] On this point Andrew Bowie concludes:

> The importance of music in the history of modernity seems to me in part at least explained by its role as part of the counter discourse of modernity, that discourse that in the face of the determination to ground the subject in rules, codes and systems always reveals the extent to which these systems cannot be self-grounding.[68]

*　*　*

Art is not about communication, it is a form of resistance against communication, against the deceit of communication.

Jean-Marie Straub

64. For the concept of a counter-history of modernity articulated around the black Atlantic see Paul Gilroy, *The Black Atlantic*, Verso, London 1993.

65. Ted Swedenburg, 'Homies in the Hood: Rap's Commodification of Insubordination', *New Formations*, 18, Winter 1992.

66. Carl Dalhaus, *Die Idee der absoluten Musik*, quoted in Andrew Bowie, 'Music, Language and Modernity', in Andrew Benjamin (ed), *The Problems of Modernity, Adorno and Benjamin*, Routledge, London & New York 1989, p70.

67. The 'underground of language' comes from Shoshana Felman, in Shoshana Felman & Dori Laub, *op.cit.*, p15; while the second voice is that of Theodor Adorno, quoted in Bowie, *op.cit.*, p80.

68. Bowie, *op.cit.*, p83.

To return to the lost harmony of the circle. In the circle of investigation we set out confident that we will return to our point of departure complete with our survey and solutions. In the ellipse we discover our decentring, and never return to our point of departure. Like a baroque column spiralling upwards in a twisting formation, we find ourselves caught in a movement in which beginning and end do not correspond. We encounter other centres, other perspectives, disseminated along the spiralled ellipse of our trajectory.

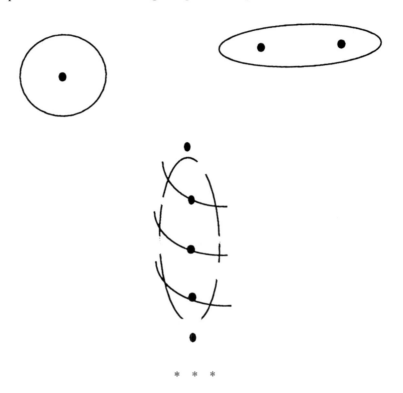

* * *

Reason is entitled to a home in the world, but the world is just that: a home; it is not totality.

Franz Rosenzweig[69]

In this exposure I encounter the judgement of the angels, the disturbing judgement of the other that resists my language, refuses my view and repudiates my history. For angels are creatures of an ambiguous provenance that move between worlds refusing allegiance. Amongst them is the allegorical angel whose wings brushed Walter Benjamin's writings: the famous figure contemplating the growing debris of the past as it is blown backwards into the future. Then there are the black and white angels that inhabit the fragmentary, dream-like cinema of Isaac Julien's extraordinary *Looking for Langston* (1989). There is also the angel that sings through the trees in the final sequence of Sally Potter's film *Orlando* (1992). These angels condense past, present and future.

69. Franz Rosenzweig, *The Star of Redemption*, trans. William W. Hallo, Holt, Rinehart and Winston, New York 1971, p13.

106   NEW FORMATIONS

Under their gaze I find myself caught between two centres: between the apparent ineluctability of time and the obscure centre of its continual crisis.[70] For the angels announce history as a perpetual becoming, an inexhaustible emerging, an eternal provocation, a desire that defies and transgresses the linearity of abstract logic with the insistent now, the body, the *Jetz*, of the permanent presence of the possible.[71]

Apparently caught in the scissors of time, a space opens up between past and future that reveals the ever-present body of language: 'The being of language – the language of being.'[72] I 'live here, forever taking leave', called upon to lend my ear and body to the miracle of the terrestrial call:

> Wasn't all this a miracle? Be astonished, Angel, for we
> *are* this, O Great One; proclaim that we could achieve this, my breath
> is too short for such praise. So, after all, we have not
> failed to make use of these generous spaces, these
> spaces of *ours*. (How frighteningly great they must be,
> since thousands of years have not made them overflow with our feelings.)[73]

70. See Mosès, *op.cit.*

71. This paragraph is a modified reprise of the coda to Chambers, *op.cit.*

72. Martin Heidegger, 'The Nature of Language', in Martin Heidegger, *On The Way To Language*, Harper & Row, New York 1982, p76.

73. Rainer Maria Rilke, from the Seventh Elegy of the Duino Elegies, in *The Selected Poetry of Rainer Maria Rilke*, Picador, London 1987, translated by Stephen Mitchell, p191. The phrase 'we live here, forever taking leave' comes from the concluding line of the Eighth Elegy, *ibid*, p197.

1. R. Barthes, *La chambre claire: Note sur la photographie*, Seuil, Paris 1980; English translation by Richard Howard: *Camera Lucida: Reflections on Photography*, Fontana, London 1982. All future references in the text are to this edition, although I have at times revised the translation. All other translations are mine, unless otherwise indicated. Other Barthes texts are referred to in the text as follows: *Le degré zéro de l'écriture suivi de nouveaux essais critiques*, Seuil, Paris [1953] 1972 (*DZ*); 'Littérature objective' [1954], *Essais critiques*, Seuil, Paris 1963 (*LO*); *Mythologies*, Seuil, Paris 1957 (*M*); *Système de la mode*, Seuil, Paris 1967 (*SM*); 'The Photographic Message' [1961], in: *Image, Music, Text*, Fontana, London 1977 (*PM*); *S/Z*, Seuil, Paris 1970 (*S/Z*); 'L'"Express" va plus loin avec ... Roland Barthes' [1970], in: *Le grain de la voix* Seuil, Paris 1981 (*E*); 'La division des langues' [1973], in: *Le bruissement de la langue*, Seuil, Paris 1984 (*DL*); *Le plaisir du texte*, Seuil, Paris 1973 (*PT*); 'Situation' [1974], in: *Sollers écrivain*, Seuil, Paris 1979 (*S*); *Roland Barthes par Roland Barthes*, Seuil, Paris 1975 (*RB*); 'Barthes puissance trois', *La Quinzaine Littéraire*, vol.1, March 1975 (*B3*); 'Sur la photographie' [1980], in: *Le grain de la voix*, (*SP*).

2. T. Clark, 'Roland Barthes, Dead and Alive', *Oxford Literary Review*, volume 6, number 1, 1983, p101ff.

THE POST-POSTSTRUCTURALIST ATTITUDE:
REMARKS ON THE AFFECTIVE PHENOMENOLOGY OF ROLAND BARTHES'S *CAMERA LUCIDA*

Neil Roughley

The fact that the publication of Roland Barthes's last book, *La chambre claire* (*Camera Lucida*[1]) in 1980 unhappily coincided with the literal death of the author, combined with the text's thematic concentration on the phenomenon of death, contributed to the interpreters' difficulties in adequately locating it in the landscape of post-war theory. These difficulties were undoubtedly aggravated by Barthes's sudden rejection of a critical idiom in whose creation and dissemination he had played a major role. An attractive interpretative strategy in this situation of simultaneous critical disconcertion and respect for the coincidence of theme and individual fate was to accept Barthes's self-propagated mythology of theoretical proteism and to mourn the demise of a liberating philosophy of anti-dogmatic perpetual motion. Tim Clark, for instance, saw no problem in the performative self-contradiction involved in supporting the dual Barthesian myths of ludic multiplicity and pure performativity by means of the remarkably coherent propositional content of quotations from a whole range of later Barthes texts.[2] Over a decade later it seems appropriate to abandon the respect for Barthes's preferred form of imaginary self-constitution and turn to the perspective *Camera Lucida* offers the reader and the argument with which that perspective is advanced.

This essay begins by locating *Camera Lucida* in the context of the sociological application of certain poststructuralist arguments. I then turn to the theoretical motivation for Barthes's return to phenomenology, which becomes clear when one recalls the philosophical aims of Husserl and the young Sartre. This leads on to a comparison of Barthes's version of phenomenological photography theory with the classical position of André Bazin. Barthes's idiosyncratic use of phenomenology is then confronted with the critique of Husserl developed by Theodor Adorno. Here I develop the contention that the individualistic phenomenology of *Camera Lucida* can be seen as the logical development of certain aporetic arguments central to the original phenomenological programme. I conclude with reflections on Barthes's reconciliation with the object of his critique in the 1950s – the sphere of 'mythology' – a reconciliation which I claim is best understood as the product of an undialectical approach to the sphere of lived human experience.

AGAINST POSTSTRUCTURALIST SOCIOLOGY

Barthes's final book, written in 1979 and published the following year – the year of his death – returns both to one of the principal themes of *Mythologies*, photography, and to the theoretical tutelage of Jean-Paul Sartre. However, instead of turning to the founder of the 'Rassemblement Démocratique Révolutionnaire', whose post-war work is strongly present in both *Writing Degree Zero* (1953) and *Mythologies* (1954-57), Barthes now turns to the young pupil of Husserl. And whereas in the 1950s Barthes viewed photography with a form of fascinated scepticism grounded in the conviction that the medium constitutes essentially 'an ellipsis of language' and is thus of its very nature 'an anti-intellectual weapon' (*M*, p161), he now drops his earlier scepticism and seeks to justify the fascination which precisely this feature continues to exert on him. *Camera Lucida*, like Barthes's poststructuralist work, affirms the specificity of individuality in opposition to the meaning imposed by external systems. However, he now adopts a new strategy to counter the flood of theories built on the complementary theses of the fictionality of the subject and the inaccessibility of reality.

The Nanterre sociologist Jean Baudrillard for instance, following closely Barthes's deconstruction of the semiological project, had developed a mode of sociological analysis based on the claim that 'reality is the phantasm by means of which the sign protects itself indefinitely against the symbolic deconstruction which haunts it'.[3] Commenting on such theoretical tendencies, Barthes states, 'it is the fashion, nowadays, among sociologists and semiologists, to postulate semantic relativity: no reality ... nothing but artifice: *Thesis*, not *Physis*' (p88).[4] In the 1960s Barthes had explained such forms of social de-realisation as the results of an intentionally steered process (*SM*, p9). Applying the critical semiology of the Tel Quel group to the sphere of the social, Baudrillard sought to explain the same phenomenon in purely formal terms: 'Reality ... is abolished, obliterated in the face of that neo-reality of the model *materialised by the medium itself*'.[5] Whilst Baudrillard went on to universalize his diagnosis in his theory of the simulacrum, Barthes's comments in his last text insist on a distinction in levels between the effect of the generalisation of the image and the pre-medial 'human world': 'We live according to a generalized imaginary. Consider the United States, where everything is transformed into images: only images exist and are produced and consumed.... In its generalisation [the image] completely de-realises the human world of conflicts and desires, under cover of illustrating it' (p118).[6] In this passage, Barthes employs the expression 'generalised imaginary' (*imaginaire généralisé*) in the same way he had criticized the production of 'a collective imaginary' by the mass media in his texts of the 1950s and 1960s. For Barthes at this stage, 'a dream' was 'something poor, an indication of an absence' (*M*, p228), a socio-cultural lack, and not, as it came to be within the Lacanian horizon, an anthropologically fundamental given. In 1980, as in 1956, *imaginaire* designates a realm of *false* interests through which subjects are constrained to live their everyday lives – ostensibly a mediation, but actually a removal of reality. The so-called advanced societies are, Barthes continues, 'more liberal, less fanatical, but also more "false" (less "authentic")' (p119). From the perspective of poststructuralist sociology, Barthes must be

3. J. Baudrillard, *Pour une critique de l'économie politique du signe*, Gallimard, Paris 1972, p189.

4. Barthes's emphasis. Translation altered.

5. J. Baudrillard, *La société de consommation, ses mythes, ses structures*, Gallimard, Paris 1970, p195. My emphasis.

6. Translation altered. Cf. J. Baudrillard, *La société de consommation*, p194; 'It is that generalized substitution of the code for reference which defines mass media consumption'.

7. J. Baudrillard, *Pour une critique ...*, p 195.

seen as having fallen back into 'the grand moralising litany over alienation'.[7]

It is in this context that the significance of the title *Camera Lucida* becomes clear. The converse image, the camera obscura, had been used by Marx and Engels as the emblem of ideology, which they represent as inverting the relations between being and consciousness in the very process of the constitution of consciousness.[8] The early Barthes had retained it as the emblem of his semiologically reformulated conception of ideology, in which the real and its representation appear upside down (*M*, p229; *SM*, p269). This dual process of signification and its naturalization, which Barthes's early work diagnoses as the central mechanism of mass culture, is also labelled the 'semiological paradox' (*SM*, p285) or, in its paradigmatic form, the 'photographic paradox' (*PM*, p19). In Barthes's structuralist and proto-structuralist writings, it appears that the function of eclipsing social processes, of 'conjuring away the political' (*M*, p161), which Marx had assigned to social processes themselves, is fulfilled simply by the technology of photography. Photography for the Barthes of the late 1950s and early 1960s constituted – for quasi-ontological reasons – the paradigm case of the camera obscura of ideology production. This brief reminder of the meaning-horizon of the image of the camera obscura in Barthes's writings demonstrates the dual movement which *Camera Lucida* inaugurates. On the one hand, it returns to the question of the relationship between the photographic medium and ideology. On the other hand, the relationship of inversion established within both spheres in the early work is itself now to be subjected to a basic reversal.

8. K. Marx, F. Engels, *Die Deutsche Ideologie, Historisch-Kritische Gesamtausgabe*, I, V, Dietz, Berlin 1932, p15.

BACK TO PHENOMENOLOGY

Whereas the early Barthes conceived ideology as located in the mechanisms of mass culture, his texts of the 1970s, following Althusser's reading of Lacan, are primarily concerned with ideology's function internal to subjectivity. In response to Althusser's 'scientific' theory, according to which 'the (defining) function of all ideology is to "constitute" the individuals as subjects',[9] Barthes develops the logical consequences of such an explanation for the internal perspective of one such subject. In 'Barthes to the Third Power', confronted with the infinite regress of reflection, which can never attain the foundations of its own constitution, he finds himself reduced to the ironic re-staging of the Cretan Liar Paradox for the modern enterprise of 'Ideologiekritik': '(bourgeois, petit-bourgeois) ideology speaks in me' (*B3*, p3). In *Camera Lucida* Barthes seeks to step determinedly out of the infinite spiral of ideological misrecognition to which the reflecting subject – trapped in the Lacanian Imaginary – appeared necessarily condemned.[10] Instead, looking for a 'science of the subject ... [which] attains to a generality which neither reduces nor crushes me' (p8) – a criterion which Lacanian psychoanalysis no longer seems able to fulfil – Barthes turns back to the phenomenological method of the early Jean-Paul Sartre. It is, of course, open to the reader to adopt a perspective on *Camera Lucida* from which 'the return of the subject' is a further

9. L. Althusser, 'Idéologie et appareils idéologiques de l'état (Notes pour une recherche)', *La pensée*, Number 151, June 1970, p29.

10. 'As an imaginary and ideological subject, misrecognition in his inevitable fate', 'Barthes puissance trois', p5.

self-fictionalisation, whose propositions are to be read in quotation marks – as *Roland Barthes par Roland Barthes* indeed recommends. Barthes does continue to invoke Lacanian concepts, but – to take only one example – the straightforward claim that the photograph is essentially the Lacanian Real (p4) is so obviously incompatible with Lacanian theory that we cannot merely be dealing with its extension or reworking. As unattainability is the defining characteristic of the Real for Lacan, Barthes is giving the same word an entirely different grammar. And the theory which provides the conceptual constellation into which such a concept fits is, as Barthes himself points out, Sartrian phenomenology.

For Sartre, in direct opposition to Lacan, 'a reflective consciousness provides us with *absolutely certain* data'.[11] For the Sartre of *L'imaginaire* (1940), to which *Camera Lucida* is dedicated, the reflexive analysis of consciousness leads the enquiring subject to certain knowledge both of the nature of its consciousness and of reality. Here Sartre is following closely the 'principle of principles' declared by Husserl to be the foundation of exact philosophy: 'Everything that presents itself to us in "intuition" originally (in its bodily reality, as it were) is simply to be accepted as that as which it presents itself'. For Husserl, whose *Ideen I* (1913) were declared by Sartre to be the most important philosophical event prior to the First World War, the validity of this principle is 'something of which no conceivable *theory* can dissuade us'.[12] It is this principally anti-theoretical impulse which has become so attractive to Barthes. In the face of sociological, semiological and psychoanalytic theories – so many systems of *explanation* – Barthes announces his 'desperate resistance to any reductive system' (p8) and declares himself a 'phenomenologist' (p33), at least for the length of these untimely meditations. *Camera Lucida* is a highly personal account of his thoughts and feelings about his mother after her death in 1978. And for a perspective which wishes to hold onto emotions *as emotions*, to personal thoughts *as personal thoughts*, the language of explanation can only be reductive.

The aim of Husserlian phenomenology was precisely to analyse the structure of those experiences which have meaning for the experiencing subject and, in doing so, to lead to those experiences which cannot further be reduced. This meant a categorical distinction between spheres of enquiry: the sphere of phenomenological enquiry is separated categorically and methodologically from the sphere of scientific explanation. The key to the distinction between the two spheres lies in the concept of 'attitude' ('Einstellung'). For Husserl the attitude of natural science is rooted in the 'natural attitude' of everyday life. Phenomenology involves first and foremost the 'bracketing out' of this natural attitude and of the scientific theories grounded in it, leaving the phenomenologist, as Barthes puts it, ' "scientifically" alone and disarmed' (p7). In Husserl's words, '... I suspend all the sciences which refer to this natural world, in spite of their solidity for me, in spite of my admiration for them, I make absolutely no use of their validity'.[13] Central for the entire phenomenological project is that the production of this 'completely altered form of attitude' is the result of a particular kind of *mental* effort.[14] Husserlian

11. J.-P. Sartre, *L'imaginaire. Psychologie phénomélogique de l'imagination*, Gallimard, Paris 1940, p13. My emphasis.

12. E. Husserl, *Ideen zu einer reinen Phänomenologie und phänomenologischen Philosophie* I, *Gesammelte Schriften* 5, Meiner, Hamburg 1992, p51. My emphasis.

13. *Ibid.*, p65.

14. *Ibid.*, p5.

phenomenology and its continuation in the hands of Sartre is a conscious attempt to renew the tradition of the *philosophy of consciousness*. Within this enterprise a key role is played by the concept of intentionality, the directedness of consciousness, which as such is always 'consciousness of something'.[15] In line with this perspective, 'reality' comes to be reconceptualized as the correlate of sense-conferring intentional acts, 'real units' as 'units of sense'.[16] Thus the analysis of the structure of consciousness appears to provide access to unmediated certainties. For Sartre, if I represent to myself my friend Pierre, 'Pierre is *attained directly*, my attention is not directed at an image, but at an object'.[17] In this way, the conceptual framework of phenomenology appears able to attain precisely what, according to Lacan, consciousness can never attain – 'the Real, in its indefatigable expression' (p4).

Sartre, like Husserl before him, is clear that the model of phenomenological reduction – the bracketing out of all existential judgements about the natural and social world – is the introspective methical doubt of Descartes.[18] It thus comes as no surprise when the fundamental problem of solipsism, into which Cartesian philosophy plunged western thought, returns in Barthes' text as it had in Husserl and Sartre. Significantly however, Barthes has no interest in avoiding the problem. For whereas Husserl explicitly aimed to provide a solid foundation for objective philosophy and was, as a result, preoccupied for the latter part of his philosophical career with an adequate mode of conceptualizing intersubjectivity, Barthes seeks a conceptual framework which will enable him both to affirm the *reality* of the object under consideration and yet to defend its essential *individuality* against conceptual subsumption. It is for this task that phenomenology – against the intention of its founders – appears suited.

A great deal of photographs can, in the phenomenological attitude, simply *have no reality*. Barthes illustrates this with an approvingly quoted passage from *L'imaginaire* – itself an interpretation of a passage from Husserl's *Ideen* – in which Sartre captures the lack of meaning such pictures have for him by means of the everyday expression that they simply 'say nothing to me' (p19). As such, they have no existence as phenomena, although they may exist as 'things' for 'normal perception' and as lines and colours in a picture for 'perceptive consciousness'.[19] The subjectivistic danger inherent in such a conception of reality-constitutive sense comes out particularly strongly in the work of Max Scheler, who was the first German phenomenologist to be translated into French, in the late 1920s. In a late text on the phenomenological method, he claimed that 'something can be true or good purely for one individual: that is, it can in its essence be characterized by *individually valid and yet in a strictest sense objective and absolute* truth and insight'.[20] This is indeed exactly what Barthes is after when in *Camera Lucida* he talks of a 'mathesis singularis (and no longer universalis)' (p8).

In the 1950s Barthes had written a series of essays on Robbe-Grillet, in which he had interpreted the *nouveau romancier*'s texts in line with standard Husserlian phenomenology as exercises in pure seeing, confronting the reader

15. *Ibid.*, p74.

16. *Ibid.*, p120.

17. J.-P. Sartre, *L'imaginaire*, p20. My emphasis.

18. *Ibid.*, p13; Husserl, *Ideen*, p65.

19. Sartre, *L'imaginaire*, p54; Husserl, *Ideen*, p252.

20. Max Scheler, *Phänomenologie und Erkenntnistheorie*, *Gesammelte Werke*, 10, Franke, Bern 1957, p393.

with 'an object without heredity, without connections and without references, … suggesting nothing more than itself, not leading the reader to any functional or substantial elsewhere' (*LO*, p11).[21] In 1980 as in 1954, Barthes could be said to be attempting to develop the utopian potential seen by Adorno in the phenomenological method: 'The key concept of intuition of essences ("Wesensschau")', Adorno states, 'appeared to provide a remedy for the growing incapacity of the subject of experience to penetrate and comprehend a complex and ideologically ever more thickly enveloped social reality'. According to Adorno, early phenomenology was motivated by the desire to break through the multiple layers of ideological distortion imposed on capitalist reality by means which do not subject the reality thus attained to the conceptual domination of instrumental reason. 'Phenomenology', he continues, 'taught consciousness to assimilate that which easily escapes it when it thinks from the top down'.[22] It aimed, in other words, to capture the non-identical by non-repressive means.

In Barthes's case, the non-identical he wishes to capture in 1979 is the individuality of his recently deceased mother. His goal is 'the impossible science of the unique being' (p71). And he sees photography as the most suitable starting point for his phenomenological investigation. Barthes now assimilates his 1961 definition of photography as a 'message without a code' (*MP*, p17) to Sartre's description of the photograph as 'an *analogon* … an equivalent of perception'.[23] The resulting arguments, interestingly, bear a striking resemblance to those of one of the classic French cinema theorists, André Bazin, who in 1945, under the influence of phenomenology, wrote an important analysis of the photographic image.

BARTHES AND BAZIN

Bazin's 'ontology of the photographic image' advances two basic propositions which recur in *Camera Lucida*. The first is that the phenomenon of photography 'has radically disrupted the psychology of the image'. Because a photograph is a mechanical reproduction 'from which human beings are excluded', Bazin states, 'we are obliged to believe in the existence of the object which is represented, literally re-presented'.[24] Barthes thus follows Bazin when he claims that the essence of photography is 'Reference' or ' "That-has-been" ' (p77). He even uses a parallel argument that it is not primarily the exactitude of the copy which endows photography with its radically new psychological force, but above all the fact that the physical process necessary for its development is a guarantee that the object depicted was actually in front of the lens. Barthes' statement, 'the photograph is literally an emanation of the referent' (p80) echoes the founding tenet of Bazin's theory, expressed in the remark, 'one could consider a photograph as a cast, an imprint of the object taken by the medium of light'[25] and repeatedly illustrated by a whole series of metaphors such as mummification, the moulding of a death mask, the preservation of a fly in amber and the sacred shroud of Turin.

21. Cf. R. Barthes, 'Littérature littérale' (1955), *Essais critiques*, p66; 'Il n'y a pas d'école Robbe-Grillet' 1958, *Essais critiques*, p103.

22. T.W. Adorno, 'Der wunderliche Realist. Über Siegfried Kracauer', in: *Noten zur Literatur*, Suhrkamp, Frankfurt 1981, p392.

23. J.-P. Sartre, *L'imaginaire*, p41. Sartre's emphasis. Vgl. *Camera Lucida*, p88.

24. A. Bazin, *Qu'est-ce que le cinéma?*, Volume I: *Ontologie et langage*, Cerf, Paris 1959, pp14-15.

25. *Ibid.*, p14.

26. *Ibid.*, p16.

The argument of the Structuralist Barthes that photography's irreducibly realist characteristics inevitably lead to a naturalization of culturally produced meaning reverts, after Poststructuralism, to a revalorization of photography's 'power of authentification' (p89). Here the Existentialist terminology, set ironically in inverted commas in *Mythologies*, according to which photography reveals a 'way of being' (*M*, p161), returns minus the textual markers of distance. Because photography is 'an emanation of past reality' (p88), it constitutes, Barthes claims, a privileged articulation of human beings' relationship to time. Again taking up observations already made by Bazin, for whom photographs represent 'the disturbing presence of lives arrested in their duration',[26] Barthes states that photography, because its essence is to capture pure ephemerality, raises fundamental questions 'of a metaphysical order' (p84). Significantly, faced with pictures of people who are, or probably are, dead, and particularly faced with a picture of his deceased mother, Barthes suddenly feels the genuine profundity of Flaubert's characters, Bouvard and Pécuchet, 'pondering over the sky, the stars, time, life, infinity, etc' (pp84-5). It is a basic characteristic of *Camera Lucida* that Barthes' shift to a hermeneutics of individual emotions brings with it an affirmation of attitudes which, under the sign of the 'mythic', had been the object of his earlier 'Ideologiekritik'. This is particularly striking in his switch of perspective on the two characters whose ironic depiction by Flaubert repeatedly appears as the paradigm of demythification throughout Barthes' earlier work.

Within the horizon of the later, dialectical Sartre, *Bouvard and Pécuchet* figures variously in Barthes' work as an articulation of the law of 'bourgeois necessity' (*DZ*, p47), as a 'veritable archaeological restauration of a mythic form of speech' demystified by an extensive use of the subjunctive (*M*, p223) and as 'stupidity' (*bêtise*), re-copied by the representatives of a 'stupid' class (*S/Z*, p105). With Barthes' own move away from the use of Marxist language without inverted commas, a move which involves a relativisation of the later position of Sartre, Flaubert's text takes on the function of demystifying any standpoint which is unaware of its own coded nature. *Bouvard and Pécuchet* becomes a set of quotations of cultural languages (*BL*, p115), a 'lexicographic artefact' (*PT*, p45),

27. M. Scheler, 'Zusätze aus den nachgelassenen Manuskripten' and 'Die Stellung des Menschen im Kosmos', in: *Gesammelte Werke*, 9, Franke, Bern 1976, p250, p41. For Scheler's conception of phenomenological reduction as the dual key to a modern metaphysics and a philosophical anthropology, see my *Philosophische Anthropologie*, Metzler, Stuttgart, forthcoming.

'the definitive farce of encyclopaedic knowledge' (*S*, p81). This movement culminates in the re-working of Flaubert's 'farce' with respect to an encyclo-paedic selection of the languages of Marxism (*RB*, p159). This development – from the judgement of the content of the speech of Flaubert's characters as 'bourgeois' or 'stupid' to the conception of their discourse as the vehicle for the reciprocal relativization of cultural codes – ends in *Camera Lucida* with the question as to whether the author Flaubert 'really did deride' Bouvard and Pécuchet (p84) and with an affirmation of 'the true metaphysics' (p85) to which they are committed. It is worth recalling at this point that Max Scheler, who also turned the methodological tools of Husserlian phenomenology to quite different uses from those intended by Husserl himself, had claimed in the 1920s that the 'possibility of a metaphysics' today depends entirely on the feasibility of the technique of phenomenological reduction, which, he claimed, provides 'the window to the Absolute'.[27]

The second basic proposition advanced by Bazin in 1945 and repeated by Barthes 35 years later builds on the first. If photography is able to capture reality 'without mediation' (p80) or, in Bazin's words, 'without the creative intervention of man', then it accomplishes by *technological* means what phenomenology aimed to achieve by the *technique* of phenomenological reduction.[28] It breaks through the conceptual and ideological mediations through which we experience the world in our everyday, 'natural' attitude.[29] As Bazin puts it, 'only the impassiveness of the lens, which strips the object of all customs and prejudices, of all the spiritual dross with which it was coated by my perception, could render it pure for my attention'.[30] Barthes uses Husserl's description of the phenomenological 'Einstellung' – which significantly means both 'attitude' and photographic 'focus' – to characterize 'photographic reduction': 'the photograph breaks the "constitutive style" [of experience]' (p90).

However, in opposition to Bazin, whose ontology of the photographic image leads on to his theory of the cinema's 'ontogenetic realism', Barthes contrasts the photographic 'époché' to the cinema, which he sees as simply copying the constitutive style of everyday experience.[31] The cinema, for Barthes, makes use of all those 'hermeneutic', 'proairetic' and 'cultural' codes which he sees as determining the way we experience the world and which are systematically developed in the genre of literary realism – 'it is ... simply "normal", like life' (p90); successful photography, on the other hand, breaks through this culturally determined realism, arriving at a 'realism [which] is absolute and, so to speak, original' (p119). Freezing the pure contingency of a singular, unrepeatable moment (p4, 20), it has the capacity to awaken the awareness of the ephemerality of human existence. In other words, against a pseudo-realism with illusory pretensions to objectivity Barthes now pits what he sees as the authentic realism grounded in individual subjectivity.

BARTHES AND THE METACRITIQUE OF EPISTEMOLOGY

It is, according to Barthes, because of photography's irreducible testimony to existential temporality – 'because each photograph always contains this imperious sign of my future death' – that the relationship of each viewer to the photographic image is absolutely individual (p97). This claim brings Barthes into opposition to the traditional phenomenology of Husserl and Sartre, for both of whom the investigation of the essential characteristics of the consciousness of an object is supposed to lead to the unveiling of a transcendental subject, a 'pure ego', which is radically distinct from its empirical counterparts. This is indeed a point at which the enterprise of phenomenology appeared trapped in an aporia from the start. The aim of the enquiring subject to achieve her or his pure consciousness contains an elementary paradox: on the one hand, if the consciousness is that of a particular person, then it must be empirical and therefore cannot be pure. On the other hand, if it is pure, then it cannot be empirical and therefore cannot

28. A. Bazin, *Qu'est-ce que le cinéma?*, Volume I, p15.

29. Cf. T.W. Adorno, *Zur Metakritik der Erkenntnistheorie. Studien über Husserl und die phänomenologischen Antinomien*, Kohlhammer, Stuttgart 1956, p204.

30. A. Bazin, *Qu'est-ce que le cinéma?*, Volume I, p18.

31. *Ibid.*, p9.

32. T.W. Adorno, *Zur Metakritik der Erkenntnistheorie*, p234.

33. *Ibid.*, pp208–9.

34. *Ibid.*, p209. Cf. Husserl's thought-experiment of the destruction of the entirety of nature, so that 'there would be no more bodies and thus no more human beings ... But my consciousness, however much its mental contents were transformed, would remain an absolute stream of mental processes with its own essences', *Ideen*, p118.

35. T.W. Adorno, *Ästhetische Theorie*, Suhrkamp, Frankfurt 1973, pp89–90; R. Barthes, 'Sur la photographie', p329.

36. W. Benjamin, 'A Short History of Photography', translated by Stanley Mitchell, *Screen*, Volume 13, 1972, p7.

37. *Ibid.*, p25.

38. T.W. Adorno, *Zur Metakritik der Erkenntnistheorie*, p42. On Adorno's concept of mediation, see M. Rosen, *Hegel's Dialectic and its Criticism*, Cambridge University Press, Cambridge 1982, pp174ff.

belong to anyone at all. One of Adorno's principal criticisms of Husserl is this impossibility of abstracting such a singular transcendental ego from 'factical egos'.[32] Morever, not only does the phenomenological unveiling of the transcendental ego abstract from the particularity of the perspective of individual selves. It also abstracts from their essential corporeality. Insisting, as always, on the futility of any attempt to separate genesis and validity, Adorno attacks the repression of human sensual nature in the 'purity of the passionless, passive phenomenological glance'.[33] Barthes's undertaking, the development of a phenomenology which takes as its guide 'an affective intentionality' (p21), his central question, 'what does *my body* know of Photography?' (p9), thus also represents an attempt to circumvent what Adorno describes as 'the "anti-nature" of phenomenological ascetism'.[34] Barthes is concerned to investigate the relationship of photography to 'the Intractable of which I consist' (p98).

The unique capacity of photography to draw our attention to the contingency of human existence was also stressed by Walter Benjamin in his pioneering 1931 essay, 'A Short History of Photography', which is praised by Adorno and Barthes alike.[35] 'The spectator', Benjamin states, 'feels an irresistible compulsion to look for the tiny spark of chance, of the here and now, with which reality has, as it were, seared the character in the picture; to find that imperceptible point at which, in the immediacy of that long-past moment, the future so persuasively inserts itself that, looking back, we may rediscover it'.[36] However, at the end of his essay, Benjamin insists on the necessity of developing captions for photographs, by means of which single moments of human existence can be located in relation to socio-historical and cultural determinations.[37] This is precisely what the Barthes of *Camera Lucida* refuses to do. In the face of photographs which move him, he proclaims, 'I wanted to be primitive, without culture' (p7). 'What did I care', he proclaims, in a rejection of the sociological perspectives, both of Bourdieu and of his own earlier work, 'about the Photograph as a family rite?' (p7).

It is at this point, in his explicit adoption of absolute subjectivity as his chosen criterion of validity (p55), that Barthes, in his eagerness to escape Adorno's critique of the transcendental subject, runs headlong into another of Adorno's major arguments against Husserl. The act of will by means of which Barthes strains to focus on the single emotional relationship established by the subject with the referent of the photographic image entails that he, in Adorno's words, 'resolutely blindfolds himself ... against all mediation'.[38] This criticism brings two spheres neglected by Barthes's reflections into consideration. The first is the causal sphere of the formation of subjectively experienced meaning behind the backs of the experiencing subjects. This is the object of those sciences – above all, psychoanalysis and sociology – whose relevance for his project Barthes, as we have seen, dismisses out of hand. The second sphere brought into play by the concept of mediation is the realm of intersubjective practice, within which meaning as lived meaning – and that is the object of Barthes's enquiry – comes into being or is upheld. It is this sphere of intersubjective practice that Wittgenstein is getting at in his question in II, xi of the *Philosophical Investigations*: 'What would be missing if you did not *experience* the meaning of a word?'[39] Meaning as a form of subjective orientation only exists as long as there is some form of (however reluctant) practical commitment to it on the part of the speakers of a language. In rejecting the radically anti-hermeneutic claim that the subject is merely an '*effect* of language' (*RB*, 82), Barthes now declares an emphatic lack of interest both in the socio-cultural determinants and in the intersubjective constitution of his own experience.[40] Instead, reactivating the Romantic topos, 'individuum est ineffabile',[41] he seeks the contours of what in the photograph escapes linguistic encapsulation, the unnamable, what he calls the 'punctum', as opposed to the encodable sphere of knowledge, the 'studium' (p51).

Here again Barthes is picking up a strand of thought which plays an important role within the phenomenological tradition. For Scheler, what can be intuited in the phenomenological attitude is 'that which is essentially indeterminable by any possible symbols'. Indeed, for Scheler, genuinely philosophical knowledge is '*asymbolic* knowledge', opposed to 'the content of the world as already selected and organized in line with the aim of universally valid knowledge'.[42] Barthes similarly invokes the 'arrest of interpretation' (p107) which he sees as imposed on the viewer by photography that *touches* her/him and which, he insists, leaves the specificity of individual experience undisturbed. Within modern philosophy, phenomenology stands at the end of that strand of thought which has given priority to *intuition* in opposition to the *concept*, the combination of which, in the Kantian conception, is necessary if we are to be able to speak of knowledge. There certainly are currents of theory, both in philosophy and in media studies, which have overemphasized the conceptual side and whose protagonists resemble 'tourists who stand in front of a building reading Baedecker and are so busy reading the history of its construction, etc., that they are prevented from *seeing* the building'.[43] On the other hand, where phenomenology sets itself up in opposition to the linguistic turn as 'a continuous *desymbolisation of the world*',[44] Adorno's rejection of such 'abdication of the concept'[45] is entirely justified. The same point had been made by Barthes himself in his Structuralist critique of his own early phenomenological interpretation of Robbe-Grillet, which had made the mistake of 'simply [believing] that there is a "Dasein" of things prior to and exterior to language' (*PRG*, p204).[46]

The world captured by phenomenology is, according to Adorno, in the last instance simply 'a tautology of the existing world'.[47] Precisely this is praised by Barthes as the characteristic of photography which is able to attain the Lacanian 'Real', which brings to a halt the succession of connotations which is fatal as soon as we enter language. Max Scheler's *Nachlass* contains a passage which is instructive in its attempt to answer precisely this criticism of phenomenology as being constitutively tautologous. Scheler discusses W. Wundt's critique of Husserl's *Logical Investigations*. Wundt had claimed that Husserl's explications of judgement, meaning etc. turn out to be nothing more

39. L. Wittgenstein, *Philosophical Investigations*, Blackwell, Oxford 1953, p214e.

40. My emphasis.

41. J.W. Goethe, letter to J.K. Lavater [1780], *Briefe* I, Wegner, Hamburg 1968, p325.

42. M. Scheler, 'Phänomenologie und Erkenntnistheorie', p412.

43. L. Wittgenstein, *Culture and Value*, Blackwell, Oxford 1980, p402.

44. M. Scheler, 'Phänomenologie und Erkenntnistheorie', p384. Scheler's emphasis.

45. T.W. Adorno, *Zur Metakritik der Erkenntnistheorie*, p42.

46. Strictly speaking, Barthes accuses Robbe-Grillet of making this 'theoretical mistake'. The mistake however is primarily to be found in Barthes' own essays of the 1950s. See note 21.

47. T.W. Adorno, *Zur Metakritik der Erkenntnistheorie*, p206.

48. M. Scheler, 'Phänomenologie und Erkenntnistheorie', p391. Scheler's emphasis.

49. *Ibid.* My emphasis.

50. *Ibid.*, p392.

51. My translation. Barthes's emphasis.

52. T.W. Adorno, *Zur Metakritik der Erkenntnistheorie*, p207.

53. *Ibid.*, p206.

54. L. Wittgenstein, *The Blue and Brown Books*, Blackwell, New York 1958, p71.

55. T.W. Adorno, *Zur Metakritik der Erkenntnistheorie*, p206.

56. *Ibid.*, p207.

than 'empty tautologies'. Scheler's answer is that in a sense Wundt is right: 'Many phenomenological discussions – not only Husserl's – do indeed take the formal course which Wundt formulates here'. However, that is only to be seen as a problem if one misunderstands the kind of text one is dealing with, that is, if the reader reads with the wrong attitude ('Einstellung'): 'One has to read a phenomenological book with a completely *different attitude*', insists Scheler.[48] Here again, it is the concept of 'Einstellung' which plays the key role in Scheler's argument: firstly as the attitude of the knowing subject towards reality – in line with the requirements of the phenomenological *épochè*; secondly as the attitude of the reading subject towards the text produced by the knowing subject at the first level. Phenomenological texts are not to be read as apophantic texts. The function of a phenomenological text can only be 'to bring the reader (or listener) to *see* something which of its essence can only be seen'. In this context, Scheler continues, all the sentences, 'inferences', 'definitions' and 'syllogisms' in the text only 'function as a *pointer*, which points to that which is to be seen'.[49] In the end 'the "tautology" instructs the reader: now look, now you can see it!'[50] The language Barthes uses here is notably similar. 'A photograph', he states, 'is always located at the end of the gesture [of the small child pointing its finger at something]; the photograph says: *that, there, like that!* but nothing more'.[51] Both Adorno and Barthes himself had, in 1956, made quite clear the conservative consequences of such advocacy of tautology. 'It consecrates present existence',[52] 'leaves everything as it is',[53] Adorno maintained. And in Barthes's own words, 'one seeks refuge in tautology ... when one is at a loss for explanation ... Tautology founds a dead world, a world of immobility' (*M*, pp240-1). Alongside the social-functional consequences of such a conception, perhaps an even more incisive criticism arises out of the problem of whether such deictic gestures, when not conceived as pointing to intersubjectively comprehensible components of a public sign system, can be made any sense of at all. One is reminded of the picture with which Wittgenstein criticizes the tautologous conception of deixis intended to pick out elements of reality accessible only to one individual subject: 'I constructed a clock with all its wheels, etc., and in the end fastened the dial to the pointer and made it go round with it'.[54]

Adorno advances the hypothesis that photography could have been the model for phenomenological epistemology. And Barthes in turn claims that phenomenology provides privileged access to the essence of photography. Adorno's description of phenomenology as 'uncritical' and characterized by 'contemplative passivity' is accepted by Barthes and simply affirmed.[55] And if phenomenology's exclusive focus on the relationship between individual consciousness and isolated objects 'imputes a condition of absolute solitude', the result of a social situation in which 'the individual has become subject to a condition of powerless acceptance, of complete dependence on pregiven reality, and of exclusive concern with adaptation', then Barthes now protests his indifference.[56] Immersed in the 'individual, under-the-breath prayer, interiorised and meditative' of his lonely viewing sessions (p97), Barthes savours the effect of certain photographs on, as he puts it, 'the religious substance out of which I am moulded' (p89). Thus, paradoxically, the individualistic phenomenology of Barthes seems to realize the personal potential seen by the late Husserl in what he had always conceived as a rigorously objective philosophical method: 'Perhaps it will even turn out that the total phenomenological attitude – and the époché which belongs with it – is, by its very essence, destined to bring about a complete personal transformation, comparable to a religious conversion ...'[57]

MYTHOLOGY AFTER POSTSTRUCTURALISM

In a quarter of a century, Barthes has come a full circle, moving from the enlightenment project of *Mythologies* to an affirmation of the essentiality of a religious understanding of experience, which the eighteenth-century *philosophes*, Marx and Nietzsche had seen as a basic obstacle to human self-liberation. As Chantal Thomas says, Barthes's 'project moves from theory to mysticism'.[58] No longer concerned with the western powers' implication in the daily mass slaughter in the 'Third World' – the photograph of a dead child in Nicaragua simply provides the occasion for formalist reflections on the association of discontinuous photographic elements (p84) – he meditates instead on 'the inexorable extinction of the generations' (p84). Photography, he claims, is to be seen in relation to resurrection (p82): it represents 'the way in which our time assumes death' (p92). The technology of photography appears to be the sphere which has taken over what Barthes sees as the essentially religious function of reconciling a society with the phenomenon of death. To Benjamin's socio-historical proposition, 'as long as there are beggars, there will continue to be myths',[59] Barthes opposes the Existentialist claim, 'as long as there is death, there will continue to be myths' (*E*, p95). It is at points such as these in the text that the ideology of the multiple, protean subject can assume the convenient function of covering up contradictions between the different positions within the Barthesian oeuvre. It is worth recalling here the young Barthes' rhetorical question, 'Do we really have to sing [death's] essence once again and risk forgetting what we can do against it?' (*M* p175) – not simply in order to demonstrate an offence against the Aristotelian canons of logic, but in order to demand more rigorous thought as to whether, and if so how, such positions can be reconciled.

Having abandoned all hope in demythification, Barthes is reduced to proclaiming that he quite simply *feels like* 'an uncertain, amythic subject' (p102). This perspective, from which cognition appears as the result of the *attitude* the subject adopts, 'dependent on the contingent mode of being of the person judging', is well captured by Adorno's comparison of the phenomenologist with early photographers. 'Like the earliest photographers, the phenomenologist wraps himself in the black cloth of his *époché*'.[60] One could see a similar *attitude* at work here to that expressed in the fact that Husserl, after being barred by the National Socialists from entering the University of Freiburg,

57. E. Husserl, *Die Krisis der europäischen Wissenschaften und die transzdentale Phänomenologie, Gesammelte Schriften 5*, Meiner, Hamburg 1992, p140.

58. C. Thomas, 'La photo du jardin d'hiver', *Critique*, Number 423-424, August-September, 1982, p803.

59. Walter Benjamin, quoted by Adorno in 'Charakteristik Walter Benjamins' [1950], in: *Prismen*, Suhrkamp, Frankfurt 1976, p290.

60. T.W. Adorno, *Zur Metakritik der Erkenntnistheorie*, p205.

61. H. Lübbe, who reports this anecdote in 'Die geschichtliche Bedeutung der Subjektivitätstheorie Edmund Husserls', *Bewußtsein in Geschichten. Studien zur Phänomenologie der Subjektivität*, Rombach, Freiburg 1972, p31f, interprets it differently: namely as a sign of Husserl's undeterred search for disinterested knowledge.

62. L. Wittgenstein, *The Blue and Brown Books*, p48.

63. See my 'In der Überlieferung sein. Eine historisch-systematische Rekonstruktion der Hermeneutik Gadamers', in *Philosophisches Jahrbuch*, 101/2, 1994.

64. Sartre, *L'imaginaire*, p44.

used the back of the official letter informing him of this to take philosophical notes.[61] Affirming an approach which he himself characterizes as 'entirely subjective' (*SP*, p332), Barthes reclaims the rights of individual experience, but in doing so shuts himself off from the rest of social reality. The fundamental perspective of the Barthes of *Camera Lucida* is less that of the child pointing at an object and exclaiming 'that!' than that of the child which, throwing a blanket over its head, believes itself immune from external influence.

Camera Lucida stands at the end of a theoretical movement whose surprising nature could only fail to be noticed by those whose perspective is clouded by the uncritical acceptance of particular authorial intentions. This movement could be characterized as the result of a justified discontentment with radically antihermeneutic theories of individual experience, which give *explanation* of that experience priority over its *understanding*; a dissatisfaction with the *reduction* of the human world of action and motivation, with the simple negation of the level of meaning which provides people with *reasons* for what they do. As Wittgenstein puts it in one passage, 'in one aspect of the matter, personal experience, far from being the *product* of physical, chemical, physiological processes, seems to be the very *basis* of all that we can say with any sense about such processes'.[62] On the other hand, the difficulty here is not to throw the baby out with the bathwater. The hermeneutic point that personal experience is in a certain sense irreducible cannot justify the refusal to look for *causes* where good *reasons* give out. This refusal marks the limits of Gadamer's – traditionalist, not individualist – hermeneutics, which insist in principle on always playing out experientially accessible 'truth' against 'method'.[63] The debate in German social philosophy between Gadamer and Habermas is essentially a debate about where understanding fails and explanation has to set in. In our context, the model of Barthes's rejection of the level of explanation is the text of Sartre to which *Camera Lucida* is dedicated. Sartre's aim in *L'imaginaire* is not only to argue that personal experience has to be the starting point of our reflections when we are interested in the meaning of personal experience. Beyond that he is concerned to demonstrate that *consciousness* is both irreducible and unitary. This leads to the outright rejection of any explanatory power which may be attached to talk of the unconscious, a position which could not be further removed from that of Lacan.[64]

Roland Barthes's last book clearly does deserve to be read in a different attitude to that in which one reads a theoretical text. The highly personal, emotional nature of its theme makes it a text with a genuine claim to articulate immediacy. When Barthes proclaims his 'naivety' (p8) in this sphere, one wants to respond with Adorno's words: that to inthrone naivety's opposite as the principle of all thought would be a sign of an 'inhumanity, which, hardly has it picked out the particular, immediately devalues it to the status of a mere transitional stage on the way to the universal'. However, one does not have to subscribe to the Hegelian idiom of Adorno to agree that even where the articulation of subjective experience is the starting point of thought, that does not free the writer from the 'work of the concept'. As Adorno puts it, the modern writer is faced with the 'demand, simultaneously to let the phenomena themselves speak – "pure seeing" – and yet to maintain for every moment their relationship to consciousness of the subject, that is the level of reflection'.[65]

65. T.W. Adorno, *Minima Moralia*, Suhrkamp, Frankfurt 1983, pp90-91.

GOOD-TIME GIRLS, MEN OF TRUTH AND A THOROUGHLY FILTHY FELLOW:

SEXUAL PATHOLOGY IN THE PROFUMO AFFAIR[1]

Gillian Swanson

1. Thanks to Ruth Borthwick, Bronwyn Hammond and Ben Worpole for their assiduous and imaginative research during the collection of materials on which this article is based. Griffith University provided the research funding to make it possible. Thanks too to Bill Schwarz for perspicacity. I am also grateful to Beverley Brown for providing incisive reader's comments and useful pointers on an earlier draft.

A PROBLEM OF KNOWLEDGE: SEXUAL DEFINITION AND NATIONAL CHARACTER

The sex scandal presents a problem of knowledge: secrecy and the reciprocality of concealment and revelation are vital to the dimension of scandal in sexual narratives. But the representation of scandals in Britain in the 1950s and 1960s became part of a larger operation of sexual debate and controversy, drawing on a public domain of sexual knowledges and bringing into focus the different ways behaviours and relationships, identities and collectivities are made sense of in such institutional knowledges as government, law, science and medicine and the popular circulation of knowledges through, for example, the press. As the co-ordinates of sexual categories were rendered uncertain in a period of changing sexual definitions, controversies worked over their gaps and incoherences, pointing to the boundaries of sexual meaning and conceptions of identity and offering a moment of rearrangement in the purchase of these discourses on the movement of everyday practices. What I am concerned to examine is the way such controversies represent, classify and categorize – even question and rework – the terms and definitions of sexuality, in particular the way in which a relation between social and sexual identity came into view as a project, or problem, of self-management in Britain following World War Two.

One of the features of the post-war period in Britain is its attention to the sexual as a matter of national concern. How is it that the modernization of sexual cultures came to assume such importance following World War Two? One problem which was identified in this context was the disruption of a spatially segregated model of sexual difference consolidated in the nineteenth century, where the conception of separate realms for men and women was not so much a literal rendering of spatial inhabitation as a motif of character: while masculinity came to be associated with public life and the attributes necessary for its effective execution, domestic and privatised femininity became a guarantor of the management of sexual and social definition, an anchor for the establishment of 'natural' sexual differences. Although this model was never absolute, so that differences existed and transformations occurred, its power resided perhaps more in its persuasive invocation of a set of objectives for mechanisms of social management, so that welfare measures could be introduced on the basis of an aspiration towards such complementarity.[2] From

2. In this respect the arguments for child welfare, nursery provision, national health measures, education etc and 'mental hygiene' programmes during the 1930s and 1940s are not dissimilar from those measures introduced during the previous moment of medico-legal management, 1860s-1880s, see, for example, Lucy Bland, Trisha McCabe and Frank Mort, 'Sexuality and Reproduction: Three "Official" Instances', in Michèle Barrett, Philip Corrigan, Annette Kuhn and Janet Wolff (eds), *Ideology and Cultural Production*, Croom Helm, London, 1979.

the mid-1940s to the early 1960s, however, the identification of differences from this model came to challenge the definition of sexual complementarity itself, as a widespread project of charting 'pathologies' informed a refigured field of social management, eventually being implemented at the level of social policy as a result of legal, medical, sociological and parliamentary inquiry.[3]

Clearly the spatial disruptions to systems of sexual difference, especially in the re-organisation of work and domestic life occasioned by the war and post-war reconstruction, helped to undermine concepts of the complementarity of sexual characters and presented a problem of redefinition. However, the emergence of 'social psychiatry' from the 1920s to the 1960s was the essential condition for this to become legible *as* disruption while the experience of war offered a field for its deployment in studies of nervous diseases, delinquency, the impact on families of evacuation, etc.[4] The connection of social psychiatry with revised forms of sexology and eugenics and their identification of the management of family life as a question of national concern, the integration of psychodynamic psychiatry (and thereby the adoption of some psychoanalytic models of neurosis) into institutionalised medicine, its impact on the management of morale in wartime and the associated determination of 'national character', created a specific field of influence whereby psychopathology could become a key mechanism for social management and the sexual a prime indicator of social equilibrium.[5] Edward Glover warned in his wartime broadcasts on morale that if a breach occurs between family and nation, women's dedication to the nation's interests may falter; he proposed the national as an object of masculine identification and the familial as one of feminine identification, both reiterating the lingering spatial model of difference of the nineteenth century and showing it to be subject to change, less than persuasive in the assumed correspondence of its two component elements. But as Glover identified a question concerning the persistence of a correspondence between two complementary realms, he also made an important assumption that it was *women* who were less than securely situated within changing national and familial arrangements and whose 'loosening' could incur a disequilibrium which would prove lethal to the community.[6] Sexual definition thus became an important feature of the changing social terrain, as G.M. Carstairs, in his 1962 Reith Lectures (commissioned as 'a review of the State of the Nation, in the light of changes which have come about in the community and in private life since the beginning of the century'[7]) pointed to the need to develop a newly modernized sexual culture, in particular one that acknowledged women's sexual identity, proposing this as a necessary part of acknowledging and contributing to the 'changing British character': the cost of not doing so would be the development of social neuroses, specifically those concerning sexual definition, which became indicative of 'social malaise' and undermining to national solidarity and cohesion.[8]

The legitimacy of nineteenth century concepts of sexual difference was thus brought under a new scrutiny between wartime Britain and the early

3. These follow reports and inquiries (which started to appear in force from the 1930s but become integrated into a concerted programme of management in the post-war period) on issues of child welfare, young people and leisure, the 'problem' family, delinquency, 'promiscuity' (often aligned to other questions, such as immigration), sexual diseases, sex education. The attention to questions of social and sexual management persisted through the 1950s.

4. I am using this term to refer to the influence of psychiatry on the development of programmes of social management, allowing the factors impacting upon individual psychological development to be identified and charted. See Nikolas Rose, *The Psychological Complex: Psychology, Politics and Society in England, 1869-1939*, Routledge and Kegan Paul, London 1986, p207.

5. The development and integration of psychodynamic psychiatry into the medical field, its association with biology and anthropology, the study of national character, and the importance of psychopathology's challenge to somatic models of disorder are outlined in Malcolm Pines, 'The development of the psychodynamic movement', and German E. Berrios, 'British psychopathology since the early 20th century', in *150 Years of British Psychiatry 1841-1991*, German E. Berrios and Hugh Freeman (eds), Gaskell (Royal College of Psychiatrists), London 1991.

6. Edward Glover was involved with various psychoanalytic institutions between the wars and helped to found the Institute for the Scientific Treatment of Delinquency. See Edward Glover, *The Psychology of Fear and Courage*, Penguin, Harmondsworth 1940, p1.

7. G.M. Carstairs, *This Island Now: The BBC Reith Lectures 1962*, Penguin Books, Harmondsworth, 1964, p7. Carstairs draws on anthropology, sociology, psychoanalysis to develop a 'scientific approach in the study of personality development' for 'studies in national character', which is indebted to psychodynamic psychiatry.

1960s. While the framework of sexual complementarity persisted it became reshaped and resituated within an enterprise of social management that identified the sexual as a means of addressing the social individual and aimed to form a more flexible and interactive model of sexual identity, one which promoted the common interests of men and women and prevented a 'too rigid' inculcation of difference which would work against family cohesion or national identification and become a cause of neuroses. As those modern forms of social – and sexual – involvement available to (or claimed by) women demanded a new conception of their familial role relations, so the 'brittle' forms of masculinity developed in the 'flight from domesticity'[9] also came under review. The traditions of both femininity and masculinity were under threat; the concern that these transformations could breed unsecured forms of sexual definition was manifested in an attention to sexual pathology.[10] In this project of defining sexual citizenships, the identification of sexual pathologies became a means to chart the forms of sexual identity which would guarantee the health of the social and so the effective individual became identified through its others: those defined as pathological and threatening to social coherence. Sociological, psychological and medico-legal studies of the 1950s showed an increased focus on the two main categories which were produced as problematic to the definition of sexual difference: prostitution and male homosexuality. It was the alliance of these two which formed the basis of one of the most longstanding debates of the 1950s, that which surrounded the Wolfenden Report published in 1957, and which informed the scandal of the Profumo Affair, in 1963.[11]

I want to use the Profumo Affair to trace the use of these two 'pathologies' identified as constitutive of, as well as produced by, social instability in a period of changing social and national definition. How did these concerns come to be mapped on to an affair surrounding the sexual indiscretions of a government minister? It is my argument that the Profumo Affair (and previous sex scandals in Britain from the early 1950s) drew on this changing field of sexual knowledges in a period during which the modernization of sexuality – particularly femininity – pointed to a specific instability: that of the articulation of masculinity with national identity. It did this by forming an association between the 'pathologies' of female prostitution and those of male homosexuality, passing from an affair concerning Jack Profumo to one which centred first the 'Good-Time Girls' Mandy Rice-Davies and Christine Keeler, but which eventually rested on Stephen Ward as a central figure of monstrous perversion damaging to the integrity of British national character.

While the disturbances made by women may have initiated a concern with national definition, then, such a concern was ultimately a question posed about the forms of masculine self-containment and authority which stood as guarantor of the social and the national, in a period during which the sexual was taken as a privileged index of character. What prostitution proposes *for masculinity* is unregulated masculine desire, operating outside the management of sexual life that underpins social cohesion. Male homosexuality came to be seen as an extension of that same lack of sexual discipline, but one which allowed masculinity to be marked *both* by the feminine *and* by an excessive masculinity antipathetic to the forms by which public life was regulated. It is this bifurcate problem of the sexual for masculinity that I wish to show was understood as symptomatic of the difficulties of achieving a secure national character untrammeled by the instabilities of sexual pathology.

In the Profumo Affair, questions raised in the House of Commons used rumours that John Profumo was involved with a 'call girl' to interrogate his political responsibility and raise concerns over the preservation of democracy.[12] This attention to the conduct of Profumo, Secretary of State for War in Macmillan's cabinet, within the parliamentary forum, was accompanied by a wave of reports surrounding Mandy Rice-Davies and Christine Keeler, as their stories of sexual exploits involving a government minister blurred the distinction between private pleasures and public persona that permits men to take up the authority of the public figure: an authority which is based on their separation from those attributes associated with the feminine; the private, the sexual, the corporeal. In the context of definitions of sexuality which segregate masculinity and femininity to public and private spheres the representation of the sexual within the public sphere disrupts the co-ordinates of sexual difference on which social order and masculine identity depend. In the political scandal, the public persona becomes inflected by the private negotiation of corporeal pleasures and desires; sexuality and the feminine enter the masculine public arena. As they shape and reshape accounts of sexual difference, these stories can tell us about the instabilities of sexual identities constructed across the public-private divide.

The statements of the 'Good-Time Girls' became the hinge of accusations of impropriety against John Profumo, centralising the accounts of the very people whose unreliability – in their potential for allowing state secrets to pass into unregulated realms – motivated public scrutiny of a potential lapse in security and hence enabled the scandal to be brought to public attention. Mandy Rice-Davies's response to the suggestion that Lord Astor denied having a sexual relationship with her, 'He would, wouldn't he?', showed the compromising of objectivity and integrity that the sexual brings to such figures.

However, the scrutiny of Profumo and his associates gave way to questions about the morality of Stephen Ward. Friend of the object of Profumo's lapse in discipline, Christine Keeler, Ward was known as a 'provider' of young girls at the parties of the famous and came to be tried on charges of pimping. Ostensibly Ward's trial had little to do with Profumo; neither he nor the person who introduced Profumo to Stephen Ward, Lord Astor, who rented Ward a weekend cottage on his estate at Cliveden, were called to testify. But in the superseding of questions of political integrity, public propriety and democratic access to the 'truth' surrounding Profumo's involvement in his affair, the attention to Ward in his trial showed a shift to questions of private conduct and moral integrity. The identification of Ward as 'culprit' thus allowed a national scandal to be displaced onto a scrutiny of private 'truths' of character,

8. 'Neurotic illness is a more sensitive indicator (than psychotic illness) of the new stresses which occur in a period of rapid social change' G.M. Carstairs, *This Island Now*, p69.

9. See John Tosh 'Domesticity and Manliness in the Victorian Middle Class: The family of Edward White Benson' in Michael Roper and John Tosh, *Manful Assertions: Masculinities in Britain now 1800*, Routledge, London and New York 1991.

10. Many of the publications of the British Social Biology Council or the Eugenics Society as well as those related directly to psychiatry for example, point to the pressures of modern forms of living, which they see as initiating a sexual confusion or form of breakdown that results in 'anti-social' sexual behaviours.

11. *Report of the Committee on Homosexual Offences and Prostitution*, Cmnd Paper 247, HMSO, London 1957.

12. *Daily Express*, 22 March 1963.

Christine Keeler and a vicar. Courtesy of the Hulton-Deutsch Collection.

intentionality and the correct demarcation of sexual relations, questions which were addressed in terms of pathological masculinity. How did this allow a scandal which was so spectacularly oriented around Profumo's relation to Christine Keeler, and her friendship with Mandy Rice-Davies, to eventually become one which spoke of the relations of men and masculinity?

THE PROFUMO AFFAIR: SOCIAL AUTHORITY AND SEXUAL PATHOLOGY

On 8 July, 1961, at Lord Astor's Cliveden estate, nineteen-year-old Christine Keeler, who was living in Stephen Ward's flat in Wimpole Mews, met John Profumo, Secretary of State for War in Macmillan's Conservative Government and they started a short affair. At the same time, it was alleged, she slept with Eugene Ivanov, the Soviet Naval Attaché in the London Embassy.

Divergent claims suggest their affair lasted between three weeks and five months.[13] On 31 July, MI5 asked the Home Secretary to warn Profumo, who had been visiting Wimpole Mews, of the friendship between Ward and Ivanov, who was probably a spy. Accounts differ about the nature of this relationship and the warning. The official version at the time, published in Lord Denning's report on the security aspects of the affair, was that Ward was dangerously under Ivanov's influence and so could not be trusted.[14] Another, later, semi-official version was that of course Ivanov was a spy – as Naval Attaché it was assumed he would be – a situation tolerated so that the British Government would have access to an unofficial and unacknowledged conduit to the Soviet Government. According to this account, Profumo was warned because Ward was working for MI5 as conduit to the Soviets through Ivanov during a period of unstable East-West relations, involving the Cuba Missile crisis and the dispute over the United States providing West Germany with nuclear weapons.[15] The more recent version, now generally reiterated in present accounts, is that Ward was using Christine Keeler to sexually entrap Ivanov for blackmail and a forced defection so he could provide intelligence about Soviet infiltration of Britain's security services at a moment when confidence (specifically that of the United States) in Britain's contribution to western intelligence was severely damaged. Profumo was simply getting in the way.[16] Others suggest that as a result MI5 attempted to enlist Profumo's aid and that he refused.[17]

Subsequent to his warning, on 8 August 1961, Profumo wrote a letter to Keeler breaking an arrangement to meet her. The affair only came to light eighteen months later, following an incident where Johnny Edgecombe, one of Keeler's lovers, slashed the face of Lucky Gordon – another lover – and in pursuit of Christine shot at the door to Ward's Wimpole Mews flat where she was staying with Mandy Rice-Davies. Christine was called as a key witess in his trial. Her anticipated evidence at the trial of Johnny Edgecombe, and her almost simultaneous offer of her story and Profumo's letter to two popular newspapers, the *Sunday Pictorial* and the *News of the World* promised a spectacle

13. Profumo said in his Commons statement in June 1963 that the last time he saw Keeler was in December 1961. Keeler agreed. In his evidence to Lord Denning's inquiry, given some months later, he brought the date forward to August. Keeler's version nowadays is that it lasted six to eight weeks (Christine Keeler and Robert Meadley, *Sex Scandals*, Xanadu, London 1985, p15), while a more recent source puts it as five weeks (David Thurlow, *Profumo: The Hate Factor*, Robert Hale, London 1992, p77).

14. *Lord Denning's Report*, Cmnd 2152, HMSO, London 1963, p85.

15. Nigel West, *A Matter of Trust: MI5 1945-72*, Coronet, Sevenoaks, London 1983, Philip Knightley and Caroline Kennedy, *An Affair of State: The Profumo Case and the Framing of Stephen Ward*, Jonathan Cape, London 1987, pp77 and 90.

16. This has recently been reiterated in Knightley and Kennedy, *An Affair of State* and David Thurlow, *The Hate Factor*, and is an assumed truth in most current newspaper references.

17. Summers and Dorril, *Honeytrap*, pp150-2.

of disclosure that initiated a flurry of activity involving Profumo in a meeting with Ward and Astor. In January Ward saw Ivanov, who left the country eleven days later, offering MI5 good reason not to pursue Profumo's breach as it could present no further danger to security. Neither the letter nor the story were published. On 26 January 1963, Christine, approached about Ward's role, told her story to the police.

Christine failed to appear at the Edgecombe trial in March and instead of adopting the common practice of adjourning in the absence of a key witness, the trial went ahead. Rumours of a judicial anomaly circulated and some suggested Profumo helped her disappear, conspiring to obstruct justice. On 22 March, Profumo read a prepared statement to the House of Commons, attesting that there had been no impropriety in his relationship with Keeler and that he had not seen her since December 1961.

On 5 June, Profumo acknowledged that he *was* guilty of improper conduct in his relationship with Keeler and contempt of the House in his lie. He resigned from office and his name was removed from the Privy Council. Three days later, Ward was arrested and after a magistrate's hearing, committed to trial at the Old Bailey the next month on charges of procuring and living off immoral earnings. The night after the first part of the judge's summing up – generally supposed to have pointed towards a guilty verdict – Ward took an overdose of Nembutal. He was found guilty while in a coma, and without recovering consciousness, died three days later.

In September, Lord Denning submitted a report on his inquiry into the security aspects of the case as a Command Paper to the Prime Minister. He declared the honourability of Profumo, the innocence of young girls 'enmeshed in a net of wickedness' and the utter immorality of the 'sexually perverted' Ward whose involvement in 'vicious sexual activities' were in aid of Ivanov and the Russians.[18]

18. *Lord Denning's Report*, pp18-9, 26, 35.

It is easy to construct a view of the public vilification of Ward as a scapegoating exercise, distracting attention from a sleazy situation that massively undermined public confidence and identifying someone to be held responsible. But this was not only an affair about adequate government; increasingly it was recognised as part of a set of conflicts surrounding faltering national security systems that had begun to affect US and UK relations in negative ways. In the aftermath of the Burgess and Maclean defections in 1951, the United States exerted pressure on the British government to follow their example in 'purging' homosexuals from prominent positions within public life, especially in the public and security services. As Leslie Moran shows, the public inquiry following this scandal did not present their homosexuality as a factor for national concern: it took until 1956 for the assertion that homosexuality was a 'character defect' to be adopted as a way of identifying figures of potential national danger within the security and public services, initiating a retrospective 'rewriting' of the scandal.[19] Nevertheless, the concept was already established in psychiatry, and the British Medical Association argued in 1955 that public hostility to homosexuality was based on 'their alleged tendency to

19. Moran argues that the conjunction of homosexuality, character defect and threat to national security is first mobilised in *The Statement on the Findings of the Conference of Privy Councillors on Security*, in 1956 (L.J. Moran, 'The Uses of Homosexuality: Homosexuality for National Security', *International Journal of the Sociology of Law*, No.19, 1991, p156-7).

place their loyalty to one another above their loyalty to the institution or government they serve ... (t)he existence of practising homosexuals in the Church, Parliament, Civil Service, Forces, press, radio, stage and other institutions constitutes a special problem'.[20] In the adoption of US measures, the use of the term homosexuality to also address relationships between women and to also subject them to purging was translated anew so that in Britain only the male homosexual was brought into the realm of scrutiny and regulation.[21] An escalation of metropolitan policing operations associated with this increased attention initiated a series of male homosexual scandals throughout the 1950s.[22]

Prior to the Profumo Affair, the trial of the Admiralty clerk, John Vassall, for spying for the USSR following his entrapment and blackmail for homosexual practices while at the British Embassy in Moscow had severely weakened confidence not just in the security services and state institutions, but in their regulation by government. Graham Mitchell, the Deputy Director-General of MI5, was himself under suspicion of being a KGB agent, as later was the Director General, Roger Hollis. Mitchell was in fact under surveillance at the very moment he went to see the Prime Minister's Private Secretary about the potential of a security breach by Profumo.

While Ward was most probably working for MI5, providing sexual 'lures' as well as diplomatic favours through his entourage of girls, the subjects of the 1950s spy scandals, including Guy Burgess, Donald Maclean, John Vassall and Barbara Fell, gave prominence to sexual identity and sexual practices in the context of Britain's international and internal relations. In a context of altering allegiances with Europe and the United States and the recasting of colonial relations, mobilities across boundaries of class, race and gender within Britain were being negotiated by the creation of alternative sexual networks. In addition to the new social mobilities articulated in post-war government rhetoric, Stuart Hall notes the increasing importance of women and black immigrants to the labour force during the 1950s. While Britain's expansion of industries catering to mass domestic consumption targetted the 'consuming housewife' it also relied upon its largest market, the working-class. It is this range of factors, Hall suggests, that informed the legislative debates of the period and against which they may be seen as situating women within British public life in a context of recast patterns of social relations.[23]

The importance of modernizing sexual relations in the post-war period, a process that started in earnest at least as far back as the 1930s, but which was understood to be part of a programme of post-war recovery of Britishness, was to address a set of problems concerning sexual development that, it was stated over and again, had arisen because of 'altered conditions' during the war years.[24] An escalation of clinical, medico-legal and sociological studies addressing the classification, treatment and prevention of socio-sexual 'problems' or 'maladjustments', especially juvenile delinquency, adolescent disturbances and neuroses, and sexual promiscuity in girls is evident following the war years, while from 1952, a series of studies linking homosexuality and

20. *Homosexuality and Prostitution, A Memorandum of Evidence prepared by a Special Committee of the Council of the British Medical Association for submission to the Departmental Committee on Homosexuality and Prostitution*, British Medical Association, London, December 1955.

21. For an account of the operations against homosexuals in the US Government services, see John d'Emilio, 'The Homosexual Menace: The Politics of Sexuality in Cold War America', in Kathy Peiss and Christina Simmons (eds), *Passion and Power: Sexuality in History*, Temple University Press, Philadelphia 1989.

22. See Jeffrey Weeks, *Coming Out*, Quartet, London 1977, p159 and H. Montgomery Hyde, *The Love That Dare Not Speak Its Name*, Little Brown and Co, Boston 1970, pp212-216, Peter Wildeblood, *Against the Law*, Penguin, Harmondsworth 1955.

23. Stuart Hall, 'Reformism and the Legislation of Consent', *Permissiveness and Control: The Fate of Sixties Legislation*, Barnes and Noble, New York 1980.

24. For example, 'The sexual excitatory effect of war is known to every student of psycho-pathological problems', George Ryley Scott, *Sex Problems and Dangers in War-Time, A Book of Practical Advice for Men and Women on the Fighting and Home Fronts*, T. Werner Laurie Ltd, London 1940.

25. 'The father may be a ne'er-do-well, the mother a conspicuously incompetent housewife ... there is often present in both parents a temperamental instability which expresses itself in fecklessness, irresponsibility, improvidence and indiscipline in the home... Illegitimacy and promiscuity are common.' C.P. Blacker (ed), *Problem Families, Five Inquiries*, Eugenics Society, 1952, p16.

26. These two concerns are merged in *Sexual Diseases and Young People*, British Medical Association, London 1964.

27. Ex-Detective Superintendent John Gosling and Douglas Warner, *The Shame of a City: An Inquiry into the Vice of London*, W.H. Allen, London 1960, p198 and p20.

28. Carol Smart, 'Law and the Control of Women's Sexuality', in B. Hutter and G. Williams (eds), *Controlling Women*, Croom Helm, London 1981, p53.

prostitution appeared, many of them publishing evidence presented to the Wolfenden Committee on Sexual Offences. While homosexuality and prostitution came to crystallise those problems of sexual management and were identified as significant categories of psychopathology, they were situated within a more dispersed and fluid range of figures and behaviours, as 'perversions' of a sexual nature ceased to be solely a condition of 'others' living outside conventional sexual arrangements and became a *potential* attributed to a range of normalised categories of person. These could be triggered by exposure to influences likely to pervert the instincts, including drinking in pubs, reading popular magazines and trashy novels, gambling, and in some accounts an inadequate family upbringing characteristic of working class communities.[25] All these factors are seen as damaging to adolescent sexual development, causing neuroses which could eventually lead to unhealthy sexual inclinations. Two associated bodies of literature proposed the importance of sex education in schools as part of an education for effective citizenship, and developed schemes training young people into disciplined sexual habits as a preparation for marriage and to address the management of venereal diseases.[26]

At the same time as this identification of 'aberrant' sexual trends in medical and sociological studies, we can see an ongoing concern with the ways new immigrants might alter the 'natural' patterns of British social life, appearing in press reports and correspondence as well as in parliamentary debates and visible in a different way in medical texts on the incidence of venereal diseases amongst immigrants and its spread to other populations. The assumption that immigration caused an increase in prostitution can be seen in statements that the notoriety of Mayfair was preceded by an 'influx of coloured girls some months before the enactment of the (Street Offences) Act', reports that a 'revival' of prostitution in Stepney could be attributed to 'an influx of womanless coloured men from the West Indies and West Africa'[27] and the assumption that 'undesirable immigrants (were) exploiting simple-minded, depraved white women' as pimps.[28] Some of the features of the Affair, and its identification of the figure of the pimp as culprit, take on particular meanings in this context. In addition to Profumo and Ivanov, Christine had two West Indian lovers, Lucky Gordon and Johnny Edgecombe, the former being spectacularly ejected from the Old Bailey by police, helmets in disarray. The stories of Ward and Keeler visiting black jazz clubs in Notting Hill and their dabbling with (and reports of her 'addiction to') marijuana offered another side to the images of an 'underworld of sin and vice' while it was of course during the trial of Johnny Edgecombe that Keeler's liaison with Profumo was placed in danger of being revealed. A feature of the Profumo Affair was, of course, not just that Profumo had shared a woman with a Soviet agent, but also with black men, and this can be understood in the context of contemporary debates over immigration and concerns over the permeabilities of not just national boundaries, but of British national identity. That sexual exchange was seen to threaten the contours of such boundaries and identities is evident in

Ludovic Kennedy's reference to Christine as 'a sort of bin for the world's refuse: Russians, West Indians, politicians, peers, all had been grist to her mill'.[29] His further comment indicates the 'spoiling' of femininity by such associations; 'the taking of drugs by a teenage girl who counted negroes among her lovers was a thing that lingered in the mind: to many people it would seem about as far in depravity as one could go'.[30]

There are, then, two aspects of the Profumo Affair that are especially revealing of the extent to which it draws on contemporary debates over the relation of the social to the sexual. The first is that representations of the sexual, and especially those of psychosexual pathology, were used to articulate a *series* of differences which were seen to be problematic to the development of national character, connecting the sexual to forms of class and racial difference but also using it to address a more dispersed and diversified set of sexual definitions that could no longer be contained by nineteenth century sexual models based on absolute categories of difference and complementarity, normality and pathology. The second feature is that 'illicit' sexual exchanges were used to present a problem of social authority: of the management of public life, models of effective citizenship, and the way these can become linked to masculinity. Britain's self-definition was being interrogated through questions of sexual identity and exchange. It is these connections which explain why the Profumo Affair was used to address the forms of public authority whereby men regulate and govern the social and which indicate why it might in particular have drawn on discourses asserting the 'pathologies' of homosexuality. When the British Medical Association asserted in 1955 that 'homosexual practices tend to spread by contact, and from time to time they insidiously invade certain groups of the community which would otherwise be predominantly heterosexual', it also showed how far it considered homosexuality to pervert the principles of public good that regulate public institutions, as it attributed public hostility to homosexuals to the alleged tendency of 'homosexuals in positions of authority to give preferential treatment to homosexuals or to require homosexual subjection as expedient for promotion'.[31] Similarly, Richard Hauser's 1962 study *The Homosexual Society* identified the problem of a 'homosexual freemasonry' and proposed the need 'to *contain* the evil' of 'spreading' homosexuality within organisations. Hauser attributes this feature to a perpetuation of 'the male society' where the belief that women 'not excluding a man's own wife, are a distinct race of beings' and the habit of sexual segregation in education created a disposition susceptible to homosexuality and prevented the development of effective sexual relations as a feature of a healthy social realm.[32] Debates over homosexuality thereby became a way of revising the relations between masculine and feminine through their pathologising of an 'excessively' masculine culture deriving from men's privileged relation to the public sphere. The association of male homosexuality with the feminine, as we will see later, allowed these instabilities to be expressed in terms of a disruption of sexual categories.

29. Ludovic Kennedy, *The Trial of Stephen Ward*, Victor Gollancz, London 1964, p39.

30. *Ibid.*, p151.

31. British Medical Association, *Homosexuality and Prostitution*, pp27 and 28.

32. Richard Hauser, *The Homosexual Society*, Bodley Head, London 1962, pp24 and 158-160.

THE PROMISCUOUS HOSPITALITY OF A DISORDERLY HOUSE

In the concern over Profumo's behaviour we can see a complicated exchange being conducted between the public and the private in the operation of political life. One key to understanding how the Profumo Affair came to take on such importance in its working over the revisions being made in this period to the relation between sexual character and the national interest, is its link to the public reaction to the Conservative Government's handling of the Vassall spy scandal, a case which has been credited with reactivating scare campaigns over homosexuality that were constellated around the figure of Guy Burgess.[33] John Vassall, a clerk in the Admiralty, had been blackmailed for homosexual activities while serving in the British Embassy in Moscow in 1956, thereafter passing documents to the KGB. Soviet informers to the CIA had revealed details of a spy in the Admiralty over a period of some months before Vassall was discovered, a period during which the CIA lost confidence in the British Security Services and its screening procedures. MI5 was considered to have been so severely infiltrated by KGB agents at all levels that Soviet defectors conspicuously chose to reveal their information to the US.

Vassall was discovered in September 1962, only four months after George Blake was sentenced to forty two years imprisonment for espionage offences over a ten year period, practices which the Lord Chief Justice Parker stated had rendered much of Britain's own intelligence ineffective.[34] The Vassall trial took place later that year and was followed by a public inquiry conducted by Lord Radcliffe. During the Radcliffe Tribunal's investigation of the security aspects of the Vassall affair, the two journalists responsible for breaking the story, Reginald Foster and Brendan Mulholland, refused to reveal their sources and were subsequently imprisoned amongst widespread condemnation. Their imprisonment was seen to be motivated by the government's embarrassment over the revelation of security failures in their key institutions. During a debate over the Government's actions surrounding the imprisonment of the journalists, opposition MPs raised questions in the House that linked the disappearance of a key witness in the Edgecombe trial, and the rumours and insinuations concerning her relation to a Cabinet Minister, to the government's apparent punishment of those journalists who allowed the Vassall story to become public. It thus spoke of the perversion of public fora for the Government's own ends.[35] In the midst of an illegitimate discourse of private gossip and speculation, the possibility that Christine Keeler's removal involved a perversion of justice produced the 'silent witness' as a sign of the supression of information whose circulation would have benefitted 'the public interest'.[36] Demands were made for an investigation into the reasons for the trial proceeding in the absence of Christine as key witness, and the conditions of her absence. Rumours about the Minister and the missing witness[37] served to question the coherence of the public individual whose identity and autonomy guarantees the viability of contractual relations governing the social – that which must place public principles over private self-interest. From their

33. Jeffrey Weeks, *Sex, Politics and Society*, Longmans, Harlow 1989, p241, Stephen Jeffery-Poulter, *Peers, Queers and Commons: The Struggle for Gay Law Reform from 1950 to the Present*, London and New York 1991, p61.

34. West, *A Matter of Trust*, p92.

35. *Daily Express*, 22 March 1963, reports Lord Chief Justice Parker as saying that 'the interests of the State must come above those of the individual'.

36. *Ibid.*

37. *Ibid.*

apparently unconnected beginnings, we can see questions of principled public conduct were focussed around an interest in the conduct of government representatives in the Vassall affair and that of the 'minister and the call girl', as the disorderly intrusions of the figures of the male homosexual and the promiscuous young woman were seen to elicit lapses in the disciplines of masculinity that guarantee a democratic body politic. The alliance of these two categories of person would come to inform the later focus on the figure Stephen Ward.

Once Profumo admitted to a sexual relationship with Keeler, the scandal refocussed on a potential breach of national security and political responsibility; the possibility of a security leak through Keeler to Ivanov. A concern that the political and legal institutions that act as ultimate guarantors of objectivity and impartiality could have been vulnerable to perversion by human self-interestedness was redirected towards Profumo's possible act of passing knowledge and his political integrity. A conflict between public interest and privatised sexual cultures, between the public representations of the national body and private embodied masculinity, was posed in terms of Profumo's ability to carry political office, for his authority could only be intelligible in terms of his public role, a subject exercising judgement unclouded by corporeal relations.[38]

Thus while Profumo's lie to the House bore testimony to a failure of his sense of duty, it was used rather as a symptom of his disordered sexuality. Should he as a public figure not have shunned such a liaison whether or not he retained security? In the development of modern liberal democracies, systems of sexual difference align the feminine with the particular, the corporeal and the familial, rather than the principle of public good. Rational civil order is founded on a division from the disorder of womanly nature: while woman becomes both antipathetic *and* foundational to the emergence of democratic citizenship and masculine rationality, men of the polis must maintain a devaluation of the private, an exclusion of the feminine and the sexual from public life.[39] Definitions of appropriate sexuality thereby become central to the techniques of self-management which maintain the distinction between public and private.

Profumo's apparent overvaluation of private pleasures and his under-valuation of the principles of discipline and self-management allowed a contamination of his character as the bodily, the sexual and, especially, the feminine, were spoken of in relation to his public persona. By allowing the sexual, the private and the personal to intrude, Profumo blurred the boundaries between public and private arenas, allowing the masculine to become contaminated by its opposite. As Macmillan later said, the problem was not that Profumo had his affair, but that he did not keep the two sides of his life separate.

It is not only 'woman's nature' which is at stake in her signification of sexual difference, but her ability to reflect *an excessive and unruly sexuality in men*, which is only restrained by relegating the sexual to the private. The presence of

38. This opposition is outlined in Moira Gatens, 'Towards a Feminist Philosophy of the Body', in Barbara Caine *et al* (eds), *Crossing Boundaries*, Allen and Unwin, Sydney 1988.

39. Carole Pateman, 'The Disorder of Woman: Women, Love and the Sense of Justice', *The Disorder of Women*, Polity Press, Cambridge 1989.

feminine voices in the reporting of the scandal thus brought into view what might be seen as the origin, or source, or disorder. The disturbances surrounding Profumo were exacerbated by the circulation of newspaper stories detailing 'Confessions of Christine'[40] and 'Men, Money and Mandy'[41]. The explosive nature of their stories was shown by a headline declaring 'Mandy TALKED – and it's DYNAMITE!'[42] Something of the difficulty of accepting testimony from such sources, and the outrage that the trial of Stephen Ward could sully the representatives of the Crown by forcing them to draw upon it, was shown in an attack on Ward on the day his death was announced by Peter Earle, the *Daily Express* reporter who covered the Ward story:

> Look at the muck the Crown had to rely on at the Old Bailey ... Lying Whores; frightened little scrubbers; irresponsible little tarts...[43]

The feminine provides a point of disturbance not only to the relations between men in public, but to the forms by which masculinity is construed. After all, in the Profumo Affair, the stories told by the girls were about *male* sexuality and *male* desire – and men's inability to embrace the principles that negate corporeality and self-interestedness. As the public figure representing democratic government becomes contaminated with questions of private conduct and the sexual, the scandal articulated the presence of those elements denoted as 'feminine' *within the construction of masculinity itself.*

It is for these reasons that the sexual can be seen to undermine the authority of public figures and institutions and is linked to a disturbance in sexual meanings and identities. The conception of authority which allows an individual to occupy political office is based on men's grasp of certain disciplines – in this case sexual disciplines. But men's sexual 'needs' are spoken of in contrary ways; in terms of bodily urges, the force of sexual passion and loss of control. As Profumo's actions brought the girls' stories into discourse, he shattered his ability to claim the authority of public office. As Rebecca West refers to the 'feeble' speeches recorded in *Hansard* in the aftermath of Profumo's resignation, she comments that 'they would not be delivered or listened to in public were it not for the charity inherent in the conception of democratic government.' 'But', she cautions, 'there is a marked difference between the proper charity offered by a hospital and *the promiscuous hospitality of a disorderly house*' (my emphasis).[44] The erosion of Profumo's authority is thus one which spreads to that of men's grasp of the principles of democratic government as the language of the improper licence of prostitution transforms it into a disorderly establishment. What followed, the trial of Ward for pimping for the girls whose stories so damaged Profumo, showed the problems of securing the social according to the intelligibility of the sexual. The parade of their stories in the press in the run up to Stephen Ward's trial therefore did more than undermine Profumo as a public figure, it also challenged the autonomous functioning of authority in public life. Hence the claim that it was a scandal which toppled a government.[45]

40. *News of the World*, 9 June 1963.

41. *Daily Express*, 24 June 1963.

42. *News of the World*, London, 5 May 1963.

43. 'The Hidden World of Stephen Ward', *News of the World*, 4 August 1963.

44. Rebecca West, *The Meaning of Treason*, Penguin, Harmondsworth 1965, p378.

45. However, while Lord Alec Douglas-Home succeeded Macmillan after his retirement in October 1963, the Labour victory in 1964 was not a convincing defeat and was only developed into a sound majority in 1966.

Instead of pursuing the problem for masculinity around the figure of Profumo, the scandal therefore shifted attention to the 'good-time girls' and Stephen Ward as they offered a relay of meanings for that which disorders masculine authority. This provides a key to the relation between male homosexuality and prostitution, in their ability to represent that which falls outside conventional masculinity. The transfer was achieved through the framework offered by a contemporary legislative focus on prostitution and homosexuality, producing feminine and feminised figures situated within a topography of current sexual debate and regulation. The Wolfenden Report, published five years previously but its recommendations still a matter of debate in the Houses of Commons and Lords, reformulated this disturbance according to the language of perversion.

THE WOLFENDEN REPORT: MANAGING SEXUAL DIFFERENCE

The Wolfenden Report, published in 1957 and first debated in the Commons in 1958, is seen as the key document in debates around the limits of sexual expression and sexual practices in the post-war period as it drew on moral and social debates at the beginning of the 1950s and was influential in framing the legislative debates and social inquiry from the end of the decade onwards. In its inquiry into the contemporary legislative apparatus for dealing with offences concerning homosexuality and prostitution, the report attempted to demarcate appropriate boundaries between public and private conduct and establish a terrain of regulation. The 'Wolfenden Strategy' has been identified as a 'shrinkage of legislative control over personal conduct combined with a more rigorous policing of the cordon representing the public domain'.[46] Wolfenden thus established the 'public good' as a principle governing the regulation of the display of sexual practices and opposed it to 'matters of private moral conduct', the 'private lives of citizens'. Sexual behaviour becomes a matter of self-management, governed within a private arena of personal conscience and self-control, according to a moral imperative located in the individual, while regulation was organised around the public protection of that individual right to privacy – including the right of occupancy of the streets without being offended by sexual activities or sights.[47] The sexual was thereby situated in the terrain of the moral and ethical as domestic principles, as opposed to the rational and political principles that inform interventions in the management of sexual behaviour in public life and which should be brought to bear in the case of a disorderly incursion of the private into the public. This enabled the report to associate the sexual with the private, the ungovernable and the *feminine*. Simultaneously, it showed the limits of the law in addressing such a realm and stated the importance of medical and psychological agencies in their management of an important component of social stability.

Wolfenden's focus on male homosexuality and female prostitution addressed two forms of sexual behaviour which in their legislative characterisation were associated with the two sexes.[48] In the report's

46. Beverley Brown, 'Private Faces in Public Places', *Ideology and Consciousness*, Number 7, 1980, p3. See also Hall, 'Reformism and the Legislation of Consent' and Bland et al, 'Sexuality and Reproduction: Three "Official" Instances.'

47. The legislative framework the Wolfenden Report defined proclaimed its principle of 'public good' as distinct from individual self-interestedness. This entailed a delicate balance between a discourse of the individual's right to autonomy and self-regulation *in private* which could only be ensured by the regulation of the *public*. The Wolfenden Report thus addressed the divide by defining public good as the protection of individual right. In doing so, however, it managed to blur the separation of spheres as the individual right to 'privacy' had to be maintained in public as well as in private.

48. This was, of course, accomplished through the erasure of the prostitute's client and the female homosexual.

49. *Report of the Committee on Homosexual Offences and Prostitution.*

prioritisation of a public arena of regulation, it focussed on the eradication of the visible signs of prostitution on the streets. The prostitute was to fall within the arena of the law to the extent that she became visible in the public realm; her bodily presence was to be removed from the streets.[49] At the same time as maintaining the distinction between public and private realms that organised sexual relations and interactions, then, the Wolfenden Report maintained the meanings and categories of masculinity and femininity and their apparently unproblematic connection to sexually differentiated bodies.

The Wolfenden Report proposed a feminine realm that it suggested lay beyond governance, absent from public discourse except by the woman's transgression. The recommendations Wolfenden made concerning prostitution displaced the body for the correct functioning of social life. It was not the access of men to women's bodies that should be reduced in legislation over prostitution, but the manifestation of the sexualised body in the public sphere.[50] Hence the displacement of women's bodies also safeguarded against the corporeal intruding *in the processes by which men regulate their relations in public*.

50. The historical specificity of a prescription to desexualise relations governing public life can be seen in David M Halperin, 'Why is Diotima a Woman?', *One Hundred Years of Homosexuality*, Routledge, London 1990.

THE PROSTITUTE, THE CONSUMER AND THE MODEL: GOOD-TIME GIRLS

The Wolfenden Report's interest in eradicating women's presence in public was not an innovation. This impulse has characterised the history of legislation concerning prostitution, whether in a framework of medico-moral management as in the British Contagious Diseases Acts of the 1860s or in one which combined a discourse of the rights of individuals to privacy on the streets with that of regulation in the case of Wolfenden's inspiration of the Street Offences Act 1959. If the segregation of social spaces is used to define a segregation of sexual identities, the sexualisation of the presence of women's bodies on the street is a result of the transgression of such definitions. Women's entry into public life, therefore, does not render them masculine, but more *'dangerously feminine'*. As they cross the boundaries of appropriate feminine restraint and modesty, they signal the lack of internal self-control that justifies women's containment in the domestic, simultaneously indicating a breach of masculine control of public space in their testimony to an effectively regulated domestic realm.[51]

51. The point about women in public becoming not more masculine but more 'dangerously feminine' is made by Mark Wigley, 'Untitled: the Housing of Gender', Beatriz Colomina (ed), *Sexuality and Space*, Princeton, Architectural Press, New York 1992.

In the late nineteenth century, the aftermath of the success in pressing for the repeal of the Contagious Diseases Act saw legislation and feminist and liberal campaigns which maintained the prostitute was a class separate from other women, enforcing their displacement from public space in a targetting of 'women of evil life' within social critique. These were the victims of the Ripper murders, located in the poor Whitechapel district and without permanent residence, of middle age and frequently having quit a previous marriage; they were far removed from the image of 'errant daughters' that had previously been the focus of liberal and feminist support for the 'rescue' of prostitutes. Their presence on the streets had brought local criticism of 'nogoodnicks, prostitutes, old bags and drunks'. Their lives were said by Canon Barnett to be 'more appalling' than the actual murders. Clearly delineated from the 'respectable' women and innocent young girls of privatized, domestic femininity, a legislative framework could thus be formed around such an object.[52]

But in the 1960s it was the 'amateur' – and the sexual delinquent – who presented the greatest object of concern, especially in the difficulties of their identification. While the 'common prostitute' could still be separated from both 'call girls' and the innocent enticed into a more delinquent lifestyle, commentators noted the difficulty of identifying women who were prostitutes. In a study of the new phenomenon of the 'car-prostitute', for example, one report recounts a case presenting such difficulties;

> There was nothing in her appearance to distinguish her from any of the growing number of women who since the Second World War had hired cars for a variety of reasons: for an evening at the theatre, to drive to a country-club, a party or a première.[53]

The writers note that this new type posed a difficulty in identifying the types who were to be eradicated; 'They were well-dressed, well spoken and intelligent. Not one could be reconciled with the prostitute of popular imagination'.[54] The question of the sexual status of the two major female protagonists in the Ward trial, Christine Keeler and Marilyn, or Mandy, Rice-Davies, was one of the central features in the investigation of Stephen Ward; the girls did not exhibit the signs that allowed a correspondence to be made between social pathology and a realm of sexual pathology. The 'perfect poppets' showed their distance from the trappings of a separate existence.[55] Their presence at the parties of the aristocracy, their affairs with men of power and influence, their lifestyles of cars, planes, holidays, furs and jewellery separated them out from other women in a more desirable way than the Whitechapel prostitutes. Their lives were built around mobility, not loitering. They visibly consumed as much as they were consumed. Rather than the 'women of evil life', their photographic presence on the front page more accurately simulated the images of stars and celebrities.

This indicates the way women's bodies become a point of dialogue between public presence and private pleasures. As prostitution is one key mode of female entry into the public realm, it is also linked to that of consumption, seen throughout the twentieth century as a distinctively feminine activity and involvement. From the late nineteenth century's address to the female shopper in the expanded consumption industries, women's claim to entry into the public realm in the twentieth century and their access to modern forms of civil life and citizenship has been associated with their definition as consumers and hence their entry has been sexualised.[56] The prostitute and the female consumer became linked in the emphasis placed on appearance, adornment and display of both the *sexual* body (with clothes, cosmetics, perfumes) and the

52. Judith Walkowitz, 'Jack the Ripper and the Myth of Male Violence', *Feminist Studies*, Volume 8 Number 3, 1982, pp566-9.

53. Gosling and Warner, *The Shame of a City*, p11.

54. *Ibid*, p11.

55. Mandy Rice Davies, *The Mandy Report*, Confidential Publications Ltd, London 1964, p35.

56. Martin Pumphrey, 'The flapper, the housewife and the making of modernity', *Cultural Studies* Volume 1 Number 2 1987, Gillian Swanson, 'Drunk With the Glitter: Consuming Spaces and Sexual Geographies', Kathie Gibson and Sophie Watson (eds), *Postmodern Spaces and Cities*, Basil Blackwell, Oxford 1994.

mobile body which exceeds its domestic place (with travel and an involvement in extra-familial leisure pastimes). In the post-war period, the association made between a derogated domain of popular leisure pursuits and the lowering of sexual standards becomes tied to the figure of the susceptible working-class girl, who it was assumed lacked appropriate family models and trainings and thus turned to a tawdry range of popular entertainments. As a wartime study argued,

> The girls … are desperately anxious for adventure and they hope for an easier life than that which their mothers have led. Their very proper desire to know more about the new world of love and sex is played upon by these magazines which feed them with such second-rate food … There is no greatness about the people or the events of their false world and nothing which makes any appeal to the idealism which is one of the lovely gifts of adolescence. If the food is low-grade it is only too likely that the mental and spiritual quality of the consumer will be the same … the sex instinct is being over-stimulated at precisely the age when this should be avoided.[57]

57. A.P. Jephcott, *Girls Growing Up*, Faber & Faber, London 1942, p110, 125.

This offers a very particular interchangeability between female promiscuity and consumption. Not only do activities of consumption take women beyond the confines of the domestic, but the 'vanities' cultivated in the forms of self-adornment they provide have been used as a framework for explaining and identifying the pathologies and temptations of prostitution.[58] As one study states that the new 'type' spanning prostitute and amateur comprises 'the children of pleasure (who) follow fashion and the playground of the fashionable', another sees such tastes as part of the disposition which led a 'type' of woman to indulge in prostitution, as 'a way of living … consciously chosen because it suits a woman's personality in particular circumstances'.[59] A dual picture emerges in both of the woman as a subject who consumes for her own unruly pleasure yet who thereby transforms herself for others' pleasure in the commodification of her sexual body.

58. The historical precedents for this are shown in Mariana Valverde, 'The Love of Finery: Fashion and the Fallen Woman in Nineteenth-Century Social Discourse', *Victorian Studies*, Winter 1989, Volume 32 Number 2.

59. Gosling and Warner, *Shame of a City*, p15.

The features of style and fashion, as motifs of consumption, thus marked out an interim range of types – the sexual delinquent, or amateur – for social critique and moral scrutiny.[60] For in the 1950s and 1960s the origin of the problems of maintaining conventional divisions of sexual roles and identities within the family and other social sites was attributed to a *sexual sickness*, characterising women of the 1950s who displayed an imperfect sense of sacrifice and duty to their families. The origins of this strain of sickness were traced back to the New Woman of the 1920s, exercising an 'over-emphasised' female desire.[61] In the commercial expansion following World War Two, a culture of consumption became seen as a *difficulty* facing women, for their desires could so easily become uncontrolled.[62] Yet simultaneously, the post-war escalation of consumption industries made leisure commodities addressed to the female consumer a key feature of discourses of femininity. The very pleasures offered to women in the move to a modernized feminine definition became a danger to their moral and sexual self-management.

This relationship between consumption and the sexual provides the context of the good-time girls of London in the early 1960s. The good-time girl's access to the means to consume – paid work – was obscured and so she was situated in relation to the sexualized, leisured and idle female body seen as characteristic of modern life from the end of the nineteenth century.[63] In the context of the 1960s this body's prejudicial association with the debased commodities of mass culture was associated with a more seductive realm of glamour, in its fashionable adornment by clothes and cosmetics. In the figure of the model (both a term used to refer to 'Ward's girls' as well as a career aspiration voiced by them) the decadent *idle* body of the sexualized figures of nineteenth century culture was replaced by one deliberately and artfully *stilled* in the adoption of the pose, the gesture. The model offered a figure which moved across work and leisure, the toiling and the decorative body; as she struck her pose she linked the work on and with her body to the domain of sexualised and commodified consumption.

The figure of the model also contained the sexual ambiguities constructed in the exchange between the consuming woman and prostitute. The permeability of classifications of the model and the prostitute was shown as Lord Denning, in his report, inferred that Christine's 'vocation' as a prostitute was clear from the newspaper photos of the 'missing model'.[64] This shows the fragility of negotiating public and private appropriations of the female body; from its public display there emerged a reading of her private 'susceptibilities' or dispositions of character. At this time, one in which Lord Astor had married the model Bronwen Pugh, modelling was a career of utmost glamour for the modern girl, giving a new form of access to social mobility. Denning's assumption that modelling was a euphemism for prostitution was not simply a social gaffe or a remnant from former times, however, but an indication of the delicacy of definitions of legitimate sexual exchange and female identity as the private arena of unlawful sexual activity became yet more difficult to ascertain.

If it could be proved that Christine and Mandy were involved in prostitution while they were living with Ward, then it was incumbent upon him to prove that he had not been living on immoral earnings. Since the disparity between his and their earnings – and Mandy's assurance that he gave them more money than they gave him – did not suggest that he was supported in any way by them, his knowledge of their activities while they lived in his flat remained the key point of proof, sufficient to satisfy that he had provided goods and services for the purposes of prostitution. The prosecution questioning pursued this line and so the two strands of the investigation were directed towards the girls' sexual practices and the extent of Stephen Ward's knowledge and responsibility for them.

While the status of those witesses who declared themselves as prostitutes was easy enough to ascertain, the press, counsel, witnesses and commentators showed a common difficulty in finding a definition of Christine's and Mandy's statuses; they became objects of contestation. Neither part of that group 'of the utmost respectability' who it was claimed Ward had propositioned or seduced,

60. C.H. Rolph (ed), *Women of the Streets: A Sociological Study of the Common Prostitute*, Secker and Warburg, London 1955, pxiv. Gosling and Warner cite statements such as the following with approval, 'the division between (the professional who sells her body for money) and the legions of amateurs, good-time girls, gold-diggers and nymphomaniacs is only a quantitative one', *Shame of a City*, p30.

61. See Elizabeth Wilson, *Only Halfway to Paradise – Women in Post-War Britain: 1945-1968*, Tavistock Publications, London 1980, pp72 and 83.

62. In 'A Report on Shopping' Mass Observation, D87/5P, Report No 3055, November 1948, one male respondent commented, 'I think it is true to say that in a good many cases shopping today has brought out some of the shabbier traits of character on both sides of the counter', p10. The concern to educate the teenage girl into desirable patterns of consumption is outlined in Lesley Johnson, *The Modern Girl: Girlhood and Growing Up*, Allen & Unwin, Sydney 1993.

63. For the practices which centered the management of the body as a feature of feminine individuality, see Michelle Perrot (ed), *A History of Private Life: From the Fires of Revolution to the Great War*, Belknap/Harvard University Press, Cambridge, Mass 1990, pp457-494.

64. *Lord Denning's Report*, p20 and 52.

65. Rice-Davies, *The Mandy Report*, p35.

66. Kennedy, *The Trial of Stephen Ward*, p25.

67. This is the very reason why, it has been argued, male homosexual practices (especially sodomy) have been so much more severely policed than other sexual offences as it may comprise a temptation away from conventional sexual practices, Jeffrey Weeks, *Sex, Politics and Society*, p240.

68. Rice-Davies, *The Mandy Report*, p36.

69. Kennedy, *The Trial of Stephen Ward*, p202.

nor part of the identifiable group of working prostitutes for whom he was charged with pimping, a definition of them nevertheless had to be found. Some of the problems of classification are shown in the proliferation of inexact terms used to describe them; models, call girls, popsies or good-time girls. Their embodiment of a clash of sexual traditions and cultures is seen in the modernized character of the American term 'party girls' and the Victorian ring of Lord Hailsham's quaint phrase 'women of easy virtue'. In her account of the case, *The Mandy Report*, published in 1964, Mandy referred to herself as the 'perfect poppet':

> I am good company for men. I listen to their problems, I sympathise with them. I build up their egos and above all I am never possessive ... I do not regret having been paid in full for all the things I have done. And when I say 'paid' I mean in the luxurious way in which I have been kept by rich men.[65]

Griffith-Jones, the prosecuting counsel, put the case that 'the women were prostitutes, not street walkers admittedly, but women who sold their bodies for money none the less'.[66] It is clear that the trial became a test not only of the boundaries of acceptable forms of exchange for sexual practices, but also of its acceptable conditions. In the course of the trial the preconditions of guilt became increasingly closer to conventionally accepted sexual models.[67] In fact the terms of the good-time girls' sexual exchanges forced a scrutiny of sexual definitions. Mandy pointed the finger directly; 'And am I so different from other women? So before you throw too many stones at Mandy, have a good look at yourself.'[68] The exact relation of the girls to the category described by the Wolfenden Report and the Street Offences Act was shown to be as uncertain as their position within the spatial demarcations employed.

While both admitted they had been left money after sex at times, the extent to which this proved a sale with a contract was unclear. One problem in ascertaining their status was their evident pleasure in their sexual practices or associated forms of sociabilities, another was their age. The prosecution and Denning referred to them as 'sixteen year old schoolgirls from their homes in the country'[69]. They thus became defined in terms of the most susceptible category of person, who the same prosecutor in the trial of Penguin Books for the publication of *Lady Chatterley's Trial* two years earlier had been at pains to assert would not be the only category of person to be harmed by reading the novel. The sixteen year old schoolgirl stood, by implication, as the paragon of innocence and vulnerability: it was *assumed* such innocence would be violated if this category of person read the book. Instead, a potential to harm a wider range of categories of person had to be proved for the prosecution to stick. It was the 'man on the Clapham omnibus' in Lord Devlin's phrase who should be used as a key test of 'normal' tolerances and thus prove the book offered abnormal, excessive offence in its public circulation. The sixteen year old schoolgirl, as vulnerable, corruptible and hence needing to be shielded from

Mandy Rice-Davies. Photo by G. Pimmer. Courtesy of Hulton-Deutsch
Collection.

the 'normal' practices tolerated in public life, was thus counterposed against the average citizen, the stable public man. Christine and Mandy could not be included in either definition. They became both objects of corruption and subjects of offence, occupying the uncertain category of both excessive innocence and excessive desire. They existed outside the norms of public *and* private sexual definition.

In their representation of a modern form of femininity, the girls entered the public realm at their cost. Christine's postcard from Spain, 'Having a Ball', hit the front page.[70] Mandy was interviewed at London Airport and arrested there.[71] Christine was met by detectives at the airport on her way back from Spain, photographed stepping down from the plane in sunglasses like an arriving celebrity. Their stories were of travelling down through France, sailing to New York, getting fed up and flying back. They were seen in cars and taxis, were constantly on the move. These bodies in motion, seeking out fun, were actively complicit in their transgressions.

> We moved in the kind of world where the normal code of morals has no place; where there is no dividing line between good and bad, only that between a gay time and boredom.[72]

While new directions in criminology and sociological studies in this period defined young women's sexual practices as a form of delinquency and marked the limits of normal behaviour against sexual 'deviance' they erased their activities from the history of changes in female sexualities. Knightley and Kennedy, for example, in their later account, assert that Christine was 'a nymphomaniac in the true sense of the term, in that she felt emotionally secure only when she was giving her body to someone'.[73] They thus impute to her a transparent psychology which sees her conduct as driven by a unified set of characterological impulses, reading her as pathological rather than situating her in a context where the practices they dub 'promiscuous' had become routinised and even fashionable; a shifting field of female sexual practices taken up for a variety of ends and pleasures. As the good-time girls showed the entry of young women into new domains, their definitions could no longer be contained by lingering nineteenth century models of spatial segregation and notions of complementarity structuring sexual difference. While the girls' delinquent scenarios were, by implication, counterposed to the normativity of passive, domestic femininity, these oppositions were reiterated with a failing confidence; the exchanges between illegitimate and emergent sexual styles disorganised the forms of difference conventional models proposed.

In a new moment of sexual and social definition, the unresolved relations of masculinity and femininity became unstable, their boundaries renegotiated. The precarious figure of Christine in these transformations in femininity shows something of the instabilities of sexual models. Her attempts at glamorous self-presentation were described in flawed terms, as 'she had little skill in applying make-up or wearing clothes and always managed to look

70. *Daily Express*, 24 March 1963.

71. Knightley and Kennedy, *An Affair of State*, p168.

72. Rice-Davies, *The Mandy Report*, p21.

73. Knightley and Kennedy, *An Affair of State*, p57.

slightly scruffy'[74], her dress

74. *Ibid.*, p57.

the sort ... that aims at being chic and looks rather vulgar ... despite the tarty high-heeled shoes, she was tiny, a real little doll of a girl, and here of course was half the attraction ... the small oval face with the high cheekbones and a hint of Red Indian blood. She was in short like an animal, and one could see at once her appeal to the animal instincts of men.[75]

75. Kennedy, *The Trial of Stephen Ward*, p35.

As her sexual relations with West Indians were used to testify to Christine's lack of sexual decorum, her sexual difference was defined in correspondence to that of race: a mysterious 'otherness' allied to a susceptibility to corruption, a 'child-like' closeness to nature and an over-representation of sexuality. The propensity to exceed conventional models of youthful femininity was presented by recourse to corporeal intrusions, 'primitive' sexualities and animal instincts; an unruly sexual realm which required more effective governance. As the irreducible difference of femininity was played out, the female body could exceed the control of culture only for a limited time. Rebecca West referred to Christine's appearance at Ward's trial as 'a pitiful sight. She remained beautiful but her beauty was now a thin veil worn by a sick and grubby child'.[76] Without the measures to regulate prostitution as emblematic of such disruptions, such 'pathological' involvements, it was asserted in one study, would become irrevocably written onto the physique as a sign of social disease beyond medical intervention:

76. West, *A Matter of Treason*, p403.

(Prostitutes) show the symptoms of that disease, unknown to medical textbooks, called degradation. Outlawed by polite society, fleeced by parasites, forced to consort with thieves and gamblers ... they slowly degenerate. Their faces age before their time, their skin coarsens, their speech turns foul until at last it is true to say that they are almost completely dewomanised in every gentle aspect of that word. This, like the mark of Cain on the brow of the murderer, is the stigmata of prostitution which none can escape.[77]

77. Gosling and Warner, *Shame of a City*, p85.

MASCULINITY AND PERVERSION: A THOROUGHLY FILTHY FELLOW

At a crucial point in the scandal, immediately after Profumo's resignation, the decision was made to prosecute Stephen Ward. The character around whom the figures of the scandal and their sexual exchanges were clustered, Ward was an osteopath, artist and 'source of beautiful women for the aristocracy', moving around the social circles of the élite with a train of young girls in his wake.[78] In the concern with prostitution shown by the Wolfenden Report and its associated legislation, the pimp – or 'the ponce' as he was frequently termed – falls within legal view as an intrusive presence in the domain of sexual transaction: while prostitution was not unlawful (only its public manifestation)

78. Lord Denning more prosaically refers to Ward as a 'provider of popsies for rich people', *Lord Denning's Report*, p84.

pimping was (even in private). Ward's prosecution juggled uneven notions of public harm and the definition of the harmful object.

What did 'modern' sexual practices, made so much of in the trial, say about the forms of government which were implicated in his scandalous connection to politicians and their own 'indulgences'? Were the methods of disciplined self-management assumed as necessary for men's assumption of political responsibility put at risk by their exercise of less restrained sexual tastes? In what ways did the foregrounding of the bodies and sexuality of men present a difficulty in the representations of the public and its personas? And where did Stephen Ward lie, in the space between sexual life conducted in private and the public figures who populated his social and sexual networks?

Ward was tried on an ostensibly simple set of charges concerning living on immoral earnings and procuring.[79] However, the routine nature of this charge was belied by an immense investigation completely disproportionate to a case of pimping. Five officers were put on overtime for six to eight weeks to interview over 140 witnesses up to fourteen or fifteen times.[80] Christine was interviewed 26 times.[81] The trial of a figure who even in the prosecution's opening address appeared as a 'libertine' rather than a criminal staged a debate over the social and sexual implications of changes in moral frameworks for self-government.[82] The representations of conflict between competing elements in the contemporary field indicated an instability in the forms by which new knowledges could be incorporated into previously established models of social and sexual definition.

Ward not only represented an intrusion in conventional modes of regulating contact between men in their exchange of women's bodies, but was shown as a figure who manifestly aided women to use sexuality as a mechanism for social mobility and an entry into the public arena.[83] Just as it was described in the Wolfenden Report, a pimp was here defined as being 'habitually in the company of', or exercising influence over, prostitutes – a too-close relation to the female body.[84]

The figure of Stephen Ward thus reformed the problem new kinds of female fashioning posed for sexual relations into a question specifically addressing masculine associations and definition. His disturbing feminine knowledge had a ready context in his profession. As an osteopath his relationship to bodies in examination and treatment was derived not from the gaze and dissection, as in the history of conventional medicine, but by manipulation and touch. In their physical contact, the bodies became joined, breaking down their separation in empirically-based scientific observation. The distinctions between different kinds of medical practice situated the meanings of osteopathy according to a historical division between *observation* which does not alter the matter under investigation, and *touch* which acts upon and has the potential to 'alter physically its object'. Osteopathy is thus positioned with the 'sciences called experimental', linking a certain sense of tampering with the natural, outside clearly established regimes of practice, with a potential for stepping outside the domain of normality; 'it is only through the stopping of a

79. Two charges of procuring abortions were to have waited until the next session. Thurlow, *The Hate Factor*, p180.

80. Philip Knightley interviewed on *The Media Show*, BBC1, Tx 1990.

81. Thurlow, *The Hate Factor*, p145.

82. Kennedy, *The Trial of Stephen Ward*, p32.

83. Ward was seen to make a hobby of 'making' working class girls into models, socialites or starlets. A 'close friend' said of him, 'People were always asking him where he got the girls. He didn't get them, he made them'. Clive Irving et al, *Scandal '63*, William Heinemann, London 1963.

84. *Report of the Committee on Homosexual Offences and Prostitution*, p98.

"normal" activity – its suppression or destruction – that the function of an activity can be known'.[85] Situated in a domain where normality and pathology meet, touch is aligned with an invasive engagement with the object – and potentially the destruction of its conventional activities. Ward appeared both dangerously near the body and threatening to its natural processes. His skills provide him with the power to render bodies obedient; 'hands had always played an important part in his life. With them he had healed the sick, sketched the famous, excited women.'[86] His sketching and his osteopathy, both of which put him 'in touch' with royalty and the aristocracy and political figures, thus became linked with a perverse, disruptive and invasive corporeality. It wasn't so much that Ward actually disrupted the bounds of masculine and feminine definition, but that what he represented for the association between masculinity and nation came to be defined by the frameworks of social psychopathology which were used to regulate their relation. Hence he was fashioned into a figure whose features were identified according to available models of disruption: a sexual *indefinability*, as the disruptions of masculinity by the feminine became linked to signs of social pathology. The sexual debates circulating around this affair helped to map such instabilities through a transformation of the body of the prostitute into that of the male homosexual. How did this occur in his prosecution for pimping?

In his discussion of sexual legislation in the 1950s, Louis Blom-Cooper refers to the attention to 'men who consort with' prostitutes given by the Royal Commission on the Contagious Diseases Acts 1864-9, where he notes that a crucial difference made between the prostitute and the pimp is that 'with the one sex the difference is committed as a matter of gain; with the other it is the irregular indulgence of a natural impulse'.[87] As he links the pimp's anti-social cultivation of bodily digressions to Lord Devlin's assertion that 'a challenge to the morality of the "average man" is a threat to the entire social order' (an argument he made against the recommendation to liberalise legislation concerning male homosexuality), we can see how the nature of Stephen Ward's threat to the social order comes to be defined by an irregular masculine subjectivity too closely associated with the indulgences of the body, whether his own, or those of others. Blom-Cooper argues that the significance of Lord Devlin's perspective lay in his view of the social order as 'being in a state of delicate equilibrium needing only a slight nudge to precipitate (it) into an abyss of chaos and a *hopelessly lost identity*' (my emphasis).[88]

Ward's 'character' was thereby established in contrast to the forms of appropriate conduct and sexual management which provided a 'self-contained' masculinity, these becoming the crux of the prosecution. What links the different accounts of 'who' Ward was is their attention to his relationship to masculine sexual tastes and behaviours, against which he became *indecipherable*. Neither absolutely acceptable nor totally deviant, he disarmed sexual categories and classifications.

In his access, control and proximity to the sexual exchanges surrounding women's bodies, Ward's persona broke down the division of public and private

85. Lisa Cartwright, ' "Experiments of Destruction": Cinematic Inscriptions of Physiology', *Representations*, 40, Fall 1992, pp137-8. Cartwright is discussing Claude Bernard's 1865 *Introduction to the Study of Experimental Medicine*.

86. Kennedy, *The Trial of Stephen Ward*, p161.

87. Louis Blom-Cooper and Gavin Drew (eds), *Law and Morality*, Duckworth, London 1976, p92.

88. *Ibid.*, p90.

behaviours and eliminated the distance from female bodies that masculinity requires for its coherence to be marked by sexual difference. While the figure of the pimp documented this infringement on a level of public harm, the discourse of homosexuality – drawn on in the stories surrounding the trial and the accounts of Ward written much later – was used to document an infringement of democratic relations and the co-ordinates of masculinity itself. In the implication of the body in the scrutiny of Ward's subjectivity, the feminine and the sexual were admitted to the public arena to unseat absolute difference as a mechanism for defining sexual categories.

Ward was repeatedly referred to as a pygmalion figure who taught working-class girls how to speak, dress and behave, remaking them into high class 'popsies' who could socialise in élite class and professional circles on the exchange value of their sexual availability. His knowingness of women, a too-close familiarity that disturbed relations of difference, opposition and complementarity, rendered him on the one hand too powerful in his broaching of irreducible gulfs and on the other emasculated and perverse in its demonstration of his capacity for feminine forms of knowledge and identification; the possession of both became constitutive of his particular inscription of a pathological immorality. By his connection to the sexual and his public attachment to women's bodies, Ward was feminized. He thereby became an ambiguous, mysterious figure; the enigma of sexual difference as an impossible fiction.

In an exchange between prostitution and homosexuality in the context of debates surrounding the Wolfenden Report, the disturbance Ward effected was thus formulated according to the language of perversion. The language of sexual offence situating Ward as a pimp was allied with that of sexual pathology, proposing a subterranean homosexuality that pitted him 'against society'.[89] Homosexuality was the second aspect of Wolfenden's reassessment of current legislation. In its de-emphasis of a concern with private conduct, it suggested that private acts of homosexuality should no longer be subjected to policing but should be addressed by other (medical and counselling) agencies.[90] Thus Wolfenden remarked the boundaries of legal purview so that homosexuality fell outside of the national public sphere and became a matter of managing character. Ward's proximity to the circulation of the bodies of women defined as prostitutes gave him a privileged position in signifying the threat of the intrusions of the feminine to masculine identity and hence he embodied the threat sexual redefinition posed to social equilibrium.

The Report's liberalising impetus therefore led it to address public regulation and private freedom across the binary categories of sexual difference. While it focused on an arena of public regulation – the prostitute's criminalised body – only the section concerning homosexuality exhibited a need to define the role of responsible civic consciousness as *constitutive* of the social. 'Homosexual identity' – and 'homosexual propensities' – were therefore given an existence beyond the corporeal realm of homosexual practices. While the prostitute's body was constructed as antipathetic to the social, simply

89. HM Government, *Hansard House of Commons Debates*, HMSO, London 1958, Vol 596:428.

90. Male homosexuality was not actually decriminalised in the UK until ten years later, in 1967.

requiring eradication from its spaces, the homosexual was pathologised by attributing to him a breakdown of masculine consciousness. It was a willed self-control which was to be exerted over the bodily 'urges' deriving from homosexual propensities; the capacity for such discipline, allowing a fully formed *social* masculinity, was to be acquired through the influences of effectively managed family, work and social life.[91]

Male sexuality was given a new emphasis in this recasting of the forms by which the relations between men were to be regulated. As part of this attention, the homosexual was not just represented through the *intrusion* of the male body, but its corporeal refashioning, understood as *disturbance*: while one symptom of a breakdown of self-management was an indulgence in public 'display', another was their 'effeminacy'. Both were features which made them identifiable as objects of medical discourse: as the British Medical Association memorandum of evidence to the Wolfenden Committee stated confidently,

> the behaviour and appearance of homosexuals congregating blatantly in public houses, streets and restaurants are an outrage to public decency. Effeminate men wearing make-up and using scent are objectionable to everyone.[92]

The homosexual body was thus reflective not only of a lapsed consciousness but also of a lapsed masculinity: falling outside models of disciplined bodily deployment, it gained physical signs that connected it to a disorderly 'feminine' corporeality. As Wolfenden shifted attention from the 'homosexual' as a person to 'homosexuality' as a flexible field of behaviour to which all men are variably disposed, it adopted Kinsey's model of grading men's sexuality across a continuum between homosexual and heterosexual desires.[93] It was this move which provided the conditions for seeing homosexual 'bodily urges' as a natural arena of disorder for masculinity, disrupting 'self control', especially in the case of diminished responsibility caused by emotional distress, mental or physical disorder or disease.

Despite Wolfenden's attempt to disavow disease models in the understanding of homosexuality, in psychopathological typologies of homosexuality, signs of effeminacy were taken to be 'symptoms'. The *British Medical Journal* greeted the Wolfenden Report by citing Barbara Hutton's argument that 'the concept of illness expands continually at the expense of the concept of moral failure'[94], adding;

> The undesirability and immorality of such acts are not in question. What is questionable is whether the present law is the best way of diminishing them, or whether more success would come from better education and the strengthening of individual responsibility... Psychiatrists have usually lent support to the majority view recorded by the Wolfenden Committee.[95]

The *Lancet* editorial endorsing the Wolfenden Report, following a further

91. *Report of the Committee on Homosexual Offences and Prostitution*, p12.

92. *Ibid*, p26.

93. *Ibid*, p12.

94. Barbara Wootton, 'Sickness or sin?', *Twentieth Century*, cited in 'The Homosexual in Society', *British Medical Journal*, May 1956, p631.

95. *Ibid*, p631.

Commons debate in 1960 in which the recommendations were again dismissed and arguing against the 'conventional' disease model, defines homosexuality as a 'deficiency disorder' comparable to the damage caused to bone formation by rickets where

> a disturbed pattern of growth and physical (mainly mechanical) pressures causes gross deformity. Thus the boney structure becomes misshapen and all the attendant disabilities follow ... It does not force the analogy to suggest that in the case of the homosexual too, it is the disturbed pattern of emotional growth due to the deficiencies in relationship formation, combined with severe social pressure, that does the actual damage.[96]

These arguments legitimise medical attention to 'relationship deficiency and subsequent character distortion'[97], allowing medical institutions to claim an enhanced role, passing between public and private, in their address to national character and the management of masculine pathology: 'everything which helps to encourage physical and mental health, social responsibility and stable family life is the concern of the medical profession, for on these factors are founded the virility and soundness of national life'.[98] The prominent psychopathologist, Clifford Allen, further endorsed the importance of psycho-sexual management in 1962 when he stated that 'the psychological basis of homosexuality is one which has been a long time coming to the front ... homosexuality is mixed inseparably with a whole host of other perversions', and suggested it should be treated with as much concern as 'some other chronic disease' which affected the population.[99]

PATHOLOGISING WARD: A FEMINISED DISPOSITION

Ward came to represent a greater problem than sexual mismanagement, then, as his prosecution posed a question concerning the efficacy of measures for desexualising relations between men and their impact on masculine character. Framed according to the features of a disordered masculine consciousness, Ward became inscribed by the *disorder of sexual difference* represented by homosexuality. In the absence of an act – for no evidence of Ward's homosexuality has ever been demonstrated[100] – the means by which this was achieved was through a construction of his as a *feminised disposition*, a corporealized subjectivity constructed both during the trial and in the thirty years since, which linked him to the female figures and their occupation of the public domain of the sex scandal. The uncertain status of the good-time girls as prostitutes and their challenge to the use of sexuality and sexual difference as a mechanism of intelligibility were thus connected to Ward's feminisation according to the pathologies of homosexuality.

The association of prostitution with the homosexual and its connection to implications of a treasonable identity had a precedent six months previously in the trial of John Vassal. Contemporary reports describe a feminised figure,

96. *Lancet*, 23 July 1960, p199.

97. *Ibid*.

98. British Medical Association, *Homosexuality and Prostitution*, p7.

99. Clifford Allen, *A Textbook of Psychosexual Disorders*, Oxford University Press, London 1962, pp170, 174. Clifford Allen acted as witness to the Wolfenden Committee and was thanked by the British Medical Association for his contribution in their preparation of evidence for submission.

100. Although Summers and Dorril attempt to chart his friendships with known homosexuals, *Honeytrap*.

'doe-eyed, soft-voiced, hesitant and ephebic', 'a much sought-after "queen", playful and girlish'.[101]

101. West, *The Meaning of Treason*, pp361-2.

> The public imagination was haunted by visions of the slender figure in sweater and tight jeans who lurks in the shadow by the wall, just outside the circle of the lamplight, whisks down the steps of the tube-station lavatory, and with a backward glance under the long lashes offers pleasure and danger. He personified the charm inherent in the idea of prostitution ...[102]

102. *Ibid.*, p382.

The use of a dual depiction of the homosexual to signify social instability in the 1950s is shown by Elizabeth Wilson in her reference to the cases of Guy Burgess and John Vassall.[103] As newspaper reports framed Guy Burgess as 'unreliable pervert, in whom one proof of his sinister nature was his sexuality, another his Communism', his determined self-definition as homosexual and Communist might be compared with the coupling of Ward's consistent refusal of conventional sexual frameworks and his sympathies for 'communist ideas', a link made in Denning's commentary. The second figure was John Vassall, whose susceptibility to blackmail was perceived as 'weak and unmanly'. The sinister, the monstrous and the controlling are drawn together around Burgess and the emasculated around Vassall, while the dichotomy of the invert (formed in his constitution) and the pervert (making a deliberate and perverse choice) was invoked in various homosexual trials, for example that of Wildeblood whose claim to inversion was his major defence. This was sufficiently part of popular currency for Wolfenden to have to argue against it in order to assert its model of the more widespread presence of 'propensities', while in 1962 Clifford Allen would still feel it necessary to challenge its appearance in the Church of England's 1954 report, *The Problem of Homosexuality*.[104] The force of these polarised figures is their reference to an undisciplined masculinity and a feminisation in similar ways to those which I am arguing are prevalent in the treatment of Ward. They contribute to not only *aligning* homosexuality with espionage and treason, but allowing it to *become an identity* (as well as an act) of treason. The evidence of 'sympathy' or commitment to communist principles may be seen in similar terms to the presence of homosexual 'propensities'[105]: the homosexual as spy, defector, enemy, thereby becomes antipathetic to the cultivation of 'sound' national character: Ward is proposed as an enemy.[106]

103. Elizabeth Wilson, *Halfway to Paradise, Women in Post-War Britain: 1945-1968*, Tavistock Publications, London 1980, p101.

104. Allen refers to their use of the distinction made by the counsel in the Montagu-Wildeblood trial: 'an invert is a man who from accident or birth has unnatural desires ... whereas a pervert is a man who from lust or wickedness will get desires for either natural or unnatural functions', Clifford Allen, *A Textbook of Psychosexual Disorders*, p172.

105. The instability of the attributes of national danger during this period are shown in *The Statement on the Findings of the Conference of Privy Councillors on Security*: 'In this paper for convenience and brevity the term 'Communism' is used to cover Communism and Fascism alike' (p2).

But while contemporary commentary on both Vassall and Ward was largely condemnatory, the newspaper reports show an attention to their elegant style and luxurious and urbane forms of living; they also offer figures of glamour and seduction. The double figure of the homosexual as tragic invert or evil pervert could not account for the fascination invoked by unknown gratifications. As the *Sunday Pictorial* series on 'Evil Men' published in 1952 shows, what the homosexual also represented were the pleasures not so much of desire as of masculine *seduction*:

106. Here I am
suggesting that
Wolfenden's model
continues to reiterate
the homo/
heterosexual divide,
even while it dismisses
the mutual exclusivity
of dichotomised sexual
categories, in its
invocation of an
identifiable
homosexuality
resulting from the lack
of control over
'propensities'. Its
model of the
continuum thereby
becomes rearranged
by this residual
dichotomisation.

107. *Sunday Pictorial*,
25 May, 1952, p6.

108. Rice-Davies, *The
Mandy Report*, p30.

109. Kennedy, *The
Trial of Stephen Ward*,
p22.

110. Rice-Davies, *The
Mandy Report*, 23.

111. Peter Earle, *News
of the World*, 4 August,
1963.

112. Both of these are
suggested in
newspaper reports, see
Daily Express, 29 June
1963.

113. Summers and
Dorril, *Honeytrap*, p37,
summarising the
retrospective
commentary of
Jocelyn Proby, Ward's
mentor in osteopathy.

(S)o many *normal* people have been corrupted and in turn corrupt others ...
once a callow youth has become enmeshed in the practices of the pervert ...
it is hard to win him back to normal life.[107]

The homosexual thus becomes positioned with the feminine as a figure of the glamour and brittle temptation of unregulated consumption, and an object of seduction. As the figure of masculinity's own exclusions, he is situated in a realm of unlicenced corporeal pleasures in a hidden world of secret sexualities. The seductive venues of spaces outside 'normal life' become sites of wayward fantasies and lethal pleasures. The motif of a lethal seduction, just as much as questions of blackmail or legislative focus, thus informs the alignment of the homosexual with the prostitute.

The 'hypnotic Dr Ward('s)'[108] charm, voice,[109] and 'fish-eyes'[110] brought those around him – including Ivanov – 'under his spell', 'mesmerising and intriguing' even those repulsed by him.[111] The 'complete control' he was supposed to have over women, especially Keeler,[112] not only rendered her malleable to the influence of his knowledge, but also suggested the possession of such knowledge was itself a perversion. His domination by the impulse of the perverse[113] and his possession of feminine skills and knowledge formed Ward into a monstrous, almost murderous figure as he was shown to move into unsurveilled spaces, stalking the backstreets in his pursuit of prostitutes.[114] His movement across masculine and feminine rendered him deviant, defiant, monstrous, as he was compared – even in a sympathetic account – to Doctor Jekyll and Mr Hyde.[115]

Even Ward's sexual skill was interpreted in contradistinction to conventional masculinity:

Stephen proved to be the most accomplished lover I have ever enjoyed. To this day I remember his prowess in bed. His skill in love-making was, I think, due partly to his dislike of normal sexual relationships. Because of this – or perhaps to make up for it – he worked particularly hard to give satisfaction to the women he slept with. (Unlike the majority of men, incidentally, who are selfish lovers.)[116]

Ward's sexual interests were described in contrast to a definition of male sexual needs around the alliance of penetration and orgasm. His postponement of the immediacy of pleasure and his refinement of the art of petting became seen as a 'perversion', 'a hint of dangerous pleasures to come... Pleasure was always to be round the corner. Never to be taken now.'[117] The contrast between this and Mandy's conception of men's sexuality as a stick of dynamite – if you light the fuse wait for the explosion – was reinforced by a description of Ivanov, published under Christine Keeler's name in the *News of the World*, ravishing Christine on a rug:

Now he had really gone mad ... There was a wild threshing about; a real

Russian romp! ... I struggled to my feet. I was gasping and saying, 'No, no. You can't ...! But I knew there was no holding him and I didn't mean it anyway.

Here was my perfect specimen of a man. And he wanted me. He couldn't have stopped now anyway ... he was just kissing me with all the power of a man in a frenzy of passion. I made one last attempt to get away. But he caught hold of me. Our very impetus carried us through the door and we half fell into my bedroom.

... he was like a God... Clumsy perhaps, but only because he so wanted me. He said so.[118]

In the face of such a classic version of complementarity as the basis of sexual difference, Stephen's concentration on other pleasures fell outside such terms of definition and his sexuality became *unreadable*. During the testimony of Christine and Mandy, Ward's 'sexual disorder' was set in the context of psychological or emotional volatility:

As she (Mandy Rice-Davies) is cross-examined in the witness box, Dr Stephen Ward sits in the dock, sketching her... Then his mood changes and he sucks his knuckles, pinches his lips or stares unseeingly... Suddenly, he smiles, shifting his tall, lithe frame in a beautifully cut dark green suit.[119]

The accounts of Ward linked his artistic temperament,[120] superficiality,[121] gregarious sociability, his capacity for talk,[122] his name-dropping, his interest in the famous,[123] his use of men to achieve upward mobility and his 'little' sexual appetite,[124] his 'precision' and a 'soft reluctance in the way he used his fine hands'[125] into a composite of feminine attributes and dispositions manifested in an exchange between his 'character' and his body. In the reporting of the trial, references were made to his elegance, his soft white skin, tall lithe frame etc. Warwick Charlton, who Ward used to record his 'own' story, comments on Ward's physiology as his 'feminine aspect'; he had 'unusually white skin', a hairless chest and a 'boyish appearance ... slim and lithe', while his 'grace and precision' were 'like ... a Dior model'.[126]

These features were presented as evidence of a hidden homosexuality. Ludovic Kennedy was the most explicit:

There was no mistaking the now familiar figure, the roué of fifty who looked thirty five, perceptive eyes set in a face rather too full to carry them, boyish hair swept back along the sides of the head to meet at the back of the head like the wings of a partridge. Ageing men who look half their years are often fairies; and one wonders whether within this screaming hetero, a homo was not struggling to be let out'[127]

The transformation of Stephen's body held certain dangers, as destructive powers threatened to exceed its physical limits. Kennedy goes on: 'All the time

114. Like the Ripper, Ward's crime indicated a knowledge of women's bodies. While it is exhibited by the Ripper in his tampering with the murder victim's internal organs, Ward's is shown in a reconstruction of bodily appearance through teaching his protegées the principles of female dress, deportment and manners as well as sexual technique (Summers and Dorril, *Honeytrap*, p55). The authors of *Honeytrap* also suggested 'the longer Ward indulged, *the less he was interested in real live women*, and the more intense his passion for the bizarre' (my emphasis) (*Ibid.*, p42). Those involved in the Ward case were questioned again early in 1964 as part of an investigation of the 'Jack the Stripper' murders of eight prostitutes between 1959-64 after an overlap was established between those involved in the sexual networks Ward moved in and the murder victims, including one who testified against Ward (*Ibid.*, pp314-5).

115. Warwick Charlton, *Stephen Ward Speaks*, A 'Today' Publication, London 1963, p13.

116. Rice-Davies, *Ibid.*, p23.

117. Charlton, *Stephen Ward Speaks*, p30.

118. *News of the World*, 16 June 1963.

119. *Ibid.*

120. *Lord Denning's Report*.

121. Rice-Davies, *The Mandy Report*, p23.

122. Kennedy, *The Trial of Stephen Ward*, pp132 and 185, *Lord Denning's Report*, 1963. Peter Earle in *News of the World*, 4 August 1963.

123. *Lord Denning's Report*, 1963, p7.

124. Summers and Dorril, *Honeytrap*, p14.

125. American journalist Dorothy Kilgallen writing at the time of the trial, cited Summers and Dorril, *Honeytrap*, p37.

126. Charlton, *Stephen Ward Speaks*, pp15 and 21.

127. Kennedy, *The Trial of Stephen Ward*, p21.

128. The comment continued, 'And at the age of fifty to have put such frequent and unusual sexual strains on himself called for more than ordinary endurance (*Ibid*., p160) placing Ward as both subject and object, an active and passive body, placing strains and enduring them.

129. *News of the World*, 4 August 1963.

130. Rice-Davies, *The Mandy Report*, p36.

one had the impression of damned waters, banked fires ... one realised that behind this bland exterior, was a man of daemonic energy ...'[128]

The hands that touch the bodies of men and women became symptoms of his depravity, a visual surfacing of evil the consequences of which he could not finally escape, in a description that suggested homosexuality in its reference to literary origin. It came from Peter Earle, on the occasion of Ward's death, referring to a meeting just prior to his trial:

> Then I found myself looking at his hands – once so lithe and clean, like a surgeon's. They were dirty, now, with ugly little marks on them ... I myself had an absurd impression that he was going rotten, that these hands of his were like the picture of Dorian Gray in Oscar Wilde's great work about a man who found perpetual youth but whose wicked life was reflected by changes on an oil portrait of himself.[129]

In a similar way to the 'stigmata' associated with prostitution, this assumption that the homosexual body would become marked by the dispositions and habits of sexual character and lifestyle used personal testimony, opinion and readings of Ward as *evidence* of a dangerous latency that ultimately social conditions could not counteract. When Mandy wrote of a 'bit of the Devil' that exists in every woman, we know she was referring to forms of promiscuous sexuality which pushed against the boundaries of the definitions of prostitution. When she wrote about the 'bit of the Devil' in every man, that environment and home-training could not mould, which in some stayed dormant and in others came out never again to be contained, she was strikingly close to the language the Wolfenden Report used to describe the existence of homosexual 'propensities'.[130]

In his double representation, as masculine *and* feminine, (homosexual) consciousness *and* (feminised) body, Stephen embodied a disorder: the available model for such a crisis was constructed in the Wolfenden Report, a masculine consciousness open to the propensities of homosexuality. But Stephen's appearance was further pathologised according to models available in medical discourse and popular representation; his perversions, seen as a latent homosexuality signified by a 'feminisation', testified to his ability to undermine social cohesion. The invasion of the male body by the 'disorderly feminine', a corporeal disruption of masculinity, translated a threat to national security into the language of an enemy within: a disturbance to national character.

It could be said, therefore, that although it was his access to women that allowed the 'discovery' and feminisation of Stephen's body, it was rather the relations between men which were under scrutiny in such exchanges. The original exchange of Christine between Profumo, Ivanov, Edgecombe and Ward was succeeded by another, as the spectacle of the trial presented the sexualised body of Stephen in the public arena – both to be exchanged by representatives of the law in the drama of prosecution and defence and to become a participant in exchange himself. The judge and defence counsel receded in the public memory of the trial in comparison to the moments when the prosecutor, Griffith-Jones, addressed the court about this 'thoroughly filthy fellow' and interrogated Ward in the witness stand, in a dialogue of masculine sexual identity. Griffith-Jones' social and moral conservatism – it was he who in the prosecution of Penguin Books two years earlier had asked the jury to consider whether they considered *Lady Chatterly's Lover* a suitable novel for their wives or servants to read – clashed with Stephen's embodiment of modern sexual libertarianism and social mobility. This masculine exchange presented a scenario of conflicting sexual frameworks.

THE ENEMY WITHIN: DISTURBING MASCULINITY

I have suggested that the stories of the Profumo Affair used the feminine as a means of inscribing a disordered male consciousness on to a male body as evidence of a lack of containment and secure classifications. The fiction of wholeness, of a unified masculine subjectivity, faltered, masculinity became divided: inscribed by sexual difference, *it took on the meanings of both terms: both* a displaced femininity *and* an uncontained masculinity.

Their contact with Ward brought the bodies of men into view, making their corporeal presence in social exchange visible. It was this 'reduction' to the body that the Cliveden swimming-pool weekend, when Ivanov and Profumo met Keeler, showed. As Ward stated in a newspaper interview, 'You've no idea how amusing it was to have the Russian and the British War Minister in the swimming pool together.'[131] His stories of treating men of power in his capacity as osteopath included one of Winston Churchill, whose bedroom he entered to discover Churchill sitting up in bed, cigar in mouth. As Churchill jumped out of bed, Ward realised he had on only his pyjama top.[132]

Ward thus marked masculinity with the stain of corporeality, rendering sexual difference visible and provisional in representations of an excessive masculinity, prone to wayward desires and beyond regulation. An 'enemy within', the unruliness wrought by femininity within a male body was a motif for disorder in the national body. The concern with defining the scandal in terms of an affliction could be seen in Harold Wilson's assurance in the Commons debate following Profumo's resignation, that the scandal should not be seen as a 'canker at the heart' of Britain but a 'diseased excrescence, a corrupted and poisoned appendix of a small and unrepresentative section of society that makes no contribution to what Britain is, still less to what Britain can be'.[133] The concern was based, then, on whether the affliction was invasive or could be excised.

The prostitute and the homosexual were situated outside of the arena of socialized identities, occupying a field of unnatural relations that showed the inadequate functioning of programmes of social management. As the homosexual was pathologised according to a breakdown of masculine consciousness by disturbances relating to unmanageable instincts, the

131. Peter Earle, *News of the World*, 4 August 1963.

132. Dorril and Summers, *Honeytrap*, p39.

133. HM Government, *Hansard House of Commons Debates*, HMSO, London 1963, Vol 679:54.

development of a capacity to control such instincts, allowing a fully formed *social* sexuality, became an aim of the programmes of sexual, marital and familial training brought together with the development of typologies of pathology in the post-war period. When Clifford Allen justified the widespread study of homosexuality amongst prisoners by reference to the habit frogs had of mating with pieces of wood in the absence of suitable partners, he suggested that the instincts of men were unruly and in certain conditions could become unmanageable: 'So strong is the instinct to copulate', he stated, 'that an animal, *and presumably a man*, will attempt to perform sexual congress with unsuitable partners if no suitable ones are available (my emphasis).'[134]

134. Clifford Allen, *A Textbook of Psychosexual Disorders*, p174.

The problems of newly modernized and public femininities disturbed the co-ordinates of sexual difference and the alignment of sexual bodies with public and private spaces, and thereby disturbed the structure of morality, discipline and authority that was implied by such relegations. The Wolfenden strategy of separating off the private sphere from an arena of sexual regulation and management underscored a problem of sexual classification. As models of domestic femininity which had underpinned men's association in the public sphere were undergoing a transformation in the post-war period, the relations between men required new forms of definition. In the Wolfenden recommendation that homosexuality in private should be removed from legislative purview, and in the following Commons debates and rejections of the recommendation, relations between men in public were placed under a new form of scrutiny; masculine identity itself emerged as an uneven and volatile category, a problem for the definition of the social and national character.

The Profumo Affair appeared at the end of a period during which a massive programme of sexual management was initiated along with a redefinition of 'normal' sexual behaviour and identity through a detailed typology of sexual pathologies. As his trial disrupted the correspondence between physiology, bodily deployment and identity, the case of Stephen Ward showed the difficulties of implementing such redefinitions in the absence of a model of sexual difference pliable enough to accommodate new forms of social and sexual being. The scandal brought forth stories of corporeal disturbance, representing an excessive masculinity, prone to wayward desires and beyond regulation. The ambivalence of Ward's sexual definition during the trial, the assumption of a foundational homosexuality held beneath a veneer, the sign of a corruption that threatened to bring about the nudge that Lord Devlin had suggested would lead British society into the 'abyss of chaos and a hopelessly lost identity',[135] ensures that Ward's trial stood as testimony to an unresolved, illicit and unaccountable incommensurability between the social and the sexual.

135. Blom-Cooper and Drew (eds), *Law and Morality*, p90.

This is an extended version of an article first published in *Law in Context*, La Trobe University Press, Australia, Volume 9, Number 2, 1991.

LISTEN TO YOUR VOICE!
AUTHENTICITY AND REFLEXIVITY IN ROCK, RAP AND TECHNO MUSIC

Johan Fornäs

Listen to your voice! This simple invitation uncovers an abyss of late modern subjectivity. Can you hear your own voice? Are you the hearing or the heard one – or both, or neither of them? To determine who you are, is it necessary to smell, feel, watch or listen to yourself? Is it at all possible to know oneself – even partly, approximately or preliminarily?

Apart from such fundamental issues of subjectivity and identity, the invitation also actualizes an ambiguity in the relation between authenticity and reflexivity – of self-expression and of self-mirroring. The authentic as the genuine or the honest expression of a subject is implied in the words '*your* voice' – a symbolic expression of precisely your own creative subjectivity. It is also hinted at in the linguistical appeal form of the sentence, that obviously directs itself towards you as a living person. The reflexive resides in the urge to hear oneself, to reflect upon one's own subject-position, to mirror one's own identity. Listening to someone else's voice might have to do with authenticity but not reflexivity, while the reflexive move does not seem possible without a certain amount of authenticity (if you use a 'false' voice, you will not hear *your* voice).

First one could argue that the most genuine voice is the non-reflective one, a spontaneously flowing and sounding existence in time and space. Listening to oneself is then repeating the Fall of Man into the unhappy consciousness of artifice and false constructions – the exit from a forever lost Edenic presence of original and innocent naivity through the gateway of imaginary mirrorings into the world of symbolic order where subjects are only sign effects and authenticity an illusion. Listening to the Siren song that tempts us to listen to our own voices forever condemns us to be inauthentic. The only possible chance would then be just to sing out, with closed ears, letting the sound waves flow out in unreflected streams. Such a position could for example value pre-modern, youthful or naive musics as more authentic than late-modern, ageing or self-conscious genres.[1] Here, authenticity is almost the opposite to reflexivity.

From the opposite corner, it could however be argued that it is exactly the unconscious voice that runs the greatest risk of getting inauthentic, steered by uncontrollable external forces in nature, culture and society. Only by carefully listening to your voice, reflecting upon one's limits and potentials, might it be possible to gain a real, active subjectivity. Reflexivity is then almost identical with authenticity, or at least its necessary condition.

1. This quasi-romantic position has both an anti-intellectual and a super-intellectual version. It can be formulated as a despisal of all theoretical reflection, but it can also turn up as a highly sophisticated longing for jouissance in experiences that escape the control of the ego by pushing symbolic textuality to its limits.

2. I am deeply
grateful to Hillevi
Ganetz for inventive
and patient assistance
in our discussions
around all these
themes.

To pay attention to one's own or someone else's voice thus opens a door to a complex field of tension between authenticity and reflexivity, related to intriguing questions of how genre, style and identity are mutually related in the use of music. To reflect upon such connections, I will use some examples to illustrate a few aspects, with the intention of generating new studies.[2]

Authenticity often appears in differentiations between genres, in highly ideologically charged discourses around aesthetic values. It is for example central in many efforts to sever plastic pop from real rock. Such demarcations often connect to the old dichotomy of high/low culture, but with varying criteria. Traditionally, art and folk music are classified as authentic in opposition to mass-produced popular music. Oppositional interpreters sometimes conceive the popular as more genuine than upper-class elite art. Within popular music, many think of rock as the real thing, in opposition to pop, disco or house, but others use the terms otherwise. Within each genre, the distinction between good and bad is repeatedly formulated in similar terms: the authentic originals versus the fake, the hype, the copies. I will mention some musical examples to see which authenticity demands are stressed within different generic spheres. But let me first make a montage of ideas around some focal concepts in my discussion, to elaborate a little a theoretical apparatus that will unfortunately have to remain more implied than elucidated.

STYLE, GENRE AND IDENTITY

Authenticity can be thought of as a special relation between style and identity. The authentic style is particularly well anchored or rooted in an identity, or at least foregrounds such style/identity-homologies. A style might be genuine if it is well integrated within a (any) genre, but a genre as a whole can also be more or less 'true' to the identities of its musicians and audiences.

Identity implies that something is identical or rather similar to something else. First, two fundamental aspects are possible, concerning time and space. On the one hand, identity is temporal continuity. The identity of an individual or a group is something that can be recognized in them for a longer period, as a somewhat stable characteristic. But there is also a spatial aspect: personal identities bind various parts of the individual together through structural patterns of consistency, and collective identities concern similarities between people as something they share though they are separate.

These examples have already also mentioned a series of other interlocking concepts separating various versions of identity: individual and collective, internal and external, subjective and objective, psychic and social. Their mutual relations are extremely complicated. For example, an individual has both a body and a soul, and both have psychic as well as social aspects. The result is an immensely multidimensional model of identities, even before it is filled with any specific content related to dimensions like gender, age, ethnicity or class.

What needs to be emphasized in this context is only that it is important not to conceive of identity too narrowly. First, if identity is understood too strictly, it completely disappears. Nothing is *exactly* the *same* as something *else*. We have to accept more vague criteria of either approximate similarity or partial identity (which is in fact much the same thing). I am never totally identical with the one I was a year ago, but we are pretty similar, or there are some important aspects of me that have remained as exactly constant as anything can be.

Second, I refuse to reduce identity to (for example) only the social or only the psychic aspect. The important thing is to keep their mutual tensions open, not collapsing them into each other. This necessitates a multidimensional model that opens up for different theorizations of the different aspects – an invitation to true interdisciplinarity (e.g. of sociology and psychoanalysis) instead of a one-eyed reductionism.

Put crudely, collective identities concern social groups, positions and patterns of norms and relations within society, while individual identities can be related to inner subjectivities, studied by psychological theories but including both mental and bodily aspects.

Social identity is however not the only intersubjectively shared aspect. A third identity form can be named – cultural identity. It is constituted by meaningful symbols and texts, while social identities act in the medium of interpersonal norms and relations. These are in fact the only identities we can perceive, since all communication takes place on this level. Subjective and social identities can only be seen and formulated through cultural identities. But this third level is not simply an effect of (one or both of) the others. In our time, it has become necessary to accept the relative autonomy of the cultural level of signs and discourses, with rules and patterns that cannot be completely reduced neither to psychic states or to social relations.

Cultural identity is the space of styles and genres. For Paul Ricoeur, cultural phenomena ('texts') can be seen as webs of meaningful symbols. They form works, as externalized units produced by human action or praxis. Genres are sets of generic rules for cultural production and reception (as a production of meaning in the appropriation of texts), potentials for generating works. If texts/works can be classified into genres this is only because these various sets of generic rules have been put into motion. No such classification is complete, fixed or unanimous, since meaning-production lets many forces interact in a never-ending process of conflicting interpretations. Genres also exist on hierarchically ordered levels, as when rock can be seen as a sub-genre of popular music but a super-genre of rock'n'roll, heavy metal and punk. Several conflicting ways of ordering genres co-exist in society, and are continuously redefined through the discursive struggles being fought. Styles are individual form patterns in singular works, but common stylistic traits can be found between single works within a genre as well as in different genres.

Now, these concepts can be used on all cultural phenomena. We can speak of genres and styles within music as well as literature, and within the institutionalized aesthetic sphere as well as in everyday life. Aesthetics might be defined as the (more or less formalized and institutionalized) reflexive discourse about cultural production (particularly around the specialized forms of art). Life styles are symbolic patterns or cultural identities shaped by people in their everyday interaction, by all accessible means: bodies, clothes, gestures, habits, language use and music. There is some confusion here, since the discussion of lifestyles or youth cultural styles has not differentiated between styles and genres. One subcultural style can be thought of either as a true style, that is an individual form pattern within the 'genre' of youth cultures or lifestyles, or as a genre – a generic set of rules of which particular groups, individuals, artefacts and actions are then instances, 'works' or 'texts', with each having its own partly unique style. Style and genre can here be seen more as mutually relative concepts than as clearcut categories. Again, a web of interlacing threads are found, rather than any stiff and unanimous hierarchical structure.

Texts have various use values in relation to different individuals and groups and in specific contexts. Use values cannot be quantitatively measured but only qualitatively interpreted.[3] Music consumption is the use of music delivered in commodity form, appropriated by an exchange with its producers. Reception is the established word for media use. Interpretation is here understood as the (re)construction of meaning in reception.

This model gives rise to many problems, since so many dimensions, levels and aspects are interacting all the time. Instead of further problematizing concepts like meaning, culture and communication, I will here use this preliminary theoretical apparatus to discuss authenticity and reflexivity in some typical present genres of popular music. If we listen carefully, authenticity and reflexivity can be heard in all late modern genre-fields. Some distinctions will be generated through this reflection upon five wide genre-spheres, offering prismatic illustrations in the music, lyrics, social settings and secondary discourses of these genres. My examples are drawn mainly from recent Swedish popular music, but there is no reason to believe that similar examples could not as well have been found in most corners of late modern global culture.

3. For a discussion of use values of rock, see Johan Fornäs, 'Moving Rock: Youth and Pop in Late Modernity', in *Popular Music*, Volume 9, Number 3, 1990, pp291-306.

ROCK/POP

The rock/pop field is a contested continuum. Authenticity is frequently used to distinguish rock from pop, as rock ideologists defend the values of folk and/or art genuinity against commercial substitutes. Rock critics sometimes turn the same dichotomy upside-down while allegedly dismissing it, as they deride the illusions of authenticity of the rock establishment and elevate the honest constructivity of the pop machinery. In both cases, authenticity is debated, but in different ways. Some of the possible criteria of value include the sincerity of the artists, the social roots of the genre, or the bodily presence expressed or experienced in the particular performance.

There seems to be a continually regenerated need for such distinctions, resulting in an ongoing struggle in discourses on musical aesthetics. Still, I think it is impossible to uphold any clear dichotomy between rock and pop. The shifts of the meanings of these terms between countries and times bear witness of their ideological character. Rock/pop is a spectrum with a range of focal points in highly complex relations to each other as well as to other (super)genres of (more or less popular) music. The relevance of certain forms of authenticity arguments is a common feature. Rock/pop is basically music conceived in and for a mass media context, with a group of electrified instruments, vocal song with lyrics, and identifiable artists with carefully constructed personae, images and cultural identities. There are important differences within the rock/pop world, but there are also fundamental continuities.

An example offered by Atomic Swing, a classical but very popular pop group from a small industrial town in central Sweden. They are explicitly anchored in the rock tradition, often referring back to musical (and visual) styles of the late 1960s and early 1970s. They are expected to deliver their own material, in their own voices, but at the same time to conform to the current versions of generic rules inherited from tradition. Here, elements of pastiche mingle with something uniquely new, as their voices at the same time grow out of a local peer group, a regional microculture and a transnational 'subcultural' genre. Here is their 'Stone Me Into the Groove' (from *A Car Crash Into the Blue*, 1993):

I woke up and the sun was dressed in blue
The Panavision colours ran out, out in my room
I wanna paint them wherever you go
I wanna thrill you but I want it slow
I wanna fly in the room of your arms
I wanna enjoy all of your charms

So just stone me into the groove
You're making everything beautiful and I think it's wonderful
Stone me into the groove
I wanna go!

Oh, my saviour, my friend, just take me away
from tonight and into today
Just take me out on a carpet ride
into a place where I mustn't hide
'cause I'm bored of the ancient truth
I'm a car crash in the blue

Again, authenticity turns out to be a complex affair: a real uniqueness, a speaking voice, a spatially, socially and temporally rooted position, but also a reflective longing for something else. The vocal, organ and guitar sounds are echoes of classical forerunners, but this does not prevent them from speaking for these four young Swedish men. We feel at once that this is music born of a real group of people working together in a living community, playing self-chosen roles as expressing subjects. These subjects sing about longing for a place where they do not have to hide, a place for sublime authenticity, but painted with Panavision colours. Signs of the real and signs of (media) reflexions intertwine.

There are innumerable variants within this genre field. Some artists emerge as individual soloists, like Madonna, Prince, Sinead O'Connor or Bruce Springsteen, backed by more or less anonymous musicians. Others appear as small and tight ensembles, from girl groups to black/death/trash metal bands – particularly but not exclusively at the rock end of the spectrum.

When Guns'n'Roses were interviewed at the MTV awards event 1992, their lead singer, Axl Rose declared, 'This has nothing to do with Michael Jackson!' They could as well have mentioned Madonna.

> 'Rock' is art. Madonna, in contrast, is 'pop' – juvenile, formulaic, artificial, shallow, self-centred, escapist fantasy, committed to making a profit. Madonna is a commodity produced by industry. Clearly, pushing Madonna to the bottom rungs of the pop cultural ladder makes a space at the top for pop music 'art'. Furthermore, despite the fact that Madonna is located in opposition to female singer-songwriters, it is Madonna and pop that are feminized … A number of music critics link Madonna, pop, and 'feminine' qualities (using adjectives like fluffy, coy, bubbly, etc.) to construct a transcoded version of the art versus mass culture distinctions within the domain of popular music.[4]

4. Laurie Schulze et al, ' "A Sacred Monster in Her Prime": Audience Construction of Madonna as Low-Other' in Cathy Schwichtenberg (ed), *The Madonna Connection*, Westview Press, Boulder 1993, p18.

5. See Richard Middleton, *Studying Popular Music*, Open University Press, Milton Keynes 1990, for a view of rock as a discursively contested terrain.

Rock/pop is a genre-field of conflicting interpretations, related to age, gender, ethnic and class conflicts. Distinctions within a genre are often made through efforts to excommunicate others from it. Some restrict rock to a male white canon of heroes, marginalizing women, African-Americans or other groups and subgenres as deviant Others. Some respond by avoiding the rock label, while others fight for the right to rock. Such discursive struggles over the definition and borders of a genre is a sign of its creative life.[5]

'I've seen the future of rock and it sucks', sings Graham Parker on 'Love is a Burning Question' (on *Burning Questions*, 1992). This can be read as a generally pessimistic rock-prophecy or a specific satirical reference to the famous statement about Bruce Springsteen as the incarnated future of rock. A more optimistic interpretation might say however that rock will continue to attract interest, or that its sucking in of various new and non-orthodox tendencies is indeed what might be able to keep it alive into the next millenium. Changes in technology (video, synthesizers, sampling, sequencers and MIDI), markets and institutions (commercialization and bureaucratization) as well as in the psychic, social and aesthetic worlds (new subjectivity forms, intensified multicultural exchange, fragmenting norms and styles) force rock to transform radically in late modernity. Its hegemony as youth music might be broken, but the present fragmented pop music field will probably not again give rise to one single heir to its throne, and neither will rock die just because it is not alone or has become reflexively aware of its history.[6]

The efforts of a strong rock establishment to claim hegemony for one tradition covers and hides various sub- and side-traditions that compete within the genre and in fact give it life. Periods of increasing openness (the explicit transgressions of gender, sexuality, age, class, ethnic and genre borders in artists like Madonna, Michael Jackson or Prince) may alternate with phases where dominant forces try to reinforce strict boundaries. It is then that the definition struggles intensify, as threatened positions defend their legitimate rights and venture new attacks on the normative efforts by what could be called the 'rock fundamentalists'. But no such purist movements can avoid the late modern flexibility and reflexivity: it is essential in grunge, heavy metal and trad rock as well, as these subgenres foster new types of hybridity in style and identity, instead of the ones they first attacked.

Rock will die, like metaphors transformed into clichés, if its hegemonic line is strong and stiff enough to repress all Others in its efforts to establish such a pure origin and canon. If and when rock can be unambiguously defined, then it will be dead. But as long as various Others ('Afro-American' soul, reggae and rap, 'female' pop, non-Anglo-American voices …) want and manage to fight stylistic wars with the male, white, western rock heroes for the right to rock, the genre survives as an open and unpredictable field. I suggest that there are enough external, psychic, social and aesthetic conditions left to make the dialectic between various positions within the rock and pop field strong enough to continue. The current struggle between rock-traditional purists, oppositional camps proposing alternative genealogies, and heterodoxical pluralists seeing rock/pop as one wide, diversified but no longer simply polarized field shows that the last words on the future of rock have not yet been said.

Artists like Madonna or Michael Jackson can be as honest in what they do (and think of themselves as true) as was ever Chuck Berry, Patti Smith or Bruce Springsteen. Genres like rock and pop can not be separated by their respective degree of authenticity, only (perhaps) in the types and forms of authentication emphasised in them.

RAP/TOAST

For some, rap is something radically different than rock/pop, for others it is a central part of it.

> Then again, rap is rock, after all, and rock has *always* been at least incidentally about pissing off the old folks … Of course, all of this is predicated on an Afrocentric understanding of the history of rock. If, like the whitebreads who program AOR radio, you believe that rock proceeds from Elvis to the Beatles and the Who to Led Zeppelin and Elton John and finally Bon Jovi and Phil Collins, then rap is not only not going to fit your

6. Allan F. Moore,
*Rock: The Primary Text
– Developing a
Musicology of Rock,*
Open University Press,
Buckingham 1993.

7. B. Adler and J. Beckman, *Rap! Portraits and Lyrics of a Generation of Black Rockers*, Omnibus Press, London 1991, pxviii.

definition of rock, it likely won't even qualify as music. On the other hand, if your hall of fame runs from Little Richard and Bo Diddley to James Brown and Jimi Hendrix and Sly and the Family Stone, to Kool and the Gang and Parliament/Funkadelic and finally to Prince and the heroes of hip-hop, then you're going to understand that rap is strictly *in the tradition*.[7]

This exemplifies genre definitions as arenas of power struggles over cultural meanings, where oppositional agents mobilize alternative canons against a dominating position. Each such reconstructed chain is problematic in trying to establish a single, clean and unitary tradition line instead of accepting the hybridity and crossings that give a genre life. A series of genealogies co-exist, pointing out different but legitimate 'origins'. All such genealogies are stakes in a power game, where their co-existence indicates that none of them alone can be correct.

The many crossovers (*viz.* Run-DMC and Aerosmith, Public Enemy and Anthrax or Ice T and Body Count) show deep affinities between rap and rock, in spite of the differences. Rap also depends on a vocal performance backed up by instruments often played by an ensemble of musicians and/or DJs. Sections with song might alternate with the rhythmical rap speech. There is today a sort of continuum between hardcore purist rap, toast and pop/soul-rap, part of it loosely associated with hiphop subculture. In this whole genre-field, the subjectivities of the artists are rather exaggerated than downplayed.

There are some successful Swedish artists here: Dr Alban, Leila K, Teddy Bear, Stonefunkers, Clawfinger, and Just D (who create Swedish texts). Many of them have an immigrant parent but are born and raised in Sweden. It is easy to find dozens of variations on the authenticity theme, in Sweden as well as by American or British groups. The quest for the real thing and the critique of 'hypes' is voiced again and again, as musical expressions stress their connections to specific social communities or individual bodies in motion. Here is Papa Dee in 'The Real Thing' (on the album *Lettin' Off Steam*, 1990):

> One thing I can't take is a media hype
> You can fool some people but I'm not that type ...
> The real is real, a hype is a hype
> You shouldn't pick the fruit before it's ripe
>
> ... I'm a raggamuffin deuce and I don't mingle with fakes
> Give them the real thing!

This toaster returns to similar subjects of origin and authenticity mixed with self-construction and hybridity on his 'Ain't No Substitute' and 'Original Black Viking' (*One Step Ahead*, 1993), where he sings in a soul/pop-tradition as much as he raps or toasts. Another mixer of rap and pop is Neneh Cherry, here on 'Money and Love' (*Homebrew*, 1992):

When I look in the mirror I see a little clearer
I am what I am. And you, you too
Do you like what you see? Do you like yourself?

Money, love and gold payments
We spend our lives thinking they are saviours
Money talks but love is for real
And you know that …

So look into my eyes, I won't tell you lies.
Who do you see? Do you see yourself?
Do you like what you see? Do you like yourself?

Again, honesty is important – that the artist's voice can be trusted, that her or his style expresses a true identity. And authenticity is again combined rather than contrasted with reflexivity. Neneh Cherry here seems to make an explicit reference to a classical British punk hit by X-Ray Spex – 'Identity' (*Germ Free Adolescents*, 1978), where the relation between authenticity and reflexivity appears to be much more problematic:

Identity is the crisis, can't you see, identity identity

When you look in the mirror, do you see yourself?
Do you see yourself on the TV screen?
Do you see yourself in the magazine?
When you see yourself does it make you scream?

When you look in the mirror do you smash it quick?
Do you take the glass and slash your wrists?
Did you do it for fame, did you do it in a fit?
Did you do it before you read about it?

Do you see the similarities, and the differences? For punk in 1977, reflexivity was experienced as painful, and it still often is. But in pop-rap today it might be easier to accept that mediated self-definitions are inescapable and that authenticity need not be the opposite of technology, communication or style. There is no pure origin and subjectivity is a construction, but this construction still exists, and the fact that no statements can be given an eternally fixed naturalized legitimacy does not imply that no claims of authenticity can be made at all.

HOUSE/TECHNO

House music is often seen as part of the same camp as rap and hiphop music, and there are parallels in the sampling techniques, rhythmic beats and

8. Moore, *Rock: The Primary Text*, p60, mentions that house music is not accepted by its fans as rock, which I find supported by many interviews and articles from within this scene, while the rap/hiphop scene is much more ambiguous in this respect.

9. Many thanks to Anti and to Elisabeth Tegner, who is a specialist on rave culture and youth dance, and who gave me this tape for my 40th birthday in March 1992.

generational settings. But in many ways house/techno is musically and aesthetically much further removed from the conventional rock/pop-field.[8]

My example here is a long mix made by the Swedish DJ Anti from Gothenburg.[9] The music is on one uninterrupted tape of 2×60 minutes, that I will treat here as if it were an excerpt from an actual rave event. Anti has mixed a number of recent house and techno numbers in a special way, to produce a continuous stream of pulsating instrumental and synthesized sounds, where human voices are mostly used as pure instruments, for example the sampled female vocals 'a-a-a'. On rare occasions, words appear, as when a male voice says 'feel the drums'. Such comments have the same legacy within the rock and rap genres' invocation of community and bodily presence. Here it works functionally as a pedagogical instruction to the dancers, reminding me also for example, of the square dance tradition and its re-use in Malcolm McLaren's 'Buffalo Gals' (on *Duck Rock*, 1983). In relation to the music itself, it appears as de-illusioning distanciation, calling attention to the process of its making and use rather than to its 'textual' world. But in relation to this very use, the instructional exclamation rather reinforces a feeling of authenticity. The voice is not Anti's, nor probably does it belong to the authors of the recording used by Anti in that specific moment, but it steps out of the flow and can be experienced as a real call to our dancing bodies.

When this recording was made, Anti was 19 years old and considered to be the best rave organizer in Gothenburg. He first met house music in England back in 1989, and since then regularly goes back there to buy new records. He describes the music on this tape as 'Acid Hardcore': 'more American techno mixed with some English, not so much British hardcore with much hiphop-drums, but more American original techno – somewhat monotonous but as much as that hard stuff, instead, with melodies on top. Mental acid-influenced techno, so to speak.' All records used on the tape were released between August 1991 and February 1992.

Many stylistic traits have been imported from rock/pop. The strictly periodic forms, the steady beat, the general sound structures and the rhythmic or melodic fragments can be traced to various rock styles (and are, indeed, often sampled from rock and pop tunes). But here, the elements taken from quite other genres (samples from jazz, classical music, folk music etc) are not only temporary inflections of a general rock idiom.

This music is clearly primarily made for dancing to. Rock/pop as well as rap/toast usually have double uses: for listening and for dancing, with different layers and parameters functionally directed towards either of these uses. Techno might first seem to lack a voice in several important ways. Firstly, although human voices are sometimes present, they are treated more like synthesized sounds than as foregrounded subjects. The description by Anti confirms my impression that this is still more so in hardcore versions of techno, where 'melodies above' do hardly exist. The music appears to be mainly background, with clearly profiled figures (*Gestalten*) lacking. This implies a very different reception than in most other forms of popular music, but somewhat similar to pure background muzak or non-diegetic film music. Even earlier non-vocal dance music usually retains foregrounded melodic figures.

Secondly, although meaningful words are sometimes heard, lyrics are extremely reduced and seemingly non-essential. Human voices and melodic lines do sometimes appear, but very seldom do they carry verbal messages. This appears to reduce the presence of subjects in the music still further.

Thirdly, the voices heard are all sampled from other sources. None of the sounds on this recording present themselves as the 'voice' of Anti. He is a candid author, hidden behind a bricolage of borrowed recordings and noises. Dancing to this music, we do not feel the immediate presence of either a band or an individual artist. In rap/toast (and recently even in rock/pop), the sampling process is used in counterpoint to the present voices of the artist or group, who demonstrate their agency by stressing their subjective authenticity in relation to a context that is like a store of borrowed material. Here, we seem only to hear the background, the store.

All this is however not quite true: it cannot really be said that Anti's music has no author. He *is* its originator, its creator (with the help of both other people and machines). And there are identifiable authors of all the recordings he uses, even when they hide between secret names and obscure identities. Anti's montage of the 'voices' of others bears his stamp. Many rave dancers know that this is Anti's work, his expression. They appreciate and distinguish his tone and sound image from other's, through his beat patterns, sound choices, formal structuration and general taste. Even if many dancers might not at the dancing moment care who made the music, this question can always again be activated. The authenticity of the musical source might be de-emphasised in the listening moment, but it does not disappear completely. New discussions and new music-making can later re-activate the attention to the speaking voices even of this seemingly anonymous stream of sounds.

This music is thus not more devoid of speaking subjects than is a futurist collage, only its mode of organizing and expressing subjectivity differs from rock/pop. In rock/pop and rap/toast one can discuss the complicated relations between person and persona, artist and image, human being and aesthetic role, but here one cannot even imagine hearing *directly* the genuine natural voice of any expressive agent. That voice is however not absent – it only appears metaphorically or indirectly, through the actual sounds of others (machines and persons).

And, even more importantly, foregrounded figures are created by all the dancing listeners in the rave, whose movements may be compared to the voices of karaoke singers or the inner interpretations of all other listening subjects, filling in the holes in the music.

The lack of a group is finally also a differing characteristic here. In the production as well as the reception of this music, there seems only to be single individuals and a large mass. On the producing side, there is this hidden Anti and a collection of more or less anonymous sounds and voices. We do not experience a rock band, not even the backing ensemble of solo artists in pop, nor is there an explicit group of DJs and rappers that can be imagined delivering this wall of sound. And in the preferred reception context of a rave, ecstatic bodies fill the space, surrounded by ever-present sounds with no specific source except maybe a singular DJ (Anti himself or someone acting as his stand-in).

It *is* possible to develop a discourse around authenticity here too. Anti is authentic in that he knows these genres, he can conform to their rules, he fulfils the normative expectations of an interpretive community, he is no fake, and he expresses some sort of subjectivity through the quality and originality that he and his fans hear in his music's ability to move their bodies in coveted ways.

AVANT-GARDE/MONTAGE

The final example mixes the last two, rap and house. Some avant-garde montages use sampling for reasons other than to produce tools for dancing. Lucky People Center is a mysterious Swedish group that produced an intriguing record full of 'musified' excerpts from non-musical 'reality' – speeches, radio sounds, sermons, police calls, storytellings and animals are mixed with 'live' instrumental rhythms and voices of rappers and singers.

One example is 'Live in the World' (*Welcome to Lucky People Center*, 1993), where the CD-booklet explains:

> this song is dedicated to a gorilla named ivan who has been imprisoned for 24 years in a small room under the supermarket 'b&i' in tacoma, washington, ivan is heard in the song, banging the walls of his cage, also heard are ex president bush, ex secretary of the state baker, the moonies, father henry nouven & a rapper from nepal.

The lyrics of this song printed in the booklet are the words introducing it, presumably by father Henry Nouven (?): 'The very process of freeing ourselves forces us to learn more & more about ourselves & the world in which we live.' Then follows a musical web of rhythms filled with the other voices and noises. 'Rodney King' uses the voices of LA cops, George Bush and many others; 'Jesus' samples a young man on a mission from god and Korean sect with megaphones, both recorded on 42nd Street in New York: 'It's Still Cloudy in Saudi-Arabia' features Bush, Truman, Schwartzkopf and other voices from television and the streets.

The resulting music is again different. Here are real, discernible voices, perceived as singular subjects but entering into a constructed dialogue staged by the LPC. The voices focus the semantics of the words, and the authors use the borrowed voices partly to create a vibrant and exciting musical sound web (suitable for dancing), but also to express ideas through these collage of lyrics. The dialogue becomes interesting only because the voices are experienced as 'real' (if actors read the different statements, the thrill would diminish considerably). And there are real instruments played here too, so even if the musicians do not sing, we hear their bodies move, seemingly expressing strong subjectivities in response to the collected noises of the world. This corresponds well to the title and the printed lyrics of the song: to live in the world – and to be 'live'/genuine in one's life – it is necessary to know the world and oneself (reflexively).

ASPECTS OF AUTHENTICITY

It is tempting to make much closer and deeper analyses of all these examples and of the genre-fields in which they take part. But within this limited context, the purpose has only been to hint at how some supergenre-specific aspects of authenticity are related to reflexivity.

Rock/pop has always had an ambivalent relation to authenticity, accentuated in the rock discourse. On the one hand, there is a dominating rock ideology with roots in a romantic mythology that honours the spontaneous and self-combusting expressions of individual artists and believes in natural origins of unity and innocence as a basis of critique against the false everyday modern life.[10] On the other hand, there has always existed a sub-text of play and dissemblance, of posing in disguises and calculating artificiality. The same is true for late modern hiphop, that first can boast of being sophisticated, and in the next moment declare itself to be the 'real' thing with street credibility. Sampling can release the voices of persons or instruments from their original tradition-contexts and combine them with technologically produced sounds, but this does not erase the search for genuine expressions, it is only given new languages. Covers and quotations can be a superficial masquerade, but they are also a way to reflexively position oneself in certain historical contexts. The return to older styles in retro-rock, or what is in Sweden called *tönt-rock* (nerd-rock), can seek to express a deeply authentic new identity-instability and a wavering between distance and devotion.

Authenticity as a characteristic of musical works or genres concerns how the musical structures (the 'texts') are constructed, how they present themselves as related to living subjectivities. Communication of meaningful symbolic forms like music involves two categories of subjects – creators and appropriators – but both are active users and (re)constructors of meaning in 'texts'. Authenticity involves a special relation between texts and subjects. Through various markers, a combined musical, verbal and visual statement is made to present itself as honest and genuine, implying a continuity or homology between textual form (style and message) and subject position (intention and desire).

The *textual authenticity* implied by symbolic expressions signals, in the production, direction of a *source authenticity*, as a specific relation between text and author (singer, rapper, musician, composer, DJ and/or producer), between the expression and the subjectivity of an artist, namely that the 'statements' of the music-makers are in some way honestly meant. Much discussion is concerned with establishing the degree of honesty that artists show in their

10. The Rolling Stones, the Doors, the Clash and Bruce Springsteen are examples of artists that often are associated with this historical line.

music-making: if pieces of music are someone's honest expression. The textual authenticity in the opposite direction also invites what could be called a *reception authenticity*, as a relation between texts and users, the listeners' experiences of emotive involvement, affective presence and acceptance of the 'statements' of the music in question. This is sometimes more central to music discourses, if a piece of music is valued regarding its ability to move its current users, to give someone a full experience. These sides can diverge: sometimes a song that dresses up as authentic can be cynically produced and be seen through as such by its audience, an honest artist's intention might fail in the ears of a listener, or an explicitly artificially impersonal song can still carry an impression of authenticity from a conscious artist to a similarly well-informed fan.

In a way, all cultural products are authentic, as they express something of their creators and/or users. Even while singing something she finds distasteful and thinking of other things, a vocalist cannot avoid putting her personal stylistic marks into her voice. And as soon as someone listens and understands something of the style or content of a musical piece, he cannot avoid relating his subjectivity to the sounds. But authenticity is more than meaning-production, understanding or interpretation. It has to do with an explicit emphasis on such subject/text-relations, in discourses around cultural forms or within these forms themselves. It is a form of identifying discourse which is not always important, but that can always be re-emphasised in all its aspects and within all genres. Authenticity thus appears as an option and a construction rather than as a given fact, and as immediately linked to reflexivity.[11]

Lawrence Grossberg distinguishes between three other forms of authenticity.[12] The most common is associated with hard rock and folk rock, and builds on the romantic ideology of rock as a construction by and expression of a magically dense community. In more dance-oriented and black genres he finds another form, localizing authenticity in the construction of a rhythmical and sexual individual body. A third form appears in postmodernist self-conscious pop and avant-garde rock, that plays with styles, well understanding that the distinctions of rock are always artificially constructed; but this very self-knowledge, in all its cynicism, shows a kind of realistic honesty.

Let me propose a modification of this model, changing the concepts a little. The one closest to Grossberg's first form I prefer to name *social authenticity* since it uses criteria taken from the level of collective group interaction. Here genuinity is based on the norms that are legitimate within a certain (real or imagined) social community of musicians and/or listeners. The next form might be called *subjective authenticity*, since it focuses the relation between an individual performer and/or listener and her own mind and body, as a state of presence. Both social and subjective authenticity thus stress either source or reception authenticity, with textual authenticity as a silent presumption. The third form could be defined as *cultural or meta-authenticity*, since it moves within (and derives legitimacy from) the level of the symbolic expressions ('texts') themselves. It is therefore here that textual authenticity itself is focused: the well-formedness of cultural works related to historically determined aesthetic

11. While authorship might sometimes be irrelevant or problematic, I do not agree with Michel Foucault or Roland Barthes that this means that the (issue of the) author is definitely dead. The same is valid for the relation of authenticity between text and reader (music and listener).

12. Lawrence Grossberg, The Media Economy of Rock Culture Cinema, Postmodernity and Authenticity in Simon Frith, Andrew Goodwin and Lawrence Grossberg (eds), *Sound and Vision: The Music Video Reader*, Routledge, London 1993, p202f.

genre rules. This third form is like a secondary or indirect authenticity mark, which is strongest when it works through (because of, rather than in spite of) obviously lacking social and/or subjective authenticity. The more plastic the music is, the more convincing would a shown meta-reflexivity of the musicians be of their honesty and consciousness.[13]

This last type has become more and more important in late modern popular music, not least so in rock/pop, rap/toast and house/techno. The two first forms have not been eroded, but an increased demand for reflexivity has forced older and more naive conceptions of authenticity to develop meta-authentic traits. It seems increasingly difficult to forget all intermediary links of social and cultural constructions between subjects and texts, between human feelings and stylistic manifestations. It is now hard to avoid seeing that social and subjective authenticity is also, so to speak, filtered through cultural authenticity. Artists and audiences can continue to strive for experiences of spontaneous community or bodily presence, but in late modernity it is almost impossible any more to repress the insight that this takes place through a complicated play of gestures, signs and strategies. Actually, unlike in earlier times, one now has the best chance to attain social and subjective authenticity if the symbolic contexts are made conscious. Modernization has irreversibly made reflexivity an inescapable condition of all cultural activities. It is through reflexivity that authenticity becomes a possible issue, and reflexivity is only interesting if the mirror shows something that can be recognized as 'I' or 'we'.

All three forms can be found in both conservative and progressive variants. The striving for community in social authenticity can long regressively for a pre-modern local deep-rootedness, but it can also be an effort to produce a late modern collectivity of choice (as in the rave-party where everyone mingles for one night). The striving for individual bodily presence in subjective authenticity can take the form of an anti-intellectual biologism that avoids all reflexivity in a mythologizing return to pure nature, or it can enjoy the heterological interplay of body and language in the praxis of dance or stylization. The striving for reflexive self-consciousness in cultural authenticity can be locked up in an authoritarian submission to the burden of convention, in a regressive obedience to traditions where music has to follow pre-determined rules. But it can also show up as a free play with newly created self-presentations that borrow historical references and reconstruct genealogical trees to subvert established power relations and search for roots as a defence against oblivion.

These conceptual tools are an invitation to trace similarities and differences between my four examples and genre-fields. Authenticity is constructed by listeners that experience musical works as pointing back towards their origins and endings in creative human agents. As Moore argues, it is a mystifying ideology to believe that these threads go back to an absolute origin, a natural, unmediated and uniform point of creation and immediate presence outside of history and sociality.[14] There is no such place. All subjects are temporally and spatially situated within history and society. All identities are necessarily

13. This argument is somewhat similar to how Ricoeur discusses deep understanding of texts to pass through a negation of the first, spontaneous surface understanding. Hermeneutical interpretation starts with a simple, primary meaning structure, proceeds through reconstructive work that uses explanatory methods that dissolve this close immediacy (comparable here to social/subjective authenticity) with the purpose to arrive at a depth semantics (cf. secondary cultural/ meta-authenticity). See Paul Ricoeur, *Hermeneutics and the Human Sciences: Essays on Language, Action and Interpretation*, Cambridge University Press, 1981.

14. Moore, *Rock: The Primary Text*, pp64, 139.

poly-dimensional, crucially split. They can never be cleared of either hybridity or unconscious levels. But these reservations do not make the issue of authenticity superfluous, as is suggested by its recurrent emergence in all the new genre fields discussed above.

Authenticity has many forms. Textual, source and reception authenticity are mostly interacting, but social, subjective and cultural authenticity refer to three different attitudes that can be held separately. The productive tension between authenticity and reflexivity seems to be a condition no-one can escape in late modernity. It can only be dealt with differently. Some people and genres stress absolute devotion, others stress conscious reflection, but no effective musical activity is in fact possible without a measure of both these sides. We find in the most extreme techno a strange mixture of total ego-oblivion in collective ecstasy (subjective reception authenticity) and calculated plays with mirrored identities (cultural textual authenticity), that parallels the different mixture of stage-diving and phoney speculation within grunge rock.

In interactive media forms like karaoke, this mixture takes new forms again, as people can listen to their own voices while diving into both the empty spaces in the pre-recorded music and the positions held open for them among their cheering friends.

ASPECTS OF REFLEXIVITY

In this context, reflexivity is understood as a mirroring of identities through cultural discourses, meaningful texts, sounds and/or images. It exists both for individuals and for collective groups, subcultures and social categories. This mirroring can be a conscious verbal and intellectual reflection, but is more often a very bodily and non-conceptual praxis using real mirrors, stylistic signs or other people as tools for defining and confirming oneself. Mass media are increasingly important to this praxis, and it would be valuable to develop further a theory of how music is used to this end. Reflexivity can be practised through lyrics as well as musical structures, and through externalized visual images as well as social interaction. In fact, self-mirroring always uses other people as well as cultural symbols, even though one of these *relational* and *symbolic* sides may sometimes be more apparent than the other.

Reflexivity concerns ideals as well as reality. In the choice of genres to play in or listen to, people mirror and confirm their identities, through various perceived homologies between these identities and some musical, lyrical and visual aspects of the music. This choice seems to have become more and more conscious and debated in late modernity, through a cultural release from naturalizing traditions and a growth in the stock of available stylistic tools. Karaoke and rap alike offer subjects opportunities to express their subjective or social ideals to others around, in a way that also works as a mirror that lets them externalize and work with these ideals in new ways, increasing the potential for authenticity. In the playing or active interpretation of pop or toast, or in the dancing to rock or house music, people also confirm themselves as human subjects and as social agents. Observing one's own movements on video, in mirrors or as reflected by fellow dancers, or listening to one's own voice, one's subjectivity or community is reinforced, which again increases one's ability to develop and thematize authenticity.

Just as authenticity might be grounded (legitimized) in three principal ways, reflexivity can also point in at least three different directions. *Social reflexivity* defines one's identity in terms of social groups, communities or categories, for example, in terms of class or ethnicity. Here, reflexive use of musical genres anchors them and by identification oneself in social collectives. *Subjective reflexivity* defines identities in terms of individual development through life stages. In this form, music is used to mirror more or less unique personal experiences through memories and various encodings of affective states. *Cultural reflexivity* is, finally, when certain musics are related to and identified with other symbolic texts, like musical, visual or literary styles and genres. There is a high degree of such aesthetic reflexivity involved in many late modern popular genres.

Many examples of these processes emerged in a study of three rock bands that I carried out some years ago. First, I found that the teenage amateur band and peer group that I investigated was very consciously working with their individual and group identities, often thinking of who they were, had been and were to become. Then, we let our informants read our first book about them and found a very complex set of reflexive mechanisms and attitudes from them towards our images of them. Some of them accepted and used our concepts and descriptions actively in their later self-thematizing, while others rejected and defended themselves against our definitions of their identities.[15] Two years after this second study was published, the complicated play with mirroring identities through us and our texts got yet a new twist, as one former band member suddenly phoned me. He had been the guitarist and main composer of the band, but now he worked at a private local radio station, playing music and making interviews on his own programme. He then made a live broadcast interview with me about our research project, why young people play rock and how it affects identity work in adolescence. He even let me tell the listeners about the teenagers we studied – including himself (which he however didn't mention on the air). Here, the reflexivity process continues several turns, without ever losing contact with a dimension of authenticity.

Neither authenticity nor reflexivity must however be seen only as positive values. There can be good reasons not to be so authentic/reflexive all the time, namely to hold back the demands for honesty and self-observation. In some spaces and occasions it can be good to find relief from these pressing demands – to sing out or play a role game without having to stand for the result, and/or without listening to one's own voice. But this cannot be done any more entirely or for long – it will soon again be necessary and attractive to relate the created sounds to one's subjectivity and reflect upon what was done.

Most theorists agree that late modern culture is increasingly reflexive, filled with demands and opportunities for self-mirroring and symbolic self-definition.

15. The original project is summarized in Fornäs *et al*, 'Under the Surface of Rock – Youth Culture and Late Modernity' is in *Popular Music and Society*, Volume 14, Number 3, 1990, pp1-25.

Sometimes this is interpreted as an irreversible loss of all authentic subjectivity. If the genuine voice is understood as something originally given, natural and spontaneous, then certainly all efforts to actively reconstruct it or reflect (upon) it can be felt as irreparable degradings.

I think, however, that this is a mistaken conclusion. In fact, reflexivity is not possible without a certain amount of authenticity. If you hide behind a 'false' voice, it is not *your* voice that you hear. And even if we accept that voices and subjects are in a continuous process of development, interfering with other subjects and voices, with the external world and with a range of symbolic systems, we need not abandon this constructed 'subject-in-process' as an illusion.[16]

16. The concept of 'subject-in-process' has been developed by Julia Kristeva.

CONCLUSIONS

To sum this up, five points can be emphasized.

1. The concepts of *authenticity and reflexivity* have been criticized but not outdated by late modern cultural theory. Certainly there are problematic and mystifying ways to use them, not least in discourses around popular music, but they *can be used* in other and less essentialist ways as well. I agree with many other critics that the old tradition of romantic rock-ideology is today luckily in decline. But instead of throwing away the concept of authenticity, I propose that we rethink it, and within all genres. Authenticity does not have to be defined as naturalness or as related to any absolute and autonomous origin, but can instead fruitfully refer to a specifically constructed relation between subjects and cultural expressions (texts, music works, genres and styles). Reflexivity need not be restricted only to intellectual reflections nor imply any total self-transparency, but may indicate any symbolically mediated reference to one's own (collective/social or individual/subjective) identity. These two key concepts have here been used and tested in relation to some illustrative examples from the four genre-fields of rock/pop, rap/toast, house/techno and avant-garde/montage.

2. There is always a very *close interaction between the authentic and the reflexive*. Even though reflexivity might be felt as inducing artificiality, it can in fact rather be shown to be intimately connected to authenticity.

3. Authenticity is a *textual* phenomenon that has *a source and a reception side*, pointing respectively to the artists and the listeners. It can appear as *social, subjective or cultural authenticity*, depending on whether it is legitimated by reference to the norms of a community, to the individual body or to the codes of a genre.

4. Reflexivity has *a relational and a symbolic side*, since it always uses other people as well as various media and/or aesthetic forms (music, words, images). It can appear as *social, subjective or cultural reflexivity*, depending on whether it relates identities to collective communities, individual histories or stylistic genres.

In *rock/pop*, authenticity is much discussed as a means to differentiate between genres, but turns up again in every subgenre too. *Rap/toast* is full of exaggerated claims of authenticity as well as extreme quests for self-definitions. In *house/techno*, strong attacks are launched against certain forms of the presence of an artistic voice, but social and subjective authenticity then reappear in new forms, for instance as secondary expressivity in montage forms or as direct appeals to dancing bodies. In *avant-garde/montage* experiments finally, similar intriguing mixtures can be found, again proving the continuing importance of my two main concepts.

Therefore my fifth and last conclusion is that it seems to me that the increasing reflexivity of late modern life and popular music does not erode authenticity – it only changes its forms. Authenticity today can not be achieved without reflexivity, nor can it be defined as a given entity. There are different types and aspects of authenticity, variously emphasised in different phases, genres and contexts, but the possibility of thematizing authenticity has certainly not disappeared or become just an ideological illusion. It is not always interesting to ask for truthfulness (towards authors, users or generic codes), but it remains possible to reactivate such discourses, through the increasingly complex reflexive prism of differentiated meta-narratives through which we live.

To listen to your voice is to be reflexive, if (and only if) you are in some way authentic, so that the style of your voice expresses your identity, reaches down to your 'heart' (metaphorically speaking). This is a strong urge for individuals and groups in late modernity, and it is a never-ending process. Or as the Swedish pop group Roxette have put it in 'Listen to Your Heart' (*Look Sharp!*, 1988): '… there are voices that want to be heard. So much to mention but you can't find the words.' Still, we can never again permanently escape the desire to search for words to understand music and to define ourselves.

C.L.R. JAMES IN AMERICA

Bill Schwarz

C.L.R. James, *American Civilization*, Anna Grimshaw and Keith Hart (eds), Blackwell, 1993, pp385, £37.50 cloth, £12.99 paperback.

In April 1965, temporarily freed from house arrest, C.L.R. James delivered a lecture on Wilson Harris at the University of the West Indies at St. Augustine, Trinidad. He began: 'I would be very much surprised if, except in a private home, there was a copy of Heidegger's *Being and Time* in the West Indies', and then went on to develop a 'philosophical' interpretation of Wilson Harris, linking the novels to Heidegger's concept of *Dasein* which James, in his inimitably colloquial fashion, elaborated in terms of 'being there', 'every-dayness' and 'authenticity'. Having demonstrated the connections he closed by saying:

> European civilization for many centuries had a fixed assumption and classification of material achievement and corresponding philosophical conceptions. Harris says that America is not like that. He insists that America is not like that, the West Indies are not like that. They have a different attitude to the world; because their whole historical and material experience has been different. But Heidegger, in my opinion, and Jaspers and Sartre, are aware that the European preoccupation or acceptance of the material basis of life, a fixed assumption – that has broken down. That is the significance of Heidegger, Jaspers and Sartre. It began to break down with Nietzsche who said that God was dead and, as Dostoevsky added, if God is dead then everything is permitted: people, especially people with authority, do anything. The whole European conception of a fixed material assumption of things and a fixed political and philosophical assumption of things – that has broken down. Harris is saying that in the Americas, in Central America and in the West Indies, that has never been. There has never been that fixed assumption of things, that belief in something that is many centuries old and solid. That is why he is saying what I interpret as the *Dasein*, the 'being there'. I find it profoundly important and viable especially for people who live in these territories.[1]

1. C.L.R. James, *Wilson Harris: A philosophical approach*, University of the West Indies, St. Augustine, Trinidad 1965, pp4 and 15.

This carries James's characteristic self-assurance. We can hear the old political militant talking, the self-taught philosopher explaining the higher abstractions to the masses. Yet for all the corners cut it presents a compelling argument, suggesting that the lived historical realities of the Americas – in some unspecified manner – have superseded the philosophical abstractions of old

Europe, and have forced into being a new epistemology, more grounded both in popular life and in the practices of everyday existence. As he had argued some seven years earlier: 'Philosophy as such has come to an end'.[2]

Such reasoning has a recognizable theoretical pedigree; it also has, in formal epistemological terms, little going for it. But James was anything but a formal philosopher. Rather it was in his sense of the historical movements of cultures and their formations that he was most astute: and consistently he is striking in charting the deepening popular dynamic at the heart of twentieth-century culture. There is a weak way of putting such arguments, itemizing the enlarged sphere of popular participation – in the mass media, in leisure – in modern societies. Or there is the more difficult, more complex task of attempting to grasp how the underlying symbolic structures of our times are in the process of re-forming, which requires us permanently to shift the key conceptual terms of the debate. To take this approach is to incline towards one reading of the postmodern – where Cornel West meets Homi Bhabha – in which a range of hitherto repressed Others articulate new voices, which in turn serves to break up the terrain of the old formations. Or to follow Stuart Hall:

> Even if postmodernism is not a new cultural epoch, but only modernism in the streets, that, in itself, represents an important shifting of the terrain of culture toward the popular – toward popular practices, toward everyday practices, toward local narratives, toward the decentring of old hierarchies and the grand narratives.[3]

Put like this, there seems a clear lineage between James and the cutting edge of contemporary cultural theory: even more so when we consider the frequency with which he is recruited into the ranks of postcolonial theory. There's an obvious truth here: after all, it's difficult to think of anyone of his generation more self-consciously 'postcolonial'. But as with Fanon, there's something too easy about this fit. Slipping him into the emergent canon and chanting the mantra does little to settle the case of James.

But there is another matter raised in the lecture on Wilson Harris. James identified a specific location where the 'fixed political and philosophical' assumptions of Europe had in reality already 'broken down': America. Or more accurately the spatial location is given various specifications: America, the West Indies, the Americas, Central America.

This too echoes arguments in contemporary discussion, particularly the idea that the cultures of modernity formed on the peripheries of the global system – in the backlands – embody within them a deconstructive momentum which anticipates and mirrors the more knowing, formal postmodern procedures of the metropolis. Such beliefs rest on a notion that the peripheries never quite underwent a proper schooling in the disciplines of a modernizing, instrumental reason. From the vantage of the State Department this can be given a normative rendering, as in Henry Kissinger's conviction that the developing world has yet to experience the benefits of a Newtonian revolution,

2. C.L.R. James, Grace C. Lee and Pierre Chaulieu, *Facing Reality*, Bewick, Detroit 1974, p65. Pierre Chaulieu is better known as Cornelius Castoriadis.

3. Stuart Hall, 'What is this "black" in black popular culture?' in Michelle Wallace and Gina Dent (eds), *Black Popular Culture*, Bay Press, Seattle 1992, pp22-3.

and thereby bears the additional burdens of epistemological underdevelopment. Or from an alternative perspective, it can be valorized as a positive escape from the unwelcome incubus of western precedents. In the 1930s a number of otherwise differing intellectuals from the metropolitan nations looked out to the undeveloped world, especially to the cultural zone where the Caribbean met and connected with Latin America, and identified an entire range of cultural forms – their links to the legacies of primitive communism still intact – which in the metropolitan purview were deemed more magical, more indigenous and more authentic than the reified, broken cultures of the imperial centres.

Even though his first historical researches on the Caribbean date from this period James never succumbed to these easy polarized essentialisms. Nor was he ever mesmerized by the magic of backwardness: to read of him in the late 1950s – whilst launching the paper of the People's National Movement in Trinidad – grubbing through junk-heaps in order to find type-face, letter by letter, is telling enough, as indeed is his reflection on the absence of books in the underdeveloped world – no Heidegger in the Caribbean. More significantly he was never convinced that the Caribbean represented a pure cultural antidote to the west, of either indigenous or African hue. To the contrary, from the time of *The Black Jacobins* on, he insisted that the contemporary Caribbean had been born in the interstices of modern industry, and that its peculiar features rested above all in its combination of backwardness and modernity. This is a constant theme. The West Indies, he claimed, have no 'indigenous civilization and culture'; they are located inside the structures of western modernity; and yet the legacies of national backwardness, 'the very limitations of the past' might still 'enable us to go further'.[4] The structure of thought here is not one which pitches a magical *indigenismo* against western reason. Its origins are more mundane: the historical thought of Lenin, and Trotsky's illuminating if halting discussion of combined and uneven development, in which he makes it possible to conceive in the mind of extraordinary historical leaps – the apparently most backward formations exhibiting the potential for creating a striking new modernity.

This is fine as far as it goes but there is an obvious problem. James identified not only the periphery as the embodiment of *Dasein* but the whole of the western hemisphere. For a marxist happy to spend the bulk of his political life as an outrider on the left extremities of the international communist movement his inclusion of the US represents a provocation. We need to see how this happens.

There is an English view of James which turns on the relationship between metropolis and colony. It begins with James's birth in the distant reaches of the empire, in Tunapuna in Trinidad in 1901. The colonial schooling, and cricket, prove decisive. The arrival in Lancashire in 1932, and immersion in the politics of Pan-Africanism, fit centrally within this scheme of things. There then appears a long caesura when, to English ears, James's voice goes quiet. It revives again with his return to England in 1953, his re-engagement with

4. C.L.R. James, *Party Politics in the West Indies*, Vedic, San Juan, Trinidad 1962, p40.

Caribbean politics in the late 1950s and 1960s, and his final triumphal incarnation as the wise old man of Brixton for another twenty years after that. It's a construction of James which privileges *The Black Jacobins* of 1938 and *Beyond a Boundary* of 1963, the lineages between the two direct and immediate.

This is a persuasive reading. It recognizes the tensions of England as an imagined community; and it centres the colonial, external dynamic. The intellectual traffic across the old empires clearly possesses a prodigious unwritten history, and James represents one moment in this larger story. In my own mind I've always thought of James in this context in parallel with Gramsci: close enough in birth to be of the same generation, moving by virtue of the structures of colonial education from periphery to centre — Gramsci an impoverished Sard nationalist, James a luminary in the largely unknown, tiny Trinidadian literary renaissance — and then, when abruptly confronted by the internal culture of the metropolis, each moving to marxism: Gramsci to the Socialist Party and thence the Third International, James to Trotskyism. In each case it is precisely the overdetermined complex set of confrontations between the new and the old, the mass and the folk, colonizer and colonized which proved so charged, unleashing for each of them within the frame of a newly acquired marxism a profound, unending interrogation of the 'home' culture and its modernity to which each had migrated.

But there is a puzzling aspect to this too. In 1937 James published *World Revolution*, a vast, epic, scorchingly critical history of the official Communist movement. If we think of James as historian, it stands alongside the two histories he published the following year: *Black Jacobins* and *The History of Negro Revolt*. Often it is ignored because of its allegiances to Trotskyism. But James wrote it; arguably it's his first serious history book; and from the mid-1930s, for some fifteen years, Trotskyism was large in James' imagination. The question then becomes this: how did he move from the conventional orthodoxies of his Trotskyism to the extraordinarily unorthodox cultural criticism of *Beyond a Boundary* twenty-five years later? This supposes, against many of his admirers, that there is no simple evolution from *Black Jacobins* to *Beyond a Boundary*, the one immanent in the other, or from James' Trotskyism to the enticing cultural thought which followed.

Of course, to put it like this takes too much for granted. Those who can divine such things spot tell-tale signs in the text of *World Revolution* which reveal that the author's credo was wobbling even at the height of his commitment to an orthodox reading of Trotskyism. Nor is it feasible to suggest that the theoretical structure of *Black Jacobins* and *Negro Revolt* exactly duplicates the more conventional structure of *World Revolution*. More to the point it is clear that there were other passions which pulled James in different directions. There was, after 1935 especially, the cause of Africa and his heterodox sympathy for Garveyism. There was cricket and his professional life as a sports-writer. And there was James the artist, a presence in the outer circles of Bloomsbury, the author of a well-received novel, of the play of the *Black Jacobins* which had starred Paul Robeson, an aesthete with radically distinctive aesthetic tastes. In the 1920s, while still in Trinidad, he listened on his gramophone to Mozart, Debussy and calypso, an impossibly hybrid conjunction within the norms of the metropolitan culture. Nor was he immune to the aesthetic and other pleasures of the good life. Fredric Warburg, the publisher of *World Revolution*, remembered him like this: 'Immensely amiable, he loved the flesh-pots of capitalism, fine cooking, fine clothes, fine furniture and beautiful women, without a trace of the guilty remorse to be expected from a seasoned warrior of the class war'.[5] Even James at his most orthodox was a figure who cut a dash.

5. Paul Buhle, *C.L.R. James: The artist as revolutionary*, Verso, London 1993, p63.

Even so, the problem is I think a real one. Its solution can be summarized in a word: America. James' period in the USA actively reordered his intellectual cosmos and, in an oblique move, gave him the means to integrate insights drawn from his own West Indian culture into his larger politics. Those aspects of James' intellect which previously had found separate outlets and which functioned as if by separate logics – cricket and marxism; aesthetics and politics; calypso and Mozart; the personal and the political; popular culture and intellectual culture – were able to find a new synthesis. There are suggestions too – from other contemporary observers – that James came more intensely to experience himself as black, the persona of the gentlemanly English aesthete relaxing. The intellectual work which made this happen was arduous, and often beyond conceptual resolution. But in all, this work – largely unknown to English audiences – pretty much resembles a protracted political and epistemological *coupure*. Or to put this in less rigorous mode, in the USA he discovered one America which brought home to him another America which historically was his: the Caribbean.

When the 1938 cricket season closed James embarked to the USA believing that he'd be back in England the following spring in time for the new season. In the event, he stayed until 1953 and even then left only under duress, at the insistence of the immigration authorities. He went originally at the behest of James Cannon and the US Socialist Workers Party – although some suspect this was a manoeuvre to 'straighten him out'.[6] In the US his existence as a Trotskyist tyro continued. Audiences loved him: they found him charismatic, charming, erotic. He travelled, spoke and wrote: with one exception all his published writings appeared under the imprint of far-left organizations, dictated by the immediate concerns of political debate. In April 1939, instead of preparing for the opening of the new cricket season, he found himself in Coyoacan in discussion with Trotsky, disagreeing in equal measure about both sport and the role of blacks in the revolutionary struggle. He was active at various moments in the cultural and political life of Harlem. He debated Hegel with Adorno in cafes around the New School on Fifth Avenue. He fell in love (more than once), married and had a son: in order for the marriage to take place he needed to divorce his first wife, which took him to Reno – a break which gave him the opportunity to draft his *Notes on Dialectics*, a nice irony of history this. Often money was short; he was ill; towards the end the Immigration and Naturalization Service and the FBI were closing in. And he went to the movies:

6. C.L.R. James, *World Revolution, 1917-36: The rise and fall of the Communist International*, Humanities Press, New Jersey 1993, pxv.

During the last years, illness and other difficulties have caused me to spend a certain amount of time at the pictures. I rather despised them – Hollywood, I mean. I don't any more. The rubbish I look at would astonish you. I can sit through almost anything. When it is very bad I see why it is bad. I have seen *Now Voyager* six times and will see it, if necessary, six times more. The reason? I work at home. At times I must stop. The only thing that keeps me quiet is the movies. So at all hours of the day or night I go where there is a picture, often the nearest. That is why I see some over and over again. I am learning plenty, I can assure you.[7]

7. C.L.R. James, *The C.L.R. James Reader*, Anna Grimshaw (ed), Blackwell, Oxford 1992, pp128-9.

Now Voyager, for those who may not recall, dealt with psychoanalysis and doomed love affairs; it starred Bette Davis [in mink] and Claude Rains. The characteristics of a high-cultural Englishness, James' ticket from Trinidad to England, were slowly breaking up. Or in different register, *Vanity Fair* was giving way to *Moby Dick*. When eventually he returned to England he wrote to friends in New York: 'It is most remarkable, but at the present moment the feeling that I have and the memory of life in the United States are expressed most concretely in gramophone records, jazz records in particular, and movies'.[8]

8. C.L.R. James, *American Civilization*, Anna Grimshaw and Keith Hart (eds), Blackwell, Oxford 1993, p17.

It would be possible to trace the mutations in James' thought through a reconstruction of his political activities: speaking in the same idiom and ostensibly remaining faithful to the same principles, he and his group – the fiery, cocksure, theoretical conquistadors of the Johnson-Forest Tendency – moved from the mainstream of Trotskyism in 1940 to an anti-Trotskyist, anti-vanguardism a decade later, ditching on the way much of Leninism, and preparing themselves to make common cause with the utopian libertarianism of Castoriadis and the group around Socialism or Barbarism. It's an important story, still largely untold, which bears directly on James' reconceptualization of the popular in the cultural formations of the mid twentieth century.

Yet it's also clear that his inherited framework of marxism, even with an increasingly diluted quotient of Leninism, was unable to offer the conceptual space he needed to explore the issues he found most perplexing. Where we can see him working through these issues, inventing what he needs as he goes from whatever was to hand, is in the text which is now published as *American Civilization*. It is a dramatic work, James' mind visibly racing ahead of his writing. It was drafted, at the end of 1949 and the beginning of 1950, at his usual ferocious pace. He wrote it for private circulation, for a small number of trusted friends and comrades. He saw it neither as outline nor abridgement: it is, more aptly, James' *Grundrisse*. The next step – which predictably perhaps never occurred – was clear. In James' words: 'The whole will be put together in one closely interconnected logical and historical exposition for the average reader, in 75,000 words, not a word more, and written so that it can be read on a Sunday or on two evenings'.

James, grisled old Bolshevik and black militant, didn't need lessons on the reactionary nature of the USA and the intensity of its systems of exploitation.

He had seen enough with his own eyes, and knew enough of Adorno and Horkheimer, to have a realistic grasp of the totalitarian potential of Americanized mass society in the opening moment of the Cold War. But in an acrobatic move, in which a renewed interest in Hegel allowed him to think his way out of Trotskyism, he arrived at the opinion that the most reactionary sector of the imperial heartlands – the USA – carried with it the possibilities for a leap into a future organized on the deepest democratization of social life. Clearly, elements of Marx and Trotsky continued in the newer theorizations: the debt to the notion of combined and uneven historical times is evident. But in arguing that the structures of the future society existed in the intersections of everyday life and the institutions of mass culture, James was at the very least calling for a necessary expansion of conventional marxist models, and maximally for a different mode of theorization altogether.

The manuscript ranges over many issues in an accelerated rhythm – until the end when it looks very much as if exhaustion set in. Individualism, intellectuals [Whitman, Melville, the abolitionists], Fordism, popular arts, happiness, with a final section on the contemporary predicaments of 'Negroes, Women and Intellectuals' – these compose the formal subject-matter, with the chapter on popular arts serving as the the thematic climax of the argument. In part I must admit the excitement of the book is historical rather than conceptual: given the contemporary overload of cultural studies James' discussion of soap operas and stars, domesticity and department stores, *True Confessions* and sexual relations doesn't immediately strike one today as daring. But that he was thinking through these issues some fifty years ago is extraordinary; it's also intriguing that a marxist of his generation was writing seriously about Bette Davis and Garbo, Cary Grant and Frank Sinatra – an impossibility in the milieu of English marxism at the time. But the manuscript is significant not only as a historical find. James never assembled the argument as planned. There were many reasons for this but one of them must be internal to the project itself: it simply wasn't possible for him to order and close his whole thesis in the manner he imagined. In my own view this is because what he uncovered could not easily be contained within the theoretical system of a totalizing marxism and Hegelianism. It was precisely the fact of a modernity in minor key that he was discovering, a modernity of the street and the home rather than of the public manifesto and the magazine, a modernity rooted in the unassuming local narratives of the everyday. Everything he discovered threatened to undermine the unity of his own theoretical suppositions. At the risk of seriously conflating what he says we need to see the bare bones of his argument, sticking only to what he has to say about mass culture.

James' premise lies in his recognition that the structure of American civilization is composed on the one hand by the imperatives of 1776 and the cult of individualism; and on the other, by Fordism and the system of mass production. The crux of his argument is the suggestion that these have now become indistinguishable: happiness has become entirely dependent on mass consumption and thus on mass production. He treats very seriously the traditions of individualism, refusing to see in them an empty rhetoric appropriate only for ventriloquist politicians. Like many Europeans before him [on arrival in the States James liked to call himself a 'black European'] he was impressed by 'the exceptional capacity for free association' characteristic of social life in America, a characteristic he found particularly pronounced in black cultures. These social instincts, grounded in the organization of a highly developed civil society, gave a true vitality to the traditions of individualism. The implication throughout is that in an age of deepening bureaucratic collectivism the revitalization of lived individualist tradition held the promise of augmenting the mainsprings of a popular radicalism.

Working against this was the mechanization of everyday life, a familiar enough theme in a wide range of literature. James offers many pages on the intensification of the labour process, extending his analysis to new forms of domesticity and housing, family life and sexual relations. 'Simply sitting in the park and watching the harried faces and manners of young married women' was enough to convince him of the depths of this social transformation. This critique of all the apparent freedoms proffered by American society – of apartments which turned out to be prisons; of modern, hygienic and Taylorized housewifery which induced silent howls of pain – was intransigent. James was not alone in formulating such a view of the realities of the postwar American dream, although he was amongst the earliest. Where he differed from many such critiques was in his refusal to espouse a commensurate impossibilist denunciation of America *tout court*, in which the only viable politics turned out to be driven by self-destructive fantasies of annihilation.

On the marxisant left the conventional step in the argument at this point would be to extend the indictment to mass culture as another manifestation, and prime cause, of the reification of social life. Quite simply, James turns this on its head: it is within mass culture, he believes, that the modest utopianism of a lost individualism is evident and where most is to be gained. 'The passionate individualistic American temperament that Melville knew so well and saw only as a danger to the organizers of society, is now stirring in tens of millions of individuals, the masses of the people, thwarted in their daily lives, hemmed in on all sides.' Mass culture, he claimed, represented not the suppression of these forces – it was neither false, reified nor escapist – but their expression; in the popular forms of commercial culture could be found a profound response to these inchoate instincts, 'dealing with the most elementary symbols and relating them to very complicated social structures'. Thus on soaps he wrote: 'these serials, ridiculous as they are, mean more than mere idle passing-the-time to the women who listen, overburdened with domestic work, the care of children, illnesses. They should be listened to and examined in the light of the fact that art has now assumed a very intimate relation to the daily lives of the great masses of the people'. It could be said that his objective in *American Civilization* was to uncover and make sense of 'the elementary symbols' of modern America; to see how they worked; and to explore how they could be transformed.

In more empirical mode, his discussion of the cultural formations of modernity parallels Benjamin on mechanical reproduction. Mass culture, James suggests, collapses the distinctions between art and culture, artists and people, and provides the possibility for imagining and bringing about a new universality. No longer are the inheritors of Whitman and Melville to be found in the modern intellectuals, philosophers and artists – for whom he has not one good word, the existentialists in particular incurring his wrath – but in the myriad forms of anonymous popular culture: 'in modern popular art, film, radio, television, comic strip, we are headed for some such artistic comprehensive integration of modern life, that the spiritual, intellectual, ideological life of modern peoples will express itself in the closest and most rapid, most complex, absolutely free relation to the actual life of the citizens tomorrow'. At which point, in a knight's move of characteristic ingenuity, James' historical imagination moves into overdrive: 'During the last thirty years *mass production* has created a vast populace, literate, technically trained, conscious of itself and of its inherent right to enjoy all the possibilities of the society to the extent of its means. No such social force has existed in any society with such ideas and aspirations since the citizens of Athens and the farmers around trooped into the city to see the plays of Euripides, Sophocles, and Aeschylus and decide on the prize-winners by their votes'. Such a futurist recovery of the past, for James, existed in the present realities of capitalist modernity.

Or not quite. His is no blithe, reflex utopianism. In all this he did not ignore the crazed, pathological dimensions of American mass culture. Time and again he refers to 'the bitterness, hate, fear and sadism which simmer just below the surface', 'the representation of murder, violence, atrocity, evil'. Here a more conventional, empirical suggestion appears. For James 1929 marked a decisive break. The great promise of American modernity, glimpsed in the early decades of the century, faltered after the Depression, turning in on itself, its utopian elements giving way ever more frequently to its opposite – to anxiety, fear and sadism. (He notes two exceptions: the Marx brothers, and – in the creation of Donald Duck – Walt Disney.) This way of thinking reflects one of his central propositions. What made American civilization unique for James was its simultaneous capacity for the expansion of subjective life – the struggle for happiness, in his terms – and, in the same moment, for its exploitation, manifest in ever more disturbed and psychotic forms. The rest, to determine which would predominate, was politics.

To summarize in this way represents a terrible reduction of James' reasoning – more often than not the insights appear in passing, and as I've suggested there are great difficulties in elaborating a finished theoretical argument from investigation of this kind. But the qualitative shift in his outlook should be clear. And so too James' insistence that Americanized mass culture carried the promise of transcending the fixed cognitive categories inherited from the abstractions of European thought. As James said of Ahab: 'He lives entirely in abstractions'.[9] He was trying to imagine the potential for a

9. C.L.R. James, *Mariners, Renegades and Castaways: the story of Herman Melville and the world we live in*, Bewick, Detroit 1978, p17.

new universalism which *began* with the popular and the everyday, in which a new integration of human life might come about. That he anticipated the current preoccupations of much postmodern theory by an insistent return to Hegel is only one of the ironies.

James' public, political writings articulate one voice. The voice in *American Civilization* is connected but very different: it's just as subversive, just as intransigent, but a deal more experimental and in my view undoubtedly of more permanent value. But from the same period there is another voice, more personal and intimate, where many of these ideas first appear, and which carries its own spirited subversion. This can be heard in those few of James' love-letters to Constance Webb which have been published. We have glimpses of a more lyrical, sensual James, brim-full of the pleasures of aesthetic life. We see him, in 1944 and 1945, in elegiac mood, ruminating on the destruction of the Europe which – all the denunciations notwithstanding – he still loves. Two years before he started on *American Civilization* he wrote: 'I feel all sorts of new powers, freedoms etc surging in me ... We will live. This is our new world – where there is no distinction between political and personal any more'.[10] Or finally we could reflect on what James might have taken for his own conception of *Dasein*:

> One day we'll have a jam session – you and me. It will begin with philosophy – the method of thought, i.e., logic, the inevitable development of ideas, and we'll reach poetry by that road. Then we'll see clear as day what the concept class means and what the absence of it has meant to poetry. Always remembering however that the poet reacts to life *emotionally* – and without that, though he were the wisest man in the world, he could not write a line of verse. But the more humanity develops the more emotional response depends upon a conception of the world which does not so much guide the poetry, but releases and expands the personality, integrates it, opens horizons, and thus gives the emotional responses a range and depth and power impossible otherwise. This, sweetheart, is to live.[11]

10. *American Civilization*, p14.

11. *C.L.R. James Reader*, p140.

REWRITING THE EVENT

David Roden

Geoffrey Bennington, *Legislations: The Politics of Deconstruction*, Verso, 1994, 302pp, £39.95 cloth, £13.95 paperback.

The fifteen essays in *Legislations* move, with no lack of rhetorical flourish, across a range of disciplinary, thematic and allegorical frontiers. The penultimate essay, 'The Frontier: Between Kant and Hegel' is occupied with the concept of the frontier and the concept *as* frontier. To understand the concept, after Frege, as a boundary is, at least implicitly, to affiliate the question 'What is a concept?' with issues of legitimacy and conduct, to operate with a certain scepticism on the border between theoretical and practical rationality.[1] Following the epiphanic title, the deceptively informative subtitle contests the boundary between something called 'deconstruction' and something called 'politics': there might, *after all*, be a deconstructive politics, despite the imprecations heaped upon the work of Derrida and his compatriots by customs officials on left and right.

The introduction introduces the frontier as theme and motif. Bennington identifies the political with those 'border incidents' in which an interlocutor puts the rules of 'my' language game in question. In such circumstances I cannot appeal to the rules in deciding whether the other is formulating a law without prejudging the other as a 'charlatan' (as opposed to a 'legislator'): 'This moment at which the legislator always might be a charlatan (and to that extent always in a sense is, can never be shown not to be), just is the moment of the political, and it is irreducible because it is undecidable.'[2]

One of the most common criticisms of Derrida and his coevals is that deconstructive readings simply foreclose any relationship to the historical particularities of a text's production and dissemination. To the extent that deconstruction is understood as ahistorical, it is possible to present it as politically and ethically irresponsible. Bennington's revisionary conception of the political allows him both to sketch the outline of a politics in which deconstruction will have a privileged role as a means of access to alterity and – as he makes clear in the introduction – to criticize those conceptions of the political whose appeals to historical or ethical particularities efface the complexity of the event of communication.

As may already be apparent, the conceptual machinery of Bennington's explicit formulation of the politics of alterity owes much to a Lyotardian account of incommensurable language games pivoting around the event-singularities which form the referents of proper names, dates, demonstratives and other indicative signs. In *The Differend* Lyotard embraces a quite radical

1. *Translations From The Philosophical Writings of Gottlieb Frege*, Black and Geach (eds), third edition, Blackwell, Oxford 1980, p139.

2. *Legislations*, p33.

contingency in the way events may be described, narrated or otherwise 'linked' to other events: the 'arrive-t-il?' is a surd, angelic and quite other to the discursive system for which it functions as referent, addressor or addressee.[3] The 'cardinal sin' for Lyotard – as it is for Bennington – is to pretend otherwise; for any one language game to claim to occupy the position of a metalanguage within which apparent incommensurabilities may be unequivocally determined or arbitrated. It is precisely for this assumption of transcendence that Bennington, in a section of the book entitled 'Refutations', takes to task some philosophical and political responses to deconstruction. Bennington cheerfully concedes that the 'refutations' will be indignant, bad-tempered and amused, inspired as they are 'by the extraordinary ignorance and complacency which [seems] to dominate critical accounts of deconstruction'.[4] The first and longest essay, 'Deconstruction and the Philosophers (The Very Idea)', is perhaps more amused than bad-tempered, finding in the attempts at systematic exposition on the part of writers such as Rodolphe Gasché, Irene Harvey, John Llewelyn and Christopher Norris a cause of some hilarity.

Bennington is, it should be stressed, far from being a philosophical Luddite (some of the best moments in *Legislations* are, as he would say, 'intensely philosophical'). However, he discerns an inevitable crudity and violence – that is to say, a 'political' moment – in any philosophical *rapprochement* with deconstruction:

> Deconstruction is not a philosophy even though it involves intensely philosophical moments. I try to show how the philosophical attempts to save deconstruction from the naiveties of 'political' or other positive approaches, though no doubt to be preferred ... always runs the risk of reinstating a philosophy of deconstruction which again closes off the opening to the other (and therefore to reading) which I have outlined.[5]

The assurance with which Bennington disposes of philosophy in this passage invites the suspicion that the name, 'philosophy', refers here to an island language game which has never entirely abandoned its imperialistic designs on the rest of the archipelago. This model replicates a Lyotardian paranoia concerning the hegemonic tendencies of theoretical discourse that is quite foreign to Derrida's writing. True, Derrida does seek to demonstrate certain *aporia* (roughly, irresolvable contradictions) attendant upon theoretical undertakings (in philosophy, psychology, linguistics, historiography etc.) but this should surely cause us to question whether violence is the inevitable concomitant of theory. Much hinges upon the vexed question of 'the event' for, in Lyotard's philosophy it is its supposed singularity (unrepeatability, one-offness) which precedes identification and hence allows the superposition of heterogeneous language games. Without this common (yet heterogeneous) element there would be little sense in talking about language games in agonistic terms. While *Legislations* contains a highly illuminating discussion of the

3. J.-F. Lyotard, *The Differend*, tr. George Van Den Abbeele, Manchester University Press, 1988.

4. *Legislations*, p3.

5. *Ibid.*, p4.

differences between Lyotard and Derrida's treatment of the event in the final essay, 'Index', these are more often elided. Bennington seems to recognize that Derrida's stress on the iterability of events (their impure repeatability) involves the abandonment of phenomenologically 'pure' singularity but seems intent on reconciling them in the teeth of this manifest incompatibility. In the final sentence of 'Index' (significantly, the final sentence of *Legislations*) Lyotard and Derrida stand reunited in 'a sort of radical passivity before the event'.[6]

This roseate vision diffracts through the passages in 'Refutations' where Bennington is suffused with the Mosaic glow of the legislator. Philosophy is, we recall, always liable to do violence to the Derridean text. The reason for this, as it emerges in 'Deconstruction and the Philosophers', is that 'Derrida's work is less a system than a series of impure "events" '.[7] Although 'pure events' might be more appropriate given the context, this metaphysics of singularities does account for Bennington's hostility to Rodolphe Gasché's positioning of Derrida within the traditions of the philosophies of reflection and phenomenology in what is possibly the most systematic account of Derrida's work to date, *The Tain Of The Mirror*. In a passage quoted at length by Bennington, Gasché writes of deconstruction as both a continuation of certain motifs in Husserl's phenomenology and as decisive breaks, not only with phenomenology but with ideas of continuity and tradition as such.[8] Bennington detects a *reductio ad absurdum* of Gasché's entire strategy in this admission. One must acknowledge that Gasché is on singularly dangerous ground when he asserts that Derrida's relation to Husserl 'is, in a certain way, radically contingent'. However, despite Bennington's occasionally rather histrionic dismissal of the Gaschean recourse to history, it is far from clear that Gasché is simply exposing the gap between his methodology and 'Derridean orthodoxy' here. If in Derrida's work we encounter a relation to tradition that also has the nature of 'a decisive break' this could equally suggest that a significant revision of our notions of tradition, continuity and historicity might be in order (though Bennington could no doubt respond that any 'revision' which took due account of 'the temporal complexities of the event' would be more *catastrophic* than significant).

Questions of historical continuity and periodization reappear in the three subsequent 'refutations', all of which are concerned with left or marxist criticisms of deconstruction, and in 'The Rationality of Postmodern Relativity' which utilizes Lyotard's non-periodizing conception of the postmodern against Charles Jencks's periodizing (postmodern as mostmodern) account of 'the continuation of modernism and its transcendence'.[9] The latter essay contains a sophisticated discussion of the relation of deconstruction to architectural theory and practice; its anti-historicist case plausible given the philosophical problems afflicting many of the accounts of modernism currently on offer. The earlier essays include a piece on Fredric Jameson's *The Political Unconscious* and 'L'Arroseur Arrosé(e)', an enjoyably caustic discussion of Peter Dews's *Logics of Distintegration* and Gillian Rose's *The Dialectic of Nihilism*. Both essays are concerned with the now familiar charge of deconstruction's effacement of the historical and reiterate the counter-charge that, under the rhetorical guise

6. *Ibid.*, p294.

7. *Ibid.*, p44.

8. Rodolphe Gasché, *The Tain of the Mirror: Derrida and the Philosophy of Reflection*, Harvard University Press, 1986, p246.

9. *Legislations*, p173.

of a concern with 'the concrete' or 'the real', an eminently metaphysical conception of history is being employed to occlude the ineluctable modalities of the text. The refutation is somewhat inconclusive, as we might expect given the entirely different presuppositions adopted by either side. There is, however, an accusation levelled at Derrida in Peter Dews's book which deserves more consideration than Bennington is inclined to allow: it is that Derrida's work, far from marking a 'decisive break' with the philosophical tradition, simply perpetuates the time-honoured German idealist language game of finding ever more inclusive 'conditions of possibility' for experience, knowledge, philosophical thought, identity and so on – a case, as Richard Rorty memorably observed, 'of Nietzschian wine in Kantian vessels'. While it can be objected that deconstructive 'conditions of possibility' (*difference*, iterability etc.) are radically finite, refractory, conditions of impossibility as well as possibility, there is no doubt that Derrida's more philosophical work can be read as articulating a quasi-Kantian categorical framework of undelimitable generality (Richard Rorty is probably correct in claiming that, for all his precautions and disclaimers, this is essentially the reading Gasché undertakes in the *Tain of the Mirror*).[10]

Bennington's somewhat peremptory response to Dews is to endorse Gasché's claim that the Derridean 'quasi-transcendental' is also 'radically empirical': that it *just is* the exposure to a certain 'contingency and historicity'. This seems to me to be insufficient if 'historicity' is exclusively an opening to contingency, however the latter is 'radicalized'. An adequate account of historicity must also deal with the *emergence* of pervasive structures and it is precisely here that (as in Gasché's heroic attempts to 'think' the relationship of Derrida's work to phenomenology) one often has the sense of a dead end, an impassable frontier. It transpires that Derrida is more sensitive to this difficulty than some of the more zealous Derrideans. This emerges with particular clarity in his treatment of 'literature' as that 'institution' which, for Derrida, institutionalizes its own precariousness and provides 'un fil conducteur' for an account of textuality as such. Thus in his essay on Kafka's parable, 'Before the Law', he explores the juridical and institutional horizon which accounts for the text becoming a *work*. It is the singularity of the work (an ambivalent and, I would argue, essentially *conventional* singularity, as distinct from that of the Lyotardian event) which puts into question the historically emergent 'borders' of the work.[11] If deconstruction cannot *avoid* the issue of social (and by implication technological, biophysical) conditions of emergence then we can no longer take the existence of a 'Lacanian bar' between something called 'deconstruction' and something called 'history' (or something else called 'politics') as self evident.

10. Richard Rorty, *Contingency, Irony and Solidarity*, Cambridge University Press, 1989, chapter six.

11. In Jacques Derrida, *Acts of Literature*, Derek Attridge (ed), Routledge, London 1992.

PARIS, TEXAS

Josh Cohen

Jean-Philippe Mathy, *Extreme Occident*, University of Chicago, 1993, 307pp. £10.99 paperback.

Recent years have witnessed the increasing hegemony of postmodern French theorizations of America. Curiously enacting his own notorious contention that theories float above, and oblivious to, the messy material practices of everyday experience, in some endlessly self-generating hyperspace, Baudrillard's rather tired aphoristic reflections on America seem to be echoed pervasively in the collective cultural consciousness.[1] Notions such as the 'fake' culture of a simulated mediascape, the 'classless' melting pot of a melancholy achieved utopia, the 'blank' locus of the death of the subject, and the 'unhistorical' space of a kind of primal modernity, sealed off from Europe's burden of tradition, often seem to be organically and unassailably embedded in the very conditions of public conversation about America. Jean-Philippe Mathy's *Extreme Occident*, a critical genealogy of France's ongoing intellectual engagement with the New World, is to be especially welcomed in this context, counteracting as it does the naturalized status of these diagnostic abstractions.

1. Jean Baudrillard, *America*, Verso, London 1988.

Mathy's central thesis, articulated through a series of chronologically and thematically organized chapters, is that the French 'intertext' of America is less a network of critical descriptions and analyses, than a ceaseless working-out of specifically French cultural anxieties. In particular, America is projected as, from its very inception, a repository of fears about the creeping erosion of the authority and autonomy of the intellectual. America, that is, emerges as the ultimate signifier of an emergent market, driven by the amoral imperatives of commercial profit and technological rationality, which threatens to supplant the aristocratic mandarin, guardian of hard-headed aesthetic judgment and philosophical reasoning, as the primary point of reference for value and action. The bitter conflation of America with the market itself has persisted, with varying intensities and inflections, through the course of the twentieth century, Mathy's central focus.

The book is at its best when it places specific representations of America in the more general context of a given writer's or movement's literary-philosophical project. Thus, George Duhamel's *America the Menace* (1931) and Celine's *Journey to the End of Night* (1934), are read as contributions to the reactionary modernism of inter-war Europe, counterparts to the German critique of Americanism as a technological assault on social and spiritual being, as posited by the likes of Junger and Heidegger. In the French tradition, this critique is distinguished, however, less by Teutonic 'blood and soil' revivalism, than by an almost hysterical cultural patricianism, as in Duhamel's vision of the American cinema. Hollywood is conceived as the demonic apotheosis of the conspiratorial manipulation of public taste for profit, a phantasmic illusion of motion, 'reducing the viewer to a "sendentary mollusc" submitted to a series of flashes, repetitions, explosions, and titillations, "this tickling, this burlesque, a kind of masturbation of the eye"' (Mathy, p81). From a contemporary perspective, it is illuminating to find that the same projection of America as the apocalyptic site of the eclipse of critical engagement, by a visual culture that disables reflection, informs both Duhamel's paranoiac polemic, and Baudrillard's wry affirmations. This sense of a lineage of representation, lent continuity by a persistent preoccupation with the status of the intellectual within a technologically-generated lifeworld, is systematically brought out in Mathy's admirably comprehensive survey of French prose.

Given his identification of the problem of agency as central to the French interrogation of America, it is unsurprising that one of the more fruitful contexts for the demonstration of Mathy's argument is that of existentialism, and in particular, the pivotal figure of Sartre. Mathy traces Sartre's miscellany of writings on America through the development of his existential system and its shifting political inflections. Thus, in the context of his post-war transatlantic journeys (commissioned by Camus for publication in *Combat*), Sartre's humanistic gaze focuses upon the American impulse to motion, to a valorization of the temporary, the unfinished, the mutable, as expressed by its adventurous, disordered, and irrepressibly modern cites. Here, America functions as a living enactment of authentic existential experience, the mobility of its people embodying 'a denial of contingency' (Mathy, p111), a refusal to yield to the metaphysics of collective destiny, in favour of the conscious assumption of individual responsibility. However, the raw material of America can be employed in the construction of a very different narrative; for American individualism is but one component in a fully systematized structure of conformity. Again, the familiar trope of social depersonalization surfaces, the repression of any articulation of individuality outside of the universalizing framework of the technological lifeworld. Thus Sartre speaks of the American's lifelong subjection 'to an intense drive to organize and Americanize him' (Mathy, p114), a drive to dissolve the tensions between individualism and conformism. It is this critique of the serializing tendencies of American life that carries forward, some twenty years later, when post-war Allied triumphalism has yielded to bitter anti-imperialism, into the damning prognosis of American genocide in his report to the Russell Tribunal.[2] Moreover, it is this very category of seriality that is at the heart of the *Critique of Dialectical Reason*, Sartre's magisterial attempt to theorize through Marxism the material degradation of existential freedom.[3] His observations on the universalizing impulse of Americanism and his condemnation of the 'total' character of the Vietnam War read like specific articulations of the abstract category of the 'practico-inert' formulated in the *Critique*, that is, the realm of external facticity that constrains existential freedom.

2. Jean-Paul Sartre, 'Vietnam – Imperialism and Genocide' in *Between Existentialism and Marxism*, Verso, London 1974.

3. Jean-Paul Sartre, *Critique of Dialectical Reason*, Verso, London 1986.

Mathy's discussion of Sartre is illuminating foremost, then, for this hermeneutic operation, one that reveals a coherent intellectual project at work within apparently fragmentary and disparate writings on America. It reveals the conceptual malleability of America, its availability for different kinds of metaphorical appropriation (the utopia of existential mobility, the dystopia of serial repression), in the service of contingent philosophical and ideological requirements. Simultaneously, it demonstrates persuasively the centrality of representations of America to French philosophies of modernity, America's haunting conceptual presence in French intellectual history. In tracing the fluid trajectory of Sartre's engagement with America, then, Mathy usefully maps the fundamental dilemmas of modernity as framed by existentialism. If his later discussion of French postmodernism seems less insightful, it may be because this sense of conceptual fluidity is absent.

The reading of contemporary French theory as expressing a more positive relationship to America produces a narrative of reconciliation, one that tends to elide the ambivalence which continues to characterize postmodern representations of America. Thus, Baudrillard's 'fatal strategy' of abandoning codes of resistance in favour of an ecstatic yelding to the simulacrum, Lyotard's assault on totalizing master-narratives in the service of generating a limitless plurality of language-games, and Deleuze's injunction to deterritorialization as the condition for the dynamic possibilities of becoming, each find themselves enacted in America. As it stands, however, this reading is somewhat partial, effacing, insofar as they are incommensurable with this reconciliatory model, the surprisingly high-modernist sensibility expressed by Lyotard's lofty condemnation of cultural comodification[4] as anathema to the sublime unrepresentatibility of the real, as well as Deleuze's seminal critique of institutionalized psychoanalysis[5] (America, after all, is the birthplace of industrial psychology, amongst other forms of collective mental systematization). Furthermore the same model excludes postmodern theorists whose work flatly refuses the reconciliatory impulse; I am thinking here of the curiously neglected figure of Paul Virilio,[6] whose apocalyptic projections of the totalized absorption of human, and especially visual, agency, by the historical conjunction of military and cinematic technologies, seem thoroughly continuous with Duhamel's earlier demonization of America's visual culture.

However, these omissions are essentially local flaws in the book's content; a more structural problem is revealed by its avowed methodology. Mathy's attempt to graft Edward Said's Orientalist framework onto his own investigations, in order 'to show the consistencies and articulations, as well as the differences and inconsistencies, that make up the complex of descriptions that forms our intertext' (Mathy, p11), seems fundamentally wrong-headed. Whilst recognizing, in his conclusion, the crucial differences in power configurations at work between the West's construction of the Orient, and France's representations of America, he fails to register fully the logical consequences of those differences. Thus, where Said's work demonstrates the continuity of the West's textual construction of the Orient with the wider forces

4. Jean-François Lyotard, *The Postmodern Condition*, trans. Geoff Bennington and Brian Massumi, University of Minnesota, Minneapolis.

5. Gilles Deleuze and Felix Guattari, *Anti-Oedipus*, Athlone Press, London 1990.

6. See, for example *War and Cinema*, Verso, London 1992, and *The Aesthetics of Disappearance*, Semiotext(e), New York 1991.

of cultural and political-economic imperialism, Mathy's book reveals the French intertext of America as an ongoing negotiation of anxieties over the latter's creeping cultural and geopolitical ascendancy. Consequently, whilst it is tenable to posit Orientalism as a legitimation of colonial power that works to appropriate and silence the voices of its subjects, it is difficult to speak in the same terms about Mathy's intertextual counterpart. Indeed, in the latter context, it can be argued persuasively that American intellectuals have functioned as participants within, as much as objects of, the creation of their own mythologies. American intellectual history, that is, is defined by a project of national self-fashioning that is as metaphorically abstracted from material reality as the French intertext documented by Mathy. In this respect, his tendency to read this intertext largely in terms of its authors' own preoccupations, whilst acute, nevertheless misses the degree to which French intellectuals have continuously, and often insightfully caught onto the inherently inorganic, self-fashioning nature of American cultural identity.

The absence of reflection on intercultural traffic between the nations only serves to underline the problematic nature of Mathy's theorization of his intertext as more revealing of France than America, as if the latter had not been instrumental in the global projection of its own identity. Despite scattered accounts of American receptions of French thought (most notably, the surprising appropriation of Continental anti-foundationalism by American pragmatism), there is little discussion of the ways in which America has both fed and fed on French culture, in forging its identity. An interesting case in point here would be Norman Mailer's appropriation of existentialism, as a way into a very specifically American auto-critique and project for a new national identity.[7] This kind of discussion would be a useful corrective to the almost exclusively French focus of Mathy's survey, in enabling America to be understood less as the objectified victim of French cultural misrecognition, than as an active agent in its own perpetual re-invention.

7. See, for example, *Advertisements for Myself*, Granada, London 1984, and *The Presidential Papers*, Panther, London 1976.

Signs of the Times present

postmodern|**times**

saturday 1 july 1995

the summer conference

city university
northampton square
london ec1

As traditional cultural, political and social formations disintegrate what is the significance of those that take their place?

postmodern **times** seeks to map the end of modernity based on subjection and subordination and charts the uneven development of a new era of critical thought on the eve of the millennium.

conference **themes**

Birth of the global or the end of the west?

Pop, techno and the poetics of place

The millennium: Critical theory for a new century

research **stream**

Towards a postmodern politics

Programme and registration details from:
Signs of the Times, 28 Wargrave Avenue,
London N15 6UD. Tel: 0181-809 5068

BACK ISSUES

1 **Peter Wollen** on fashion and orientalism / **Denise Riley** on 'women' and feminism / **Dick Hebdige**'s sociology of the sublime / **Laura Marcus** on autobiographies / **John Tagg** should art historians know their place? / **Franco Bianchini** on the GLC's cultural policies / **Homi K. Bhabha, Stephen Feuchtwang** and **Barbara Harlow** on Fanon / Reviews – **Cousins** on Foucault, **McLennan** on Norris, **Schwarz** on Englishness and **O'Pray** on Powell and Pressburger.

2 **Mary Kelly, Elizabeth Cowie** and **Norman Bryson** on Kelly's Interim / **Greil Marcus** on subversive entertainment / **Georgina Born** on modern music culture / **Geoffrey Nowell-Smith** on popular culture / **Ien Ang** on 'progressive television' / **Alan Sinfield** on modernism and English Studies in the Cold War / **Tony Bennett** on Eagleton.

3 *TRAVELLING THEORY* – **Julia Kristeva** on the melancholic imaginary / **David Edgar** on carnival and drama / **Kobena Mercer** black hair – style politics / **Jacques Rancière** on journeys into new worlds / **Peter Hulme**'s Caribbean diary / **Bill Schwarz** on travelling stars / **Ginette Vincendeau** on chanteuses réalistes / **Steve Connor** on Springsteen / **Christopher Norris** on Gasché's Derrida.

4 *CULTURAL TECHNOLOGIES* – **Simon Frith** making sense of jazz in Britain / **Griselda Pollock** on Doré's London / **Colin Mercer** on entertainment / **Tony Bennett**'s exhibitionary complex / **Ian Hunter** setting limits to culture / **David Saunders** on copyright and literature / **Jody Berland** on television.

5 *IDENTITIES* – **Homi K. Bhabha** on the commitment to theory / **Philip Cohen** on Tarzan and the jungle bunnies / **Glenn Bowman** on Palestinian nationalist consciousness / **Kristin Ross** on Rimbaud and spatial history / **Kaja Silverman** on liberty, maternity, commodification / **Adrian Rifkin** on Carmenology / **Margaret Sotan**'s epistemology of the wandering woman / **Andrew Benjamin** on psychoanalysis / **Gill Davies** on heritage / **Les Back** on soundsystems.

6 *THE BLUES* – **Jacqueline Rose** on Margaret Thatcher and Ruth Ellis / **James Donald** how English is it? / **Benita Parry** on Kipling's imperialism / **John Silver** on Carpentier / **Mitra Tabrizian** and **Andy Golding**'s blues / **Barbara Creed** on *Blue Velvet* / **Joseph Bristow** on masculinity / **Graham Murdock** on Moretti's *Bildungsroman* / **Edmond Wright** on post-Humptydumptyism.

7 *MODERNISM/MASOCHISM* – **Victor Burgin**'s Tokyo / **Linda Williams** on feminine masochism and feminist criticism / **John Tagg** on criticism, photography and technological change / **Geoff Bennington** l'arroseur arrosé(e) / **Emilia Steuerman** on Habermas vs Lyotard / **Paul Crowther** on the Kantian sublime, the avant-garde and the postmodern / **Mark Cousins** on Lévi Strauss on Mauss / **Iain Chambers** being 'British' / **Adrian Forty** on lofts and gardens / **Lisa Tickner** on Griselda Pollock.

8 *TECHNO-ECOLOGIES* – **Peter Wollen** cinema: Americanism and the robot / **John Keane** on the liberty of the press / **S.P. Mohanty** on the philosophical basis of political criticism / **David Kazanjian** and **Anahid Kassabian** naming the Armenian genocide / **Paul Théberge** the 'sound' of music / **David Tomas** the technophilic body / **Félix Guattari** the three ecologies / **Margaret Whitford** on Sartre.

9 *ON ENJOYMENT* – **Slavoj Zizek** the undergrowth of enjoyment / **Peter Osborne** aesthetic autonomy and the crisis

Back issues cost £14.99 each
Make cheques payable to *Lawrence & Wishart* and send to:
Lawrence & Wishart, 144a Old South Lambeth Road, London SW8 1XX

FORTHCOMING

MICHEL FOUCAULT: J'ACCUSE

new formations 25

EDITOR: JUDITH SQUIRES

In association with *Signs of the Times*

Based on the highly successful conference held in London on 25 June 1994 to mark the 10th anniversary of Michel Foucault's death, the articles in this issue testify to the continuing and profound impact of Foucault's ideas on contemporary theorising.

Foucault's biographers, David Macey and James Miller, question the legacy of Foucault's life and work, whilst leading theorists from a wide range of disciplinary backgrounds use Foucauldian themes and images to explore current theoretical and political issues.

Contributors include:

Colin Gordon, David Macey, John Marks, Doreen Massey, James Miller, John Rajchman, Alan Schrift, Kate Soper, Wendy Wheeler, Robert Young.

new formations

FREE!
2 issues of
New Formations
Worth
£30!

To mark the start of a new year we are pleased to be able to offer two of our most popular issues **FREE** to all new subscribers. These issues alone are worth £30 – they are yours for **free when you take out a new subscription**.

Your two **free** issues, *The Question of 'Home'* and *Hybridity* feature Ariel Dorfman, Doreen Massey, Simon Frith, Christopher Norris, Jenny Bourne Taylor and others exploring the clash between globalisation and localisation via the cultural-political syntheses that characterise the post-colonial era.

Take out a 1995 subscription, receive these **two issues free**. Plus… you will receive your *New Formations* delivered to you, pre-publication, direct to your home address and at a **special discount price**.

To apply, complete the form below – not even a stamp is needed – but do hurry, stocks are limited and we don't want to disappoint.

PS *If you don't want to cut up your issue, a photocopy is acceptable.*

The Expanding Vista
American Television in the Kennedy Years
Mary Ann Watson

"An exceptional piece of scholarship that adds significantly to the literature of the field .. gracefully presented in a highly readable form. This book is a model for other broadcast historians who have yet to treat many important developments in the history of a medium that has greatly defined the modern era."
- Everette E. Dennis, Columbia University 273pp, 38 b&w photos, £13.95 pb.

House / Garden / Nation
Space, Gender, and Ethnicity in Post-Colonial Latin American Literatures by Women
Ileana Rodríquez

Focusing on the nation as garden, hacienda, or plantation, Rodríquez shows us five Centro-Caribbean women writers debating the predicament of women under nation formation from within the confines of marriage and home.
272pp, £15.95 pb, £47.50hb

Still Life in Real Time
Theory after Television
Richard Dienst

Drawing lessons from television programmes like *Twin Peaks* and *Crime Story*, television events like the Gulf War, and t.v. personalities like Madonna, Dienst produces a remarkable range of insights on the character of the medium and on the theories that have been affected by it.
256pp, £15.95 pb, £47.50 hb.

Complimentarity
Anti-Epistemology after Bohr and Derrida
Arkady Plotnitsky

Many commentators have remarked in passing on the resonance between deconstructionist theory and certain ideas of quantum physics. In this book, Plotnitsky rigorously elaborates the similarities and differences between the two by focusing on the work of Niels Bohr and Jacques Derrida.
328pp, £16.95 pb, £47.50 hb

Extended Play
Sounding Off from John Cage to Dr. Funkenstein
John Corbett

"Corbett has honed in on some of the most intriguing music happening today and his discussion is never less than lively, intelligent and politically concerned. . . his scope is much wider and more discerning than most academic cultural theory. His analysis of REM as "corporate avant garde" and his history of anti-censorship strategies are striking and original." - *The Wire*
408pp, 25 b&w photos, £16.95 pb.

Sex Workers and Sex Work
Anne McClintock, editor

Protesting the stigmatized public image of sex workers as hapless victims, the contributors to this volume debate the politics of female representation and agency and claim a place for sex workers at the feminist front line.
260pp, 33 illustrations, £7.50 pb

Inventing High and Low
Literature, Mass Culture, and Uneven Modernity in Spain
Stephanie Sieburth

Stephanie Sieburth suggest, no division between "high" and "low" culture will stand up to logical scrutiny. Why, then, does the opposition persist? In this book she questions the terms of this perennial debate and uncovers the deep cultural, economic, and psychological tensions that lead each generation to reinvent the distinction between high and low.
288pp, £16.95 pb, £37.95 hb.

Feminism and Postmodernism
Margaret Ferguson and Jennifer Wicke, editors

This collection of essays explores the significant agreements and tensions between contemporary feminists and postmodern theories and practices. Contributors include Toril Moi, Linda Nicholson, Andrew Ross, and Marjorie Garber.
304pp, £14.95 pb, £32.95 hb

Cracked Coverage
Television News, the Anti-Cocaine Crusade, and the Reagan Legacy
Jimmie L. Reeves and Richard Campbell

"An intricately researched investigation into the various distortions, idiocies and hypocrises of the US media's roll-over-and-die acquiescence to Reagan-Bush's opportunism and doomed "war on drugs." A book, I imagine, that will go down like a cup of cold sick in Normal, Illinois." - *The Guardian*
360pp, £18.95 pb, £57.50 hb

Eloquent Obsessions
Writing Cultural Criticism
Marianna Torgovnick, ed.

This collection offers models for writing eloquently about culture - models that are intellectually and socially responsible, but attuned to the critic's voice and the reader's ear.
328pp, 12 b&w photos, £16.95 pb.

Rethinking Objectivity
Allan Megill, editor

Allan Megrill has gathered essays from fourteen leading scholars in a variety of fields to gain critical understanding of the idea of objectivity as it functions in today's world. 352pp, £14.95 pb, £43.95 hb

DUKE
university press
c/o Academic & University Publishers Group
1 Gower Street, London WC1E 6HA